C000300597

'Margaret White has spent a lifetime in and reflect written a wise and fresh book that all those connected teachers, governors and administrators, and above a profit and delight.'

Sir Anthony Seldon, Vice-Chancellor, University of Buckingham

'This is a beautifully written book, marrying the personal with the practical set into a system-level approach to education. The central focus of the book will provide new leaders across the education system with a memorable representation of ensuring that children thrive at school. This is a wonderful distillation from a wonderful and career-long teacher.'

Brett Wigdortz, Founder and CEO, Teach First

'Margaret White has written a compelling account of why ethos-based education, which puts the individual pupil at its core, really does matter. Her educational ideals, articulated so clearly, are rooted in the best kind of evidence – her direct experience of children based on her many years' teaching.'

Keith Budge, Chair, HMC and Headmaster Bedales Schools

'This book is a breath of fresh air, arguing forcefully for a fresh vision of education. We all know that something crucial is lost in human and spiritual terms between primary and secondary education; we all know what difference is made by personally supportive, ethically alert, close-knit educational communities. Traditional prep schools may seem an unexpected place to look, but many of them have developed exemplary practice in all these respects, which deserves to be taken very seriously as a resource. A timely, wise study.'

Rowan Williams, Master of Magdalene College Cambridge
and former Archbishop of Canterbury

'Margaret White's superbly constructed arguments are logical and sound. This is a book of worth that makes a significant contribution to educational debate on this subject that must, in my opinion, be considered as a leading work in its field. It is a "must read" essential for all school leaders.'

Sally Eaton, Executive Head, Langley Hall Primary
Academy, Berkshire

'This is a wonderful book. It is clear that Margaret White has been an outstanding teacher who has managed to capture and distil the key features of a good education. It is refreshingly honest and written without pretention and anyone who cares about the education of our children should read it.'

David Hanson, Chief Executive, IAPS

'A passion for education, in the fullest sense of the term, and a lifetime's teaching experience are evident on every page of this inspiring, creative and insightful book. It should be read by anyone directly or indirectly concerned in the great enterprise of ensuring children of all backgrounds are able to benefit from schooling that provides a truly rich and coherent personal formation.'

James O'Donnell, organist and Master of the Choristers,
Westminster Abbey

'This book touched me. It is, in the best sense of the word, utopian. That is, it sets the highest possible standards. And then it makes us – it made me – feel those standards can be reached. Not simply. Not without hard work. Not without disappointments and fall-backs and worries. But doable – and doable by all us ordinary everyday sinners. It is an odd thing to say but this book made me happy! It shaped inchoate hopes into a clear vision. I think it will have a wide readership, and it will give many people hope, and a clearer path forward.'

Lisbet Rausing, science historian and philanthropist

'This book will raise the spirits of any practitioner who wants to do more than just prepare for tests and exams. An inspiring vision for our children's education, supported by a practical model to make it happen.'

Mark Hayes, Chair, Saffron Academy Trust

'Insightful, inspiring, and effervescent, this book distils the substance of what counts as a good education. At the heart of her reflections lies respect for the uniqueness of each individual student. This is compelling reading for practitioners of education and indeed for anyone who cares about education.'

Violet Lo, social innovator, Director and Founder, Inclusive
Business Lab, Hong Kong

'In my experience, the voices of policy-makers are nearly unanimous in support of education. But, whatever does that mean? Margaret White defines a good education so well that her four-dimensional principles create a framework that should prove useful for crafting public policy. Margaret remembers, as a young teacher, she "loved the puzzle of having to work out how to explain something in the best possible way so that it was simplified but not distorted, how to lay rigorous and stable foundations on which to build, how to engender confidence in those who were less certain and yet cater for the brightest. . .". That love endures throughout this beautifully-written volume.'

John A. Maher, member and speaker pro tempore,
House of Representatives, Pennsylvania

'A "must-read" for educators, policy-maker and parents. Margaret White has delivered a magnum opus addressing many of the crucial issues facing our schools today.'

David Saunderson, Chief Executive, Cantab Asset Management

'Margaret White has carefully distilled the wisdom of her decades of teaching and leadership experience into an insightful and very readable book. She has some key messages for students of education, teachers, leaders and parents alike as she sets out her vision for what constitutes a high quality and broad primary education.'

Anna Vignoles, Professor of Education, University of Cambridge

'It's wonderful to see a book that focuses on the whole and individual child. Healthy, engaged children who are connected to the world around them are better equipped to learn, and this book explains how teaching with vision, purpose and empathy for the whole child could bring extraordinary benefits.'

*Dame Fiona Reynolds, Master of Emmanuel College Cambridge, and
former Director-General of the National Trust*

'Margaret White has married a lifetime of experience as a teacher with an outstanding gift for explaining what really good education is. Her four-dimensional vision is inspiring, thorough and practical. It combines a wise approach, that could be applied in any school, with perceptive and persuasive responses to possible objections. She has achieved something extraordinary, and all stakeholders in education should learn from it.'

*David Ford, Emeritus Regius Professor of Divinity, Cambridge University,
and Chair of Church of England Vision for Education group*

'It's a fascinating view of education that will be invaluable to teachers and to parents. In a time of Academy governance it's also a unique, riveting and taboo-busting inquiry into what the state sector can learn about independence from the private schools system. I wish Margaret White could be drafted into government as Education Secretary.'

*Peter Florence, Director and Founder of the Hay Festival
of Literature and Arts*

A Good Education

This book provides an answer to one of the key questions of our time: namely, what constitutes a good education. Presenting a 'four-dimensional' model, it directly considers the essential elements a good education should include. Through forging this framework and outlaying its origins, implications and practice, the book explains how a good contemporary education can be defined and implemented. From the premise that such educational essentials are neither the preserve of the elite nor a minimum standard, White's exploration keeps the child at the heart of the discussion, focusing on every pupil's worth, identity, interactions and development.

The author offers a detailed and rigorous perspective reflecting on extensive professional experience, starting with a consideration of the current educational climate and progressing through the book's three parts:

- looking for a good education
- creating a model of good education
- applications, implications and implementation of the model.

A Good Education recognises the transformative power of education and reflects on the importance of human factors: teachers' provision for their pupils and students' ability to flourish. This book is addressed to those actively engaged in or concerned about educational provision: graduates entering teaching, school leaders, policy-makers and parents. It also speaks more broadly to all those who know that a good education really matters.

Margaret White is Deputy Head Academic at St Faith's School, Cambridge. She studied Natural Sciences and Education at Cambridge University and has over twenty years' experience of teaching and school leadership. Her passion for education draws on her experiences as a pupil, student, teacher, parent, governor and school leader.

A Good Education

A New Model of Learning to Enrich Every Child

Margaret White

Routledge
Taylor & Francis Group

LONDON AND NEW YORK

First published 2018
by Routledge
2 Park Square, Milton Park, Abingdon, Oxon OX14 4RN

and by Routledge
711 Third Avenue, New York, NY 10017

Routledge is an imprint of the Taylor & Francis Group, an informa business

© 2018 Margaret White

The right of Margaret White to be identified as author of this work
has been asserted by her in accordance with sections 77 and 78 of
the Copyright, Designs and Patents Act 1988.

All rights reserved. No part of this book may be reprinted or
reproduced or utilised in any form or by any electronic, mechanical,
or other means, now known or hereafter invented, including photocopying
and recording, or in any information storage or retrieval system,
without permission in writing from the publishers.

Trademark notice: Product or corporate names may be trademarks
or registered trademarks, and are used only for identification
and explanation without intent to infringe.

British Library Cataloguing in Publication Data
A catalogue record for this book is available from the British Library

Library of Congress Cataloging in Publication Data
Names: White, Margaret, (Principal), author.
Title: A good education : a new model of learning to enrich every child /
Margaret White.
Description: Abingdon, Oxon : New York, NY, 2018. | Includes
bibliographical references.
Identifiers: LCCN 2017047131 (print) | LCCN 2017060095 (ebook) |
ISBN 9781351270137 (ebook) | ISBN 9781138576315 (hbk) |
ISBN 9781138576322 (pbk) | ISBN 9781351270137 (ebk)
Subjects: LCSH: School autonomy—Great Britain. | School improvement
Programs—Great Britain.
Classification: LCC LB2822.9 (ebook) | LCC LB2822.9 .W45 2018
(print) | DDC 371.2/07—dc23
LC record available at https://lccn.loc.gov/2017047131

ISBN: 978-1-138-57631-5 (hbk)
ISBN: 978-1-138-57632-2 (pbk)
ISBN: 978-1-351-27013-7 (ebk)

Typeset in Bembo and Helvetica Neue
by Florence Production Ltd, Stoodleigh, Devon, UK

For Ian
in appreciation, gratitude and love

Contents

Illustrations

Figures

Tables

Summary boxes

Vision boxes

Foreword

'Education, education, education!' was the political clarion call of the incoming Labour government in 1997. It was one that resonated with many, and successive Secretaries of State made considerable progress in subsequent administrations. Yet delivery of early years' education still remains an unresolved, contentious, politically and ideologically divisive issue today. Why?

Surely, the mountain of academic publication and genuine commitment of so many to the cause, alongside considerable fiscal investment, should have delivered a perfect solution by now. Unfortunately the scale and nature of the need and the sheer variety of proposed solutions bedevil the systematic 'one size fits all' approach. And education by its very nature, like delivery of healthcare, is a human process which is subject to enormous variation in the way those delivering education at different ages can interface effectively with a system and deal with the individual needs of students at different ages. It is also a process where the impact of changes take decades to achieve fruition and a measurable outcome, with surrogate measures needed to satisfy understandably impatient parents and policy-makers.

As in healthcare, these surrogate measures mean that there is an ever-increasing evidence base for what works and what doesn't, and much of it is objectively assessed and analysed. Is this not sufficient? What is the role of the individual teacher's experience? We are taught that such evidence is weak in comparison, yet to ignore it flies in the face of logic.

At the heart of education is the individual child/student, and her early experience will determine her future approach to education in later years. This is something we all have to be committed to in an ever-more technologically complex and unpredictable world. This must be coupled with the critical role of the teacher. The influential 2014 UNESCO report on *Education for All* collated data from around the world and identified that, regardless of economic circumstances, the quality of the teacher is critical to educational outcome.

In this volume, Margaret White draws on her own experience, as a state school pupil and independent school teacher, and challenges us to think again. The child is placed centre-stage and the education process must revolve around a clear understanding of who they are. She eschews simplistic outcome measures but seeks solutions that are required for holistic development of a well-rounded individual whatever the environmental circumstances. But this is not just another series of important personal observations, as it is drawn together in a framework that warrants further study and consideration.

So please read on, but with a warning. In the finest academic tradition, your prejudices will be challenged and at times you will question, but whatever your perspective, be it policy-maker, academic, educationalist, teacher, student or parent, the time spent will be well rewarded.

Sir Leszek Borysiewicz, Vice-Chancellor,
University of Cambridge
September 2017

Acknowledgements

This is a book about learning, and I must start by thanking and acknowledging all those from whom I have learnt myself. First thanks must therefore go to my parents who have taught me so much and from whom I continue to learn, along with my siblings and wider family. Through church, school and university, numerous teachers stand out, but especially those who took a personal interest in my learning, who were especially encouraging and kind. As we continually learn through life, everyone with whom we come into contact teaches us something, so I am grateful to those people who have engaged me in conversation about education through chance encounters whether on the train, at conferences or over dinner. In the realm of teaching, my colleagues at St Faith's have been a continuous source of inspiration – I owe them an enormous debt of gratitude.

Specific individuals have given most generously of their time and expertise to support this particular project. I must thank the Vice-Chancellor of the University of Cambridge, Sir Leszek Borysiewicz, for his willingness to write the Foreword. I am also most grateful to Professor Madeleine Arnot for her enthusiasm and encouragement from the outset, without which this project would not have started, and to Professor Anna Vignoles, for her active interest, support and advice, both of the University of Cambridge Faculty of Education and Jesus College.

I am most grateful to Nigel Helliwell, Headmaster of St Faith's Cambridge for his most generous support, and to all my colleagues there from whom I learn daily; I am particularly grateful to Alison Price, Claire Thurlby and Jane Greaves for generously reading the manuscript and for their helpful comments on it, as I am to David Hansen, Chief Executive of the IAPS, for his support and enthusiastic interest.

My father, Dr Robert Hunt, was among the first to read an early draft and I am very grateful to him for his tremendous positivity at that important stage, and his perceptive and detailed comments. I am similarly grateful to Janet Purvis and John Cornwell for reading an early-stage draft and for their enthusiastic responses and helpful insights. I am most grateful to Dr Michael Minden and The Revd Dr Paul Dominiak, both of Jesus College Cambridge, for their helpful and detailed comments on the manuscript, and to Dr Jonathan Nichols and Dr Jennifer Barnes who shared most informed insights resulting from their significant roles in Higher Education. To Judith Bronowski, Mark Hayes, Helena Renfrew Knight, The Rt Revd Martin Seeley and Ross Wilson, I extend my appreciation and gratitude for their input as experts in their fields, as I do to Victoria Herrenschmidt for her valuable perspective as someone about to embark on a teaching career. I am very grateful to Lisbet Rausing for her generosity in allowing me to reproduce the inspiring words of her grandfather from her memoire, and for her helpful insights as a parent. As well as to numerous members of the teaching profession with whom I have consulted, I am of course also very grateful to Bruce Roberts and Alice Gray at Routledge, with whom it has been a pleasure to work, for their support, enthusiasm and advice, and for the members of the editorial and production teams.

Final thanks must go to my immediate family, to Emma and Luke, and to James and Lucy for their constant interest, encouragement, support and forbearance. As members of the generation who will undoubtedly be concerned with education in the future, their engagement and willingness to discuss these significant matters are highly valued, as well as their personal support, kind interest and loving positivity. Finally, I must thank my husband, Ian, for his belief in me and his constant loving commitment to me, without which I would not have entered teaching in the first place or reached the level of responsibility that I now have; his unflinching support for this project and the time that he has given to it are all the more remarkable given the levels of responsibility that he shoulders himself. This book is dedicated to him in appreciation, gratitude and love.

Abbreviations

GCSE	General Certificate of Secondary Education
GDP	Gross domestic product
HMC	Headmasters' and Headmistresses' Conference
IAPS	Independent Association of Prep Schools
ISC	Independent Schools Council
IT	Information technology
MP	Member of Parliament
NSP	National, school, personal
OECD	Organisation for Economic Co-operation and Development
PE	Physical Education
PISA	Programme for International Student Assessment
PSHCE	Personal, social, health and citizenship education
PSHE	Personal, social and health education
SMSC	Spiritual, moral, social and cultural education
STEAM	Science, technology, engineering, art and maths
STEM	Science, technology, engineering and maths
VLE	Virtual learning environment

Introduction

I see that it is by no means useless to travel, if a man wants to see something new.

Jules Verne, *Around the World in Eighty Days*

A good education is said to be the challenge of our time. It is the concern of parents, teachers and governments. This book aims to describe a model of good education which can be widely applied, accessible and available for many. It does so by looking for what is educationally good, analysing it, describing it and applying it.

The educational principles are drawn largely from my reflections as a teacher in the independent school sector, although the practices described are also to be found in many state-funded schools nationwide, and elsewhere further afield. It is my hope that these reflections might make a real contribution for the next generation, towards the shared goal of securing for them a good education in whatever context that education might take place.

Like many aspects of education, this is politically charged and potentially controversial, which may make some readers wary. Surely independent schools cater for the elite, have impossibly vast financial resources at their disposal and have no relevance to the real world, we might expect to hear. While such a critique may be understandable, I believe that this venture has a legitimacy which can be explained and defended.

First, I believe that all children are equally deserving of access to the best possible education, irrespective of family background, financial circumstances, neighbourhood of birth or any other such spurious differentiators. This suggests that a good education needs at the very least to be sought, identified and articulated, precisely what the model set out in this book seeks to attempt. I therefore believe the goal is not merely legitimate, but also essential.

Second, I believe that the process is legitimate. The reason for this may seem counter-intuitive: it is because every single element of this independently inspired model can in fact be found within the state-maintained sector currently. Some examples speak for themselves: a trustee of a newly opened state-funded London primary school asked me how important character education is, and when I replied that it is absolutely central, he urged me to look at his school's website where, indeed, it securely sits at the heart of their practice. Another London school, in a poor area, determined to match the best-known private schools in the country, has succeeded in providing the opportunity for its pupils to pursue competitive rowing at the highest level. Elsewhere across the city, another primary school has links with the local music conservatoire whereby every pupil has access to music tuition. The chaplain of a church state-school I spoke with explained how her school is organised into manageable pastoral units, each of a few hundred children, so that everyone can be cared for individually in sub-schools within the school. Still another school in a deprived inner-city area offers additional optional lessons in the holidays ahead of public exams (as well as seeking to generate pride and distinctiveness in written work by having all its pupils writing in fountain pen); as a teacher from that school commented to me, it's all about culture.

A culture of excellence already exists in many schools across different contexts, supported by the vision and hard work of those who provide it. Tenacious care of individuals and the pursuit of community life are neither confined to, nor guaranteed in, the private schools of leafy suburbs. Opportunities to pursue academic excellence, artistic endeavour and sporting success can be found in maintained schools in the most deprived of neighbourhoods, as well as in some independents. Education of the whole person can be, and is, provided in some of the most troubled, as well as some of the most privileged, communities. Gathered together under one roof, these characteristics form the essential core of England's traditional independent school system,[1] wherein, in practice, they may be evident to varying degrees – as well as finding expression across state-funded provision.

Third then, and by extension, provision of a good education is not principally about context. Nor is it primarily about levels of resource or parental cooperation. Rather, it is about setting priorities based on clearly articulated values and principles. Whether funded by the state or the paying parent, all schools have to establish their priorities. Limited resources, external priorities and over-emphasis on measurable results in English and maths can be distracting obstacles standing in the way of a good education in a private or state school. On the other hand, clear values and sound principles which create a rich culture of excellence can be found in both sectors too.

What this book seeks to do is forge a rich framework of educational essentials and describe how they can work in practice. Such essentials should neither be considered the preserve of the elite, nor some kind of ineffectual minimum standard. Rather, we should consciously seek to provide them in a positive and structured way for all children – because a good education matters. It matters right now for our very own generation of children in every school across the country.

But although we know for sure that good education matters, it seems difficult to state with equal certainty what matters for an education to be good. Even if a school provides excellent educational elements, such as those outlined above, would we know for sure whether the education received by a child in such a school is as good as it could or should be? This book speaks to the heart of this question by offering a description of what good education is and what it means to be well educated in today's world.

An initial search for the 'best education' tends to lead to one of two places: league tables of examination results, or Finland (or sometimes both, concurrently). Finland's educational success story came to light with the publication of the first PISA[2] test results in 2000;[3] scores in maths, science and reading have continued to be high ever since. As a result, every new initiative coming out from Finnish schools receives the scrutiny of the world's education correspondents.[4] Much research, involving numerous trips to Finland, has been conducted by educationalists from other countries to try to ascertain the reasons behind the success, and almost as many theories seem to have been proposed. But under the heading 'Why Are Finland's Schools So Successful?', LynNell Hancock quotes a Helsinki principal with 24 years of teaching experience as saying, 'If you only measure the statistics, you miss the human aspect'.[5]

Theoretically, it may be possible to describe and define a good education which does not have the child at its heart, but I am convinced that not only is the human aspect of education absolutely essential, but that it lies at the centre of the best educational practice. As a result, this book presents a model of education which has a clearly defined view of the child at its very core. It is also full of the human aspect of education. Anecdotes, incidents, examples and personal experience are relayed as the model of good education unfolds, because, at its heart, education is about each unique child and how individually and together they can best be provided for.

While many care passionately about the educational grand challenge, for all of us, our personal experiences contribute significantly to our attitudes towards the educational endeavour. I remember my feeling of surprise the first time I met someone who had clearly loved his school and the time he spent there. He communicated a warmth and affection for school that was all the more striking and memorable for it being, frankly, slightly bewildering. I suppose I knew this was a theoretical possibility, and that the old adage about school days being the best days of your life must have its origins somewhere, but until that time I do not think I had actually believed such joyful and genuine loyalty to be a plausible reality. My own school experience had been so very different.

It had always seemed to me that there was no reason why schools should not be wonderful places for children, but that was not what I had known myself. While I enjoyed pin-prick star-like memories of good moments and events at school, these stood out against a somewhat bleak background of a grim, grey, Greater London post-war primary school, vast and impersonal, or so it seemed, perhaps partly due to the stark contrast it formed with the nurturing environment of a warm and happy family home. My secondary school experience was somewhat chaotic, as the introduction of comprehensive education brushed aside my formal all-girls grammar school mid-breath and reinvented it overnight as a liberal-minded mixed sixth-form college, old values – good and bad alike – unceremoniously cast aside, as the new ideals of education reforms were deferentially ushered in.

Over the years, I have been deeply influenced by and taken inspiration from many quarters. To my own personal reflections as a pupil, I add those arising from my years as a school governor and parent, and lessons learnt from inspirational teachers and school leaders. But while these provide useful context and balance, most of the reflections in this book arise from my own professional practice.

My teaching career took me into a whole new world, a school not unlike the one my friend had been to, of which he had spoken with such warmth: a community which cared about the individual, and which aspired to excellence in various different guises. And although it has never claimed to be perfect, it remains a school which works hard to provide a good education, and is successful in doing so. The experience of working in what remains one of the largest independent junior schools in England, for children from the ages of four to thirteen, has provided the opportunity to reflect deeply on what a good education *could* be and, with the increasing responsibility of years and roles, the freedom – and duty – to try and implement what it *should* be.

My twenty-year journey from junior teacher to senior leader has granted me the opportunity to develop educational practice on the basis of established *ethos*: a set of values and principles which underpin policy and practice but are not primarily determined by an external agenda, political constraint or preconceived dogma. This ethos runs through the school like blood through veins. It brings passion and compassion, aspiration and inspiration, excellence and innovation.

Working in this environment has enabled me to concentrate on thinking through educational provision that encourages and enables individual children to experience maximum development and success in their areas of strength, while also supporting them to develop in areas where they feel less certain. There is nothing easy about achieving this: irrespective of resourcing levels available, these things do not just happen, but require intense commitment and immense effort – mental, physical, emotional and intellectual. In order for every individual experience gained inside and outside the classroom to meld together into an effective education that achieves these aspirational objectives, a secure and rigorous framework of thought, planning and preparation is required, informed by a clear and fitting vision. The construction of such a framework is facilitated by strong leadership that brings individual teachers together into supportive, collaborative teams, articulating and adopting appropriate goals. These goals translate into agreed practices and are achieved through commitment and sheer hard work: culture, again.

I went into teaching because I thought at the very least I should be able to make children's school experience better than mine had been. There was no reason, I thought, why schools could not be humane, caring, happy places where it was pleasurable to learn and the individual was appreciated and valued. I continue to believe that learning can and should be a thoroughly enjoyable, positive and worthwhile experience for all those involved. Children need to be provided with educational opportunities through which they are inspired, encouraged and equipped to reach high and to contribute fully to their own success and that of others: this really is what a good education is all about. Parents need to have assurance that their children will be equipped in the best possible way to face the future with all its opportunities and challenges. Teachers, educational providers and elected representatives need to have confidence that they are making provision for this to happen as successfully as possible.

It is only after reflecting on many years of teaching that these ideas have crystallised into the model presented in these pages. The model elucidates that the key characteristics of a good education which supports these goals can be expressed as four dimensions of education: height, breadth, depth and length, as shown in Figure I.1.

In the pages that follow, this four-dimensional education is defined and its origins explained. Its constituent parts are described – the foundational values at its core, the character traits which grow from these, the all-important educational

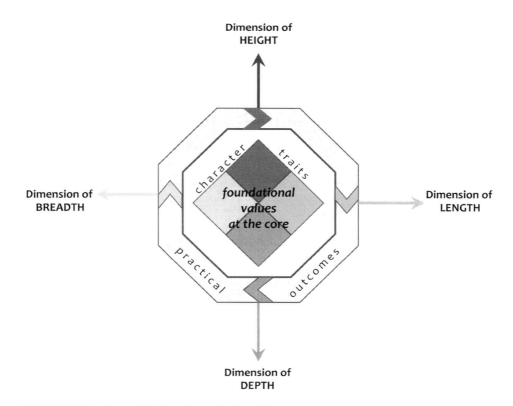

FIGURE I.1 The shape of the four-dimensional model

principles which form the four dimensions, and the practical outcomes that result. The practicalities surrounding its provision are identified and articulated. The implications, based on experience, are made clear.

Based primarily on work with seven- to thirteen-year-olds, this writing is intended to be supportive and helpful for all those with a direct interest in educational practice, particularly in the pre-public examination years, especially those who teach, wherever and whatever that may be. It is also intended to be a helpful point of reference for those outside the teaching profession but who share interest or concern in how we should best provide for the next generation, whether as parents, school governors or policy-makers.

This model has the child at its heart because it rests on my belief that good education is not primarily about cohorts, classes, statistics or standardisation, nor is it about state or independent funding. Rather, it is about a culture which promotes the passionate and tenacious care of individual children and young people. Its goal is for these individuals to flourish in their own right, as members of a community and as contributors to society.

These ideals can – and I believe should – be embraced across the range of existing educational contexts. To do anything else would be to miss the human aspect of education, and to do that would mean that we miss the point entirely.

Notes

1   Education is devolved within the United Kingdom, each of the four countries (England, Scotland, Wales and Northern Ireland) having similar but separate systems. The traditional independent schools of England have their counterparts in the other countries within the Union.

2   The Programme for International Student Assessment (PISA) is a worldwide study by the Organisation for Economic Co-operation and Development (OECD) in member and non-member nations of 15-year-old school pupils' performance in mathematics, science and reading.

3   www.oecd.org/edu/school/programmeforinternationalstudentassessmentpisa/33690591.pdf, accessed 28 July 2017.

4   See for example, www.independent.co.uk/news/world/europe/finland-schools-subjects-are-out-and-topics-are-in-as-country-reforms-its-education-system-10123911.html, accessed 28 July 2017.

5   *Smithsonian Magazine* (September 2011) www.smithsonianmag.com/innovation/why-are-finlands-schools-successful-49859555/, accessed 28 July 2017.

Looking for good education

"Begin at the beginning", the King said gravely, "and go on till you come to the end: then stop."

Lewis Carroll, *Alice in Wonderland*

1

What is a good education?

It is always timely to consider what is meant by good education. But as every generation of parents, schools and nations seeks to provide for the next in the best possible way, in a rapidly changing world this becomes increasingly challenging. Where should we begin?

Starting out

The first thing I remember learning at school was how to draw the number 8. To my surprise I discovered that an 8 did not consist of one circle sitting on top of another circle, as I had previously thought. With a sense of marvel that I can recall to this day, I learnt that an 8 is correctly constructed by forming the shape of a capital letter S (starting at the top) and then joining the two ends together, all in one movement without taking the pencil off the paper. I must have been three at the time.

That first lesson, learnt under the watchful eye of my indomitable nursery school teacher, reveals a great deal. First, I gained some crumbs of knowledge: there was a right way to construct an 8 – and I knew what it was.[1] Second, I had acquired some understanding: things are not always as they appear – the 8 did not consist in a circle sitting on a circle. Third, I had acquired a skill (of limited extent, true): I could actually construct the figure myself. Fourth, I was intrigued: if I had misunderstood the 8, what else might be out there for me to comprehend? There was a whole world of things that I did not know, that I did not begin to understand, that I could not do, waiting to be explored. It was exciting, and rather daunting.

I still believe that the acquisition and development of these four things – knowledge, understanding, skill and appreciation – form the foundation of every good lesson: I was served well, albeit within rather narrow parameters. Undoubtedly that was the beginning of my formal education, the culmination being my final university examinations. But what happened in the interim, and particularly in those years which preceded scrutiny through formal public examination? Was my education simply one lesson after another, day by day, week in week out, term on term, year after year? Does it matter what those lessons were and how they fitted together? Was everything necessary; were some things missed out? Was it particularly good, or could it have been better? And is that all there is to it anyway, just a great pile of lessons, or is there more, a bigger picture of what we mean by education, which enables us to determine how good it is?

Education, education, education

We all know that education matters. As Prime Minister Tony Blair famously announced in 2001, 'Our top priority was, is and always will be education, education, education',[2] with Arnold Schwarzenegger, speaking as Governor of California, putting it even more directly: 'Nothing is more important than education'.[3] Both were echoing Aristotle's reputed words, even if some of his poetic beauty had been lost *en route*: 'Education is the best provision for the journey to old age'.[4] Across continents, across centuries and across cultures, education has been recognised as the most powerful human force there is. Its energy is waiting to be harnessed.

Acknowledging the importance of education in words, apparently we are not shy to provide fiscal back-up for the rhetoric either: in 2017, Her Majesty's Treasury budgeted education spending at £87.2 billion in the United Kingdom,[5] well over 10 per cent of total public expenditure. And while UK figures show 6.7 per cent of GDP being spent on educational institutions (primary to tertiary), the figure is comparable elsewhere – 6.5 per cent in New Zealand, 6.4 per cent in Denmark and 6.2 per cent in the United States of America.[6] Not only do we commit to making this huge investment in education, but there rarely seems to be a dissenting voice suggesting that it should be any other way.

It is helpful to stop and consider for a moment why this is the case. We invest in education not because we really believe it to be an end in itself, although it sometimes seems to act as such. Rather, we invest in education because we believe it to be an enabler. Education provides opportunities otherwise impossible, for individuals, communities and whole societies. It is the transformational power of education in the lives of persons, families and nations that is so alluring. The UK government's consultative paper of 2016 reflected this, in stating that its 'overriding objective is to create an education system that will allow anyone in this country, no matter what their background or where they are from, to go as far as their talents will take them'.[7] Looking at the broader impact, Nelson Mandela put it this way: 'Education is the most powerful weapon you can use to change the world'.[8] Education is the primary determiner of the future of society: we believe it can make us better, and in our hearts we all know that matters.

Outcomes and input

A good education, then, is one with good outcomes. Those with an interest in education, from parents to politicians, can see the long-term effects of a good education by the life and career opportunities that it brings the individual, along with the opportunity to flourish as a member of various communities within a competitive world, and the means to make a positive contribution to society. Integral to living a fulfilling life we might include the ability to make good decisions and a certain appreciation of aesthetic beauty, and we may suppose that education will have some part to play in the acquisition of these too. In order to achieve these life-goals, examinations generally need to be successfully navigated, and since these are the most easily monitored educational measures, they receive great attention and close scrutiny.

Good educational outcomes are therefore seen to take two forms: the quantitative (measurable) outcomes such as examination results and career outcomes which can be collated into performance tables if desired, and the qualitative (harder to measure) outcomes including a sense of well-being, opportunity and positivity. The former typically act as prerequisites of the latter, at least to some extent, because quantitative outcomes are the most common gateway to further education, subsequent employment, prosperity and choice. In practice, they may also tend to be prioritised over the latter because school performance is typically assessed on the basis of quantitative data. About both there is relatively strong agreement, however: they are desirable outcomes of the educational process.

Good education exists within the United Kingdom across a whole range of types of schools, as indeed is also the case elsewhere globally. As a country, we can generate some excellent examination results. Individuals leave our schools to attend many of the world's most prestigious higher education institutes. Many of our pupils and students go into fulfilling and worthwhile jobs. We can build reliable aeroplanes, create beautiful gardens, invent new technologies and make progress in understanding diseases. By any global measure, we remain relatively prosperous. We also know that the best of our education is itself a global commodity, highly respected and in demand at home and abroad. Yet even apparently objective measures of educational outcomes vary. In 2014, Pearson's league table ranked the United Kingdom's education sixth best in the developed world and second best in Europe[9] while the 2016 PISA tests placed the UK a disappointing 27th in maths, 22nd in reading and 15th in science worldwide.[10]

Even if we could be certain where we sit in the rankings, what exactly is it that contributes to these desired outcomes, that makes the best of our education, really good? Because if we can answer that question, then we can hope to ensure even wider and wiser educational provision generally, and make better informed choices personally. True, we can observe and monitor ultimate outcomes, but it would be very helpful to find a complementary approach which attends to the all-important question of input. Such an approach would ensure the creation of conditions necessary for the cultivation of success, and enable us to recognise them when we see them.

Confidence in what we mean by good education at the point of input would help schools to decide how to respond to the demand that they start teaching computing, or reintroduce craft – should it be one or other, or both (or neither)?

It would help us to know whether we should be timetabling lessons on resilience, mindfulness, grit or happiness, whether we need to attend to learning styles, or teach using IT, or introduce philosophy – all variously and vigorously promoted by different interested parties. If as parents we knew what we meant by a good education, we would know whether it matters if our children know about Chaucer and Coleridge, or can name the capital of Canada, or understand the composition of calcium carbonate, any or none of which may have featured in our own education. And we would know how much manners matter, whether respect should be caught or taught and just how important competitive sport really is. All educational stakeholders, from policy-makers and providers, to practitioners and purchasers, need clarity of thought regarding what makes an education a good education.

Shoes, for example – and why we were right not to get a hat

We know what we mean by a good pair of shoes. Most of us will not buy a pair of shoes at a billionth of our educational price tag unless we are certain that the fit, feel and form are sufficiently good as to serve the desired function – be that fell-walking or high fashion. How much more, when it comes to educating the next generation, should we be certain that the education we provide has the necessary fit, feel and form to fulfil its function? We know what that function is: good outcomes – 'allowing anyone to go as far as their talents will take them'.[11] But what form should education take? What will it feel like in practice, and how can we be sure that it fits the context it is serving?

Over the last fifty years or so, rather than addressing these questions directly, in seeking to achieve better educational outcomes the characteristic response of government, at least within the United Kingdom, seems to have been a commitment to improvement through structural change. The UK government's 2016 consultative paper on education was entirely concerned with expanding the 'number of good school places available to all families'[12] rather than addressing any question as to what an education looks like within such schools. While educational systems and structures are necessary to provide, protect and promote good educational opportunities, our shoe analogy would suggest that an over-emphasis on structural arrangements within our educational system is rather like concentrating attention on the details of the shoe boxes and the way in which they are stacked rather than on the shoes inside them: the boxes may well be orderly, robust and even beautiful, but it is what is inside that matters.

I remember going with my mother on the train to London, aged eleven, armed with an inordinate sense of anticipation, to buy my navy-blue school blazer, regulation navy-blue skirt, salmon pink blouses (a colour combination I have not been keen on since), gabardine mac, blue gym skirt and various other sundry items. I still recall the adrenalin-pumping sense of excitement, the feeling of being so grown up, and the sense that soon I would belong to an institute that had its name indelibly and beautifully carved on imposing wooden gates, that seemed (from my perspective) to have been there forever.

We did not buy the school hat (a navy-blue, dome-shaped felt ensemble, with a narrow brim and salmon pink band), my mother guessing correctly that not only would I never wear it, but it would shortly become an obsolete part of the uniform. What we did not realise was that the entire uniform would soon become obsolete as my school changed within a couple of years from being a blazer-wearing girls' grammar school to a be-jeaned mixed sixth-form college.

The wind of change continues to blow relentlessly through the corridors of education as a good education is sought for successive generations. In my day, the wind blew us from selective to comprehensive education. Now it would seem to be blowing from state-controlled to independence.

It was the United Kingdom's Labour government of Tony Blair which, through The Learning and Skills Act of 2000,[13] introduced 'academies' to England (known at the time as 'city academies'). Within fifteen years, despite differently coloured political parties being in office, there were over 5,000 open, this including over 65 per cent of all secondary schools country-wide,[14] and in some areas, all secondary schools. Academies are defined by the government as 'publicly funded independent schools';[15] they do not have to follow the National Curriculum and can set their own term dates. Funded directly from central government, academies are run by trusts that employ the staff. Some academies have sponsors such as businesses, universities, other schools, faith groups or voluntary groups. These are explicitly responsible for improving the schools' performance – which is measured quantitatively. Many existing schools have now adopted academy status, but the term also includes 'free schools', which were founded as academies from the outset.

In 2015, Prime Minister David Cameron stated his vision that every state school in England should become an academy, not run by 'bureaucrats', as he put it, but instead with the head as 'captain of the ship'.[16] The same year, in a speech entitled *How Autonomy Raises Standards*, Nick Gibb MP, outlining the recent time-line of autonomy among state-funded schools in England, stated: 'The idea of school autonomy was of course reborn with the first city academies created by Lord Adonis in 2002, and by 2010 there were 203 academies in England. Since then, our government has been guided by the idea that school autonomy should no longer be a status enjoyed by a select group of schools, but an opportunity for all'.[17]

As this indicates, the change to academy status, and the resultant autonomy enjoyed by schools, is seen by these advocates as being the best way to equip schools for the challenges ahead, such as the introduction of what are seen as tough new minimum standards required by the government in reading, writing and maths. Other problems, which so-called 'academisation' is believed to address, range from funding cuts and teacher shortages to the problem of recruiting heads. According to their advocates, academies bring better support for teachers and the opportunity to focus on teaching and learning, rather than administration.

The public funding of independent schools is not confined to the United Kingdom. The right to create private schools in Germany is protected by law which cannot be revoked, even in a state of emergency, and all *Ersatzschulen* (literally 'substitute schools') receive substantial federal funding.[18] In the Netherlands, while all schools are publicly funded, over two-thirds are independent.[19] In Australia, where around 35 per cent of children attend independent schools (including the Catholic systemic schools) which receive state support, the Independent Schools Council of Australia states that 'Independent schools are a significant, large and growing component of the Australian schooling system'.[20] In the United States, a 'public charter school is a publicly funded school that is typically governed by a group or organization under a legislative contract (or charter) with the state or jurisdiction. The charter exempts the school from certain state or local rules and regulations'.[21] Since the first law allowing the establishment of charter schools was passed in Minnesota in 1991, 42 states in the US have followed suit, with 6.2 per cent of all American children being educated in charter schools by 2013, that figure rising to 43 per cent of all children in Washington, DC.[22]

While this pursuit, or at least endorsement, of independent schooling is seen globally, an additional trend to emerge over the past decade has been the increasing number of English fee-paying independent schools (identified from here onwards as 'fee-paying', 'private' or 'traditional' independent schools to distinguish them from the newer publicly funded independent schools or academies) opening branches abroad. In 2009, for example, Sherborne School Qatar opened at the invitation of Qatar's Supreme Education Council as part of its Outstanding Schools Initiative. Expertise and ideals travelled quickly from Dorset to Doha and seemingly made the journey well: despite there being over 1,000 pupils at the school, demand for places continues to outstrip supply. The first such school to open was Harrow in Thailand in 1998 (it also opened in Beijing in 2005 and Hong Kong in 2012), with many other traditional independent English schools having since opened branches in the Middle East, the Far East, Central Asia and North America. Overseas campuses totalled 59 in 2017, an increase from 46 the previous year.

And while numbers attending traditional independent English schools abroad are evidently rising, the same seems to be true at home. By 2017, the number of children being educated in member schools of the Independent Schools Council (ISC) was at its highest since records began in 1974, a rise partly due to an increase in international students and partly due to the 18 per cent of pupils over the age of sixteen attending such schools.[23] In at least one London borough over half the children are privately educated.[24] Surveys published by the ISC regularly suggest that over 50 per cent of parents would send their children to traditional independent schools if they could afford to.[25]

Allied to this expansion of the fee-paying sector at home and abroad, and the increase in the number of publicly funded independent schools within England, the last decade has seen an increasing expectation and assumption that the traditional independent schools should share expertise and facilities with state schools[26] or even, as it has been put, their 'DNA'. This final demand, first coined in 2007 by Lord Adonis,[27] the architect of the academies, seems to arise from an intense desire to improve parity of outcome, the highly disproportionate degree of success achieved at university level and beyond by pupils from fee-paying independent schools continuing to be widely reported as a matter of concern.[28] In a speech at the Brighton College Education Conference in 2013, he repeated the phrase saying, 'Everything about academies is in the DNA of the successful private school: independence, excellence, innovation, social mission'.[29] The message promulgated is clear enough: both at home and abroad, in the eyes of both politicians and parents, independent education is to be desired and pursued (whether paid for by the state or by parents).

Three voices to be listened to

Even among those who are generally supportive of the academies programme, however, there remains a range of opinions as to how far independence is to be valued as an end in itself, particularly since it is now widely acknowledged that the level of success enjoyed by academies has been varied. An increasing trend is to see the value of academies as lying in their formation into self-improving chains. One think-tank report states that academy status is not 'some sort of panacea which will automatically lead to improvements'.[30] The report continues by quoting a regional schools commissioner who endorses academisation on the grounds that each academy 'will be part of a wider family and the independence this brings creates opportunity for innovation and choice'. In practice, multi-academy chains prove to be financially beneficial, and at least one has now grown to include over fifty schools.[31] Although the political opposition in England continues to endorse the academies programme, in 2015 the Shadow Education Secretary signalled that she would 'reverse some of the school freedoms promoted by successive Labour and Conservative governments and give back more power to local councils and mayors',[32] the chief argument being the need for greater local oversight, particularly, perhaps, as local governing bodies are being replaced by more distant advisory committees in the larger trusts.

Others, supportive in general of the move to greater independence within state education, nevertheless argue that the case for state school improvement being achieved through closer imitation of private independent schools is misled. Jon Coles, chief executive of United Learning (a chain of academies that forges collaboration with a group of private independent schools) and a former director general for education standards at the Department of Education, argues that because educational contexts vary so much, 'an atmosphere of mutual respect'[33] is what is needed. In his view, free but judicious borrowing of ideas in a two-way flow is desirable, rather than one-way imitation. Schools are different and contexts are different; the best progress will be made through ensuring a 'rigorous, evidence-based appreciation of excellence' and developing networks and relationships through which excellent practice can be developed, he argues.

Of course there are others who are entirely opposed to this trend, desiring an alternative educational provision, which is more fully 'comprehensive, democratic and progressive'.[34] Some opponents see the international move towards independence as the unhelpful and inappropriate imposition of a business model on education.[35] The results, they argue, are an increased focus on competition and test-based accountability, a destruction of teacher professionalism and an increase in privatisation of education. These critical voices worry that education is being viewed as an opportunity to 'maximise human capital, abandoning [its] role of creating cultural good and social cohesion'; it is being developed as a 'commodity which can be traded globally'. This, they say, is evidenced in England in the growth of academies, standardised tests and league tables of results.

My sense is that each of the three voices in this debate is saying something profoundly important which needs to be heard and heeded.

The proponents of universal independence are seeking to improve opportunities for all by imitating what they see as the chief characteristic of the highly successful private independents – the very fact of their independence. They point to the disproportionate ability of pupils educated in these traditional independent schools to secure places at the most competitive universities and achieve success in everything from professional sport to careers in the City. Independence clearly works, they say, and its benefits must be shared by being made available to all, irrespective of a family's income or the wealth of a neighbourhood. Parity of opportunity and outcome must be provided: the success created by independence must be available to all.

Second, the proponents of sharing best practice emphasise that we must all learn from each other, but avoid making any generalisations because every context is different. They sound a cautious note against thinking that one system that operates successfully among a minority can possibly provide all the answers, or have a monopoly on educational wisdom.

Finally, the proponents of centralisation argue that it is essential that all pupils have equitable access to the same type and standard of education that should be supplied and protected by government: market-led independence must be eradicated because it leads to fragmentation and inequality of provision, and at worst to children being treated as mere statistics in league tables, a crude bottom-line in a market economy. Rather, every child must be given a fair and equal chance of a good education.

At first sight, it may seem that we have to make a choice between these three ideals. But I believe that we need to seek a way to ensure that the benefits of independence are not confined to a minority, while also ensuring that the needs of individual contexts can be met appropriately and yet that there is good educational provision for all. In order to reconcile these three ideals, I think we first need to ask and answer a different question: not how can a good education be delivered to all, but rather, how can a good education be defined for all? Or, to put it another way, what is a good education?

Extrapolating from experience and returning to shoes

I have already argued that a good education is one with good outcomes, both quantitative and qualitative. The successful outcomes of the traditional independent sector are a key reason why independence is advocated more widely. The government says that the UK's independent schools 'have a long history and the best have a worldwide reputation for excellence. They produce excellent exam results and well-rounded citizens who go on to excel in a variety of fields'.[36] To help identify and define a good education, although success is to be found elsewhere too of course, I want to start at this place of acknowledged success and find out what lies at its heart. Looking beyond outcomes, I also want to peel away the obvious layers of tradition and social privilege, and put aside outward idiosyncrasies and – at least initially – discrepant levels of resourcing, in order to identify and focus on the *educational* elements that contribute to this evident level of achievement.

In doing this, my first goal is to identify some essential underlying educational principles. Having identified them, my second step is to extract and isolate these principles from their traditional independent school context so that they stand alone. Having identified and then isolated them, my third step is to use these principles as the constituent parts to build a theoretical 'model' or idealised construct of good education, formulated without reference to context or specific practice, but containing the essential elements of a good education. This resultant model is described using the phrase 'four-dimensional education', reflecting and describing its most distinctive characteristics. Finally, the four-dimensional model can be utilised in different ways as appropriate in either the maintained sector or the independent, leaving room for freedom of interpretation according to local need, identified priorities, availability of resources and specific circumstance.

In undertaking this exercise, the principles underlying the strengths of traditional independence can be both identified and applied more widely; local contextual differences can be recognised and accommodated; and some uniformity of provision can be attempted through a dedicated commitment to articulated and shared goals. In other words, all three voices above can be heeded through the construction and application of the model.

The creation of the four-dimensional model is thus an attempt to identify the substance behind the packaging of good education. To return to our analogy of the shoe purchase, the proposed model provides a framework of a good education that could be used to ensure that education takes the 'form' needed to fulfil its function. But this is not a crude transference of DNA or simplistic imitative cloning of a school. Rather, once the essentials have been distilled, the model described can be interpreted generously and freely to allow for appropriate 'feel' as determined by circumstance, need and resources. It can be used as a point of reference when considering elements of whole-school policy and practice, the overall curriculum, specific subjects and even individual lessons. It is thus a highly practical framework for use on a day-to-day, term-by-term basis. In this way it helps to ensure a good educational 'fit' with the needs of the time in which we live and different specific contexts in which we may find ourselves.

This book and the four-dimensional model of education described in it arise from personal reflections of a life in education. Educated in the state sector during a period of flux (causing the previously mentioned loss of hat), being a parent at a church-run state school (where I also served as a governor) and an independent Methodist school, and being a teacher at an independent junior school, my reflections are based on a necessarily limited, but nevertheless eclectic, mix of personal experiences.

My starting point however, is to consider the final place that my own educational journey has taken me, that is, the quaintly privileged world of the English 'prep' school. Prep (or to give them their full name, 'preparatory') schools are those traditional private junior schools which in the past catered for boys aged between seven and thirteen. Morphed, to a greater or lesser extent, into their twenty-first century guise, these remain the hidden powerhouses of the traditional English independent school system.

Now it is more customary for them to educate both girls and boys, and often they educate them from the age of four (in what may be called 'pre-prep' years), or even younger (in 'nursery' years). Thus a child going right through the independent school system in England could spend nine or more years in a prep school; they will typically spend five years (and possibly as few as three) at their senior school. The prep school years then typically account for the great majority of a pupil's schooling, and unless more than three years are spent in university education, the majority of all their educational years put together.

These seldom-heard-of independent junior schools are the feeders for mighty Public Schools like Eton, Harrow and Winchester. What exactly occurs in these 'preparatory' schools, in which pupils are indeed 'prepared' for the major senior schools? These prep schools are key educational players in the system, but surprisingly little attention seems to be directed towards their work. They bear close scrutiny.

Prep schools provide a rich, interesting and sometimes surprising source from which we can attempt to extract the essence of the best of what traditional independence offers, particularly for children aged between seven and thirteen. The purpose in doing so is to distil this education into a more widely applicable framework of principles. This can then be interpreted, if so desired, into practices suitable for local need in different contexts, whether state or privately funded, or used as a point of reference for anyone with an interest in educational provision.

In doing this, there is absolutely no presumption that such schools are necessarily the best, are uniformly good, or do not themselves have lessons to learn from others. It is reassuring, and not surprising, to note that many schools outside the prep school system, both private and state, within the United Kingdom and further afield, hold similar principles dear and implement them effectively. Nor am I suggesting that a comparable exercise could not usefully be undertaken by closely examining any good, successful system of education. There is always plenty to be learnt from the experience of others with a different approach. I believe it would be a helpful addition to the debate for those who are familiar with other contexts and approaches to do just this, not least so as to identify the extent of overlap and understand any areas of difference. The contribution made by this book is merely a starting point, an offering of personal reflections on personal experiences and observation; it is of necessity informed and limited by them, but it tries to make something useful of them.

In doing so, this book does not advocate any new initiatives: there has been a plethora of those of late. It does not prescribe a systematic restructuring: that has been done many times. It does not even really suggest anything new: everything here has been tried and tested in many contexts. Rather it simply tries to distil the essence of what it is about a good education that makes it good, in order that we might be able to see it more clearly and implement it more consciously, more confidently, more consistently and more widely.

Notes

1 Ironically, it turns out this is not a universally acknowledged rule, as I thought at the time.
2 Labour Party Conference, 1996.
3 Introducing his coalition for education reform, 2005.
4 Diogenes Laertius's *Lives of Eminent Philosophers*, 5.1.
5 Public spending figures published at www.ukpublicspending.co.uk/year_spending_2017 UKbn_17bc1n_20#ukgs302, accessed 28 July 2017.
6 *Education at a Glance 2016: OECD Indicators* page 205 figures for 2013, at www.keepeek. com/Digital-Asset-Management/oecd/education/education-at-a-glance-2016_eag-2016-en#.WXreDNQrK9I#page3, accessed 28 July 2017.
7 https://consult.education.gov.uk/school-frameworks/schools-that-work-for-everyone/ supporting_documents/SCHOOLS%20THAT%20WORK%20FOR%20EVERYONE%20 %20FINAL.PDF, accessed 28 July 2017.
8 In a speech delivered at the launch of the *Mindset Network*, Johannesburg 2003.
9 http://thelearningcurve.pearson.com/index/index-ranking, accessed 28 July 2017.
10 www.bbc.co.uk/news/education-38157811, accessed 28 July 2017.
11 https://consult.education.gov.uk/school-frameworks/schools-that-work-for-everyone/ supporting_documents/SCHOOLS%20THAT%20WORK%20FOR%20EVERYONE%20 %20FINAL.PDF, accessed 28 July 2017.
12 *Ibid.*, p. 5.
13 www.legislation.gov.uk/ukpga/2000/21/contents, accessed 28 July 2017.
14 www.parliament.uk/documents/commons-committees/Education/report-education-academies-and-schools.pdf, page 5, accessed 28 July 2017.
15 For an overview of types of schools in the UK, see www.gov.uk/types-of-school/academies, accessed 28 July 2017.
16 www.bbc.co.uk/news/education-33944203, accessed 28 July 2017.
17 www.gov.uk/government/speeches/how-autonomy-raises-standards, accessed 28 July 2017.

18   www.ecnais.org/wp/wp-content/uploads/2012/10/Anke_Tastensen_private_schools_in_
        Germany.pdf, accessed 28 July 2017.

19   www.ncee.org/programs-affiliates/center-on-international-education-benchmarking/top-
        performing-countries/netherlands-overview/netherlands-system-and-school-organization/,
        accessed 28 July 2017.

20   http://isca.edu.au/about-independent-schools/, accessed 28 July 2017.

21   National Center for Education Statistics: https://nces.ed.gov/fastfacts/display.asp?id=30,
        accessed 28 July 2017.

22   *Ibid.*

23   www.isc.co.uk/research/, accessed 28 July 2017.

24   www.rbkc.gov.uk/pdf/pic_community_ch7achieving.pdf, accessed 28 July 2017.

25   www.isc.co.uk/media/2589/2012_attitudessurvey_isc.pdf, accessed 28 July 2017.

26   See, for example, Sally Morgan, former Ofsted chairwoman speaking at the Headmasters'
        and Headmistresses' Conference (HMC) annual meeting in Newport, South Wales,
        September 2014; or Charlie Rigby, founder of the Challenger Trust, a government-backed
        organisation providing learning outside the classroom writing in the *Times Educational
        Supplement*, October 2014.

27   Lord Adonis, Labour Education minister, speaking in 2007 at the Headmaster Headmasters'
        and Headmistresses' Conference (HMC) 2007.

28   See, for example, Sutton trust at www.suttontrust.com/research-category/professions/,
        accessed 28 July 2017.

29   www.brightoncollege.org.uk/college/college-news/item/3283, accessed 28 July 2017.

30   Reported in *The Guardian*, www.theguardian.com/education/2014/sep/23/state-schools-
        academies-report-thinktank-michael-gove, accessed 28 July 2017.

31   REAch2 Academy Trust has 51 primary schools, http://reach2.org/, accessed 28 July 2017.

32   Reported in *The Financial Times* on 18 September 2015, with similar views reported on
        26 September 2016 in *The Independent*.

33   www.independent.co.uk/news/education/schools/jon-coles-michael-goves-ambition-to-
        tear-down-berlin-wall-between-independent-and-state-schools-is-9124679.html, accessed
        28 July 2017.

34   See, for example, http://antiacademies.org.uk/, accessed 28 July 2017.

35   See, for example, the website of the (English) National Union of Teachers, which opposes
        the so-called Global Education Reform movement (GERM), www.teachers.org.uk/edu
        facts/germ, accessed 28 July 2017.

36   https://consult.education.gov.uk/school-frameworks/schools-that-work-for-everyone/
        supporting_documents/SCHOOLS%20THAT%20WORK%20FOR%20EVERYONE%20
        %20FINAL.PDF, page 12, accessed 28 July 2017.

2

In search of educational ethos

An examination of traditional independent education, particularly that offered by the prep schools, provides the opportunity to see beyond notional stereotypes. In doing so, an understanding can be gained of some key underlying characteristics, or what might be described as 'ethos'.

A brief excursion back in time

It was more than a uniform which was lost in the transition my secondary school underwent. Despite the obsolete name obstinately remaining carved into the gates, my school's identity was removed: the core, the ethos, the rationale, the heart was lost. Everything changed. It became a different school.

It had been founded in 1914, and survived for fifty-nine years before closing in 1973, two years after I joined, in a reorganisation of the borough's educational provision which saw it reopen the same year as a mixed sixth-form college. This new sixth-form college lasted just fourteen years, itself closing in 1987, and being replaced by a tertiary college when the borough's post-16 education was reorganised. The tertiary college closed twelve years later when the borough's tertiary provision was reorganised in 1999, the site becoming one campus of a larger further-education college. So there is still an educational establishment on the site of my school, but its website is silent on its old-school history. It is possible that some of the original buildings remain, but if they do they are not featured in any publicity. There is no sign of the wooden gates, with their carved lettering, or the Latin motto which we loved to translate as 'Don't frustrate the teachers' (*Nisi dominus frustra*: without the Lord you strive in vain)[1] or the carefully tended areas of lawn where we sat and ate sandwich lunches on sunny days. I cannot really claim that my school still exists.

The school where I currently teach was founded a generation before my own, in 1884. It was named after the daughter of the founding headmaster. I recently met an elderly gentleman who had been a boy at the school many years ago; he told me that as a very young boy, he had met a very old lady. This lady was the daughter after whom the school was named over 130 years ago. I was touched by the extraordinary sense of continuity spanning the generations and the centuries. The school moved to its current site a few years after its foundation and the three nineteenth-century houses that make up the original part of the school fabric are still used for teaching purposes. The school motto is the same as at the time of foundation, and elements of the school uniform remain unchanged.

It would be easy to draw the conclusion that independence provides unchanging stability elusive in state-controlled schools. However, the last fifty years have seen an extraordinary pace of change in all sectors of education. Typical of many prep schools, the school in which I teach has changed from being an all-boys' boarding school from age seven, to a mixed day school from age four. What would seem evident is that some establishments have been adept at adapting, retaining a strong sense of identity, while others have disassociated themselves from any earlier version. For unlike my own school, despite these significant changes, it remains the same school, its name unchanged.

This raises the question as to what it is that constitutes a school and, more importantly, and perhaps more elusively, the education that it provides. For the purposes of this study, more precisely, what lies at the heart of independent prep school education?

Similarities and differences

Consideration of independent, fee-paying schools may lead some to think of the so-called 'Public' schools, which are typically perceived as being old, well-endowed schools with outstanding facilities and small classes – and perhaps flamboyant, anachronistic uniforms. However, there are more than 2,500 private independent schools in England, just over 10 per cent of all schools. As independent schools, by nature they are different one from another. There is no uniformity among them: they are independent of each other as well as of the state. Some are day schools and some are boarding schools; some are single-sex and some are mixed; some are enormous and some are tiny; some are old and some are new; some are very well-off financially and others have extremely limited resources; some have no outdoor space, others are situated in vast country estates; some are highly successful, others very much less so. Operational contexts also vary considerably.

Around 1,200 of these independent schools belong to the Independent Schools Council (ISC), and between them they educate over half a million children. ISC schools, their heads and bursars, each belong to one of seven associations;[2] with strict membership criteria, the ISC claims that its schools rank 'among the best in the world'.[3] Among these seven associations is the Head-masters' and Headmistresses' Conference (HMC). The 279 schools within this organisation are known as Public Schools, and include some of the most historic and best-known names: Eton College, Rugby School, Charterhouse, and so on. Its junior school equivalent, the Independent Association of Prep Schools (IAPS), has around 650 schools. Membership of both these bodies is tightly regulated.

For Heads to qualify for full membership of the HMC, as well as their schools having to meet a specific academic standard, 'other qualitative criteria are borne in mind such as the school's ethos, philosophy and discipline; the range and balance of the curriculum; the quality and effectiveness of the classroom teaching; achievements in co-curricular activities; arrangements for pastoral care, boarding and careers guidance'.[4]

The IAPS also has strict membership criteria, which include 'teaching a broad curriculum, maintaining excellent standards of pastoral care and keeping staff members' professional development training up to date'. In a pithy summary, the Association states that 'although each of our schools is independent, and has its own ethos, they are all committed to delivering an excellent, well-rounded education to the pupils in their care'.[5] So rather than focusing on small class sizes and fancy blazers, these membership criteria, straightforwardly enough, suggest a rather more relevant and fruitful starting point in establishing what exactly the characteristics are of prep schools. The premium placed on pastoral care is paramount – that is, looking after and ensuring the personal well-being of each member of the school community. A second essential is the provision of a broad, or rounded, curriculum which enables excellence for all – this will include both the regular curriculum delivered through timetabled lessons and learning beyond it. While individual prep schools vary greatly, these two characteristics provide the linchpins for prep school education, and the requirement to keep staff training up to date serves to ensure that in both respects standards are kept as high as possible. Each characteristic bears close examination in the attempt to identify and isolate the principle elements of what prep school education looks like at its best.

Individual pastoral care

When I first started teaching, even some of the seven-year-olds boarded in the school. Following national trends, boarding ceased altogether at the school twenty or so years ago but many positive characteristics of boarding school culture remain.

Despite there no longer being boarding houses as such in this school, the structure of 'houses', each headed by a teacher, and supported by other teachers who are allocated to the house, remains. This structure breaks the larger community down into smaller, more manageable groups, the aim being to foster a sense of belonging, of shared purpose and a context in which every individual pupil is known. It is hard to describe the sense of kinship which exists in such a setting, pupils typically having a sense of rootedness which makes them feel – literally – at home. Having a house structure is typical of traditional prep schools, as well as their senior counterparts: as the five-hundred-year-old Giggleswick School in Yorkshire characteristically puts it, 'The House system is at the heart of Giggleswick life'.[6]

As well as creating a shared identity and common sense of purpose, through proactive care, houses can help ensure that individuals do not slip through the net or get overlooked. House staff, as well as children, often remain within the same house for many years. Children from the same family may be allocated to the same house, building up loyalties within families, even from one generation to the next. Houses enable the community to operate successfully by ensuring that every individual is a valued and known member, and has a personal sense of belonging.

The result of this is enhanced pastoral provision for each child. Just as in a family, different children's needs have to be met in different ways, so this is the case all the more in larger groups within schools. A pupil may need some special encouragement, such as a word of individual commendation or to be provided with an opportunity to exercise service; one individual may need a brief reminder quietly spoken to help them on their way in the right direction, while another may need a firmer, stronger and more persistent steer. This level of care can only be made available if pupils are known and looked after as individuals, if differences are recognised and welcomed.

For all children, school must be a place of safety and unstinting care; sadly, for some it will be the only such place. Safeguarding concerns, of course, must always be addressed immediately, but it is important to note that pastoral care is not only about stepping in when there is a problem (or trying to avoid problems), but rather it is about showing love, care and commitment to each pupil whether or not they have a problem to be resolved at that particular time.

Allied to this ongoing care of each pupil is the involved approach typically taken in the development of personal character. Charles ('Skipper') Lynam was headmaster of the Oxford Preparatory School (known as the Dragon School, now among the biggest prep schools in England) from 1886 to 1920. Regarded as being ahead of his time, his view was that boys and girls should enjoy school and be positive and independent. In an extraordinary speech in 1908, now rather wonderful to our ears, he addressed the Association of Preparatory Schools (to become the IAPS) on the subject of character development:

> We have failed, unless we have helped the boy to develop his mind and his capacities in his own way, unless we have given him full scope for all of the imagination and originality that is in him, unless we have let him know the causes of sin and suffering in the world, unless we have made his heart beat with the heart of mankind, unless we have made him scorn to do what others do because they do it, unless we have made him try to right wrong whenever he sees it, unless we have shown him the falseness of all the gods of society, gold, sham religion, conventionality . . .[7]

The proactive development of character and the development of a genuinely critical faculty continue to be seen as intrinsic aspects of pastoral care within prep schools, fostered as they regard themselves as being *in loco parentis*, hence assuming, alongside parents, responsibility for the development of the whole person. In the school in which I work, this is through encouraging every pupil to be 'their best self', and taking time and energy to explain to each exactly what that means.

Pastoral care of course is at its most visible when problems do occur, as they inevitably will at some time for every pupil. Problems may arise from difficult situations at home, from health or friendship issues, or from academic worries. Relationships of trust which have built up during the good times, the sense of the whole family being part of the school, and strong channels of communication already in place, together enable the best provision to be made in caring for the pupil when times are hard. Just as in any relationship, trust is built up gradually, day by day over a period of time, so that when concerns arise or calamity strikes, relationships that are already strong and in place enable the provision of appropriate support and care.

The emphasis on community life

While care for the individual is the starting point of pastoral care, it is not the end. The most overwhelming difference from my own school experience that struck me when I started as a prep school teacher was the palpable sense of community in the school. I believe this characteristic to be fostered particularly within traditional independent schools partly because of their roots in so many cases as boarding schools, perhaps even going back to their origins in early religious communities.

When working well, the upshot is that the school is a place where teachers, children and their families feel a sense of belonging, not just to the place but also to each other. Community is not just about the pupils, but is much wider, including support and teaching staff, and whole families – siblings, parents and grandparents – who are known and cared about in person. A genuine community is a place where individuals are made to feel that they are wanted, for themselves, for who they are. There is nothing impersonal about community: everyone is addressed by name. While undoubtedly this element of school life may be encountered in many different contexts, the first time that I encountered it was when I came into contact with the prep school system.

Community life, like individual pastoral care, may also be fostered through the house system, especially in a large school. Houses may play sport together, make music or put on plays together, raise money for charity together or eat together. In this sense they are a subset of the bigger community, bigger than a family but smaller than a school.

A community has the dual sense of being a group of people who live together (and therefore share both experiences and space) and a group of people who hold values in common (and therefore share ideals and goals). Houses facilitate both elements, each house within a school typically having a slightly different character from the others, often reflecting the interests of the teachers in charge.

In some prep schools, houses may be distinguished by variations on the school uniform, already touched on as being a quintessential element of the traditional

English school (both state and independent). It is worth stopping for a moment to ponder the impact of the classic school uniform. It seems to me that uniform promotes not uniformity but unity, the chief benefit being exactly that of reinforcing the concept of community. Every pupil in a school wearing uniform implies a sense of belonging (as reflected in my childish excitement about going to buy my uniform). If you wear the uniform, you belong – as is also the case with fashion among young people, where the chosen 'casual' dress code is every bit as important as school uniform in signifying a sense of belonging to a particular group. This, incidentally, is another benefit of school uniform, in signifying that everyone belongs equally to the whole group, not to a more or less fashionable subset within the whole.

Traditionally, an English school uniform (noun) is not merely uniform (adjective), but also smart. Prep schools typically sport coloured jackets known as blazers, sometimes in an alarming range of colours and stripes. (The original sense of the word blazer was indeed 'a thing that blazes or shines'.[8]) These are most usually accompanied by smart trousers (or skirts), and shirt-and-tie, sometimes including for the girls, with sensitive interpretation allowing for different faith traditions. Such uniforms also signify the school being a place of high standards, where it is not enough simply to look the same and hence belong, but it is important to look the same *well* and hence belong *well*. A smart uniform conveys a sense of aspiration to excellence – even if it is not always very practical. (Stripy blazers, it turns out, make perfectly adequate football goals at break time, even if afterwards the smartness has literally worn a little thinner.)

The phrase 'old school tie' of course has pejorative overtones. Interestingly, while the *Oxford English Dictionary* defines the phrase to mean first 'a necktie with a characteristic pattern worn by the former pupils of a particular school, especially a public school', and, second, states that it is 'used to refer to the group loyalty, social class, and traditional attitudes associated with people who attended public schools',[9] the *Cambridge Advanced Learners Dictionary* somewhat brutally defines the old school tie as 'the way in which people who have been to the same expensive private school help each other to find good jobs'.[10]

What is undisputed, however, is the way in which the community of a typical traditional independent school, especially an older, larger one, such as an IAPS or HMC school, extends beyond its current pupils back to its former pupils – in many cases even including those who have long since passed away. Community in this sense is marked and distinctive. For better or worse, this sense of belonging marks out pupils who have been to particular schools, at its best creating a lasting loyalty both to the school and to each other.

Perhaps the occasion each year when I see this community spirit at its most palpable is in the school annual remembrance service. Poppy wreaths are laid by the children in front of the war memorial boards on which are poignantly inscribed the names of those former boys (as it was then) of the school who lost their lives in the two world wars and in subsequent conflicts. As the entire school stands in silence, those of its number from years gone by are remembered as the current school community stands as one, the present body united with its former members in a moment of respect and deep solemnity.

The significance of heritage

For those schools which do retain connection with their past, there can be a significant richness and sense of strength. It is not just the traditions of school songs and in-house language, but a sense of continuity with our past, our dependency on it and its dependability, which I think are most valuable. The sense too that we are laying down a legacy for future generations, and have a duty and responsibility to build with care, means that heritage should breed a most healthy mix of confidence and humility.

To have a sense of heritage means to know something of our alumni and take inspiration from the lasting contributions that they made to society. According to their websites, neither my primary school nor my secondary school (if anything remains of it) would appear to consider that they belong to, or share a part in, a lasting community of members. In contrast, the school where I teach is pleased to note that it educated the inventor of the hovercraft, a well-known name in British economics, and more than one rugby international, to mention but some. Such alumni are regarded as inspirational role models who help current pupils to feel proud of their school and encouraged that they too might in some way contribute, coral-like, to the great reef of achievement and service built up over the years by previous generations. All schools have inspirational alumni, whether well known or not, but some choose to celebrate and value them, while others seem to prefer to live in the moment and go it alone.

One additional factor strikes me as being significant in the heritage of many traditional independents, especially the older ones, and that is the inherited sense of commitment to the service of others. The chapel of the independent senior school that our children attended is lined with individual memorials to former members, 'old boys', whose lives were lost in the world wars. When the Year 9 pupils go on a school trip to Flanders, they hold a memorial service at the battlefield site, recognising their solidarity with their counterparts of previous generations who gave their lives for the greater good. This attitude of service is reflected in the school's CCF (combined cadet force) in which all pupils are encouraged to take part, at least for a while, more general community service also being encouraged. The attitude of serving the community, whether through fundraising for charity, offering practical support or singing carols in a care home at Christmas, is also an important part of a school's heritage: you care because you are part of a caring community.

Perhaps none of this is surprising given the number of traditional independent schools whose origins lie in the provision of education for the least privileged members of society. In the city where I live, Free School Lane still indicates the origin of the oldest school in the city, now a highly competitive and sought-after fee-paying independent, but founded to provide free education for any boy in the city. Perhaps it is something of a harking back to this earlier ideal that lies behind the reintroduction of 'free schools', even if government now foots the bill rather than the generous private benefactors of the past.

Heritage may include names and mottos, buildings and spaces, uniform and jargon. But most importantly, heritage is about people and ethos, a continuity of commitment to values and to caring for the individual both within and without the school community. A sense of heritage implies recognition of there being something of additional significance in making a school, which lies beyond the immediate physical constituents of buildings and bodies.

Individual pastoral care, which sits in a context of community life and heritage, is the first of the distinctive characteristics of prep schools. The second is the provision of a broad and rounded curriculum which facilitates excellence for all.

The aspiration to excellence for all

As Lord Adonis identified, traditional independent schools unashamedly, openly, consciously aspire to excellence. Academic excellence is often cited as a reason for choosing a school, or is closely bound up in its view of itself. Cheltenham Ladies' College, founded in 1854 early on in the struggle to introduce education for girls in the second half of the nineteenth century, states its vision as being 'to embody excellence, independence, inspiration and empowerment in the education of women'.[11]

It would be hard to find an independent school which does not use the word excellence somewhere in its website. Statistics regarding university places gained, scholarships awarded, prizes and competitions won are frequently rolled out as evidence in support of such assertions.

What this means in practice is an ambitious attitude towards qualifications (particularly in A-Level exams, taken at the age of eighteen). Exceptional performance is regarded as a realistic aspiration, and indeed an essential require- ment, and hard work will be expected in order to achieve it. Although some independent schools are academically selective, not all are. Excellence for all in this context cannot therefore mean that all pupils will achieve in the same way, or at the highest academic level. Rather I understand it to mean that a standard of excellence in teaching and learning is expected for all pupils, and that success in one or more areas should be accessible and attainable for all, even if those areas are quite diverse. Fee-paying schools require considerable financial commit- ment (and usually sacrifice) on the part of parents, who will want to see a return on their investment. In practice, this means schools working hard to find the gifts or talents that each of their pupils has, in order that they all may be encouraged to reach as high and go as far and as well as they can in these areas, and so experience success for themselves in some or other sphere of activity.

At the prep school where I teach, strong provision is made across all areas of learning. Not only are English and maths lessons generously timetabled, but there is also a full programme teaching other academic subjects – the sciences, humanities, languages and technologies. In addition to this, significant time is dedicated for the arts (art, music and drama), sport and pastoral work.

It is of note that when the IAPS was founded over a hundred years ago, by a group of prep school headmasters, the purpose of their meeting was to discuss a matter of great educational importance to them: not the curriculum, examination syllabus or pupil attainment, however, but the evidently rather troubling matter of determining the appropriate weight of a cricket ball for boys under the age of thirteen to use in play. The prep school curriculum is not just a matter of academic learning, let alone hot-housing or exam preparation, but facilitates breadth of opportunity for every child.

Learning beyond the curriculum

Breadth of opportunity enables excellence to be achieved in any number of different areas. This is typically realised through the provision of both a broad curriculum as described above, and extensive co-curricular activities (learning opportunities that take place outside of normal lesson time, including after-school clubs, for example). The King's School Canterbury, the oldest school in England, quotes a former headmaster describing a King's education as 'resting on the simultaneous pursuit of academic and co-curricular excellence'.[12]

Perhaps for these reasons, our prep school day is relatively long, with an extensive co-curricular programme that may provide up to ten hours of additional learning time, in addition to thirty hours of timetabled lessons each week. Every full-time member of staff is required to lead an after-school activity, and many freely and willingly run several each week. The result is that for the five hundred or so pupils on roll, there are over eighty extra-curricular activities per week. These range from extending curriculum subjects such as sports, music and drama, to non-curriculum activities such as chess, online debating and craft. Teachers opt to share their particular enthusiasm or interest and children opt to share it with them.

The ways in which prep schools seek to ensure excellence for all vary, but where I currently work, in addition to optional after-school activities, all pupils participate in up to ten off-timetable days per year. Here opportunities may be taken to visit a mosque or a museum, to listen to an outside or in-house speaker or to visit a local university department or botanical garden. Five of these days fall within one week each summer term, where one or two year groups may go away on residential trips while others remain in school working on longer-term off-timetable projects.

Such co-curricular activities, whether immediately at the end of the school day or during the long summer holiday, enable a relaxation of standard classroom formality. Making cakes with pupils, joining in a sponsored walk or abseiling down cliffs enable those important relationships to develop in a different, fuller and richer way than is possible in a formal classroom situation, and so help to build the pastoral work of the school.

Imitation, the highest form of flattery?

The overall, and problematically disproportionate, success of the independent sector of education continues to be reported widely. A report published by Durham University in 2016[13] found that even taking differences of home background into account, differences in reading and maths scores were found in favour of independent schools at ages four, eight, ten and at age 16 (GCSEs). The report states that the difference 'suggests that attending an independent school is associated with the equivalent of two years of additional schooling by the age of 16'. The results would place England's private independent schools at the top of the PISA[14] league table in Europe and on a par with (or close to) Japan and Korea.

A Sutton Trust report,[15] also published in 2016, analysed what it described as the UK's top professions, and reported that 71 per cent of the top military officers, 74 per cent of top judges, 51 per cent of leading print journalists, 61 per cent of top doctors and 32 per cent of MPs were educated privately. Fee-paying schools also educated 67 per cent of British Oscar winners and 63 per cent of British Nobel Prize winners. As has already been noted, it is only about 7 per cent of pupils who attend these independent schools overall.

It is not surprising that over the last decade considerable debate has been generated concerning how valuable or desirable it is for state-funded schools to emulate the practices of the fee-paying independents. Should, or could, successful independent schools simply be replicated in the state-funded sector, or do contextual differences render this too simplistic to be effective? Such contextual factors vary enormously from school to school, but include prior attainment of pupils, family resources, parental support and expectations, school resources, selection procedures and so on, all of which can vary vastly within the range of independent schools, and all the more so beyond.

Perhaps because contextual differences make simple imitation less than straightforward, one repeated alternative proposal has been that private schools should sponsor academies. 'Every successful private school, and private school foundation, should sponsor an academy or academies, in place of existing underperforming comprehensives. They should do this alongside their existing fee-paying school or schools, turning themselves into "federations of private and state schools"' is how Lord Adonis said he would like to see it.[16] Sir Michael Wilshaw, chief inspector of Ofsted,[17] went further, saying that private schools 'should lose their tax subsidies and the reliefs they get from the Charity Commission unless they sponsor an academy'.[18]

Another suggestion, put forward as an amendment to the Charities Bill going through parliament in 2016, was that private schools should lose their charitable status unless they shared their facilities and resources with state schools. Images of vast acres of private school sports fields lying fallow for large parts of the school week, while a local school makes do with a few square metres of tarmac, readily suggest obvious opportunities for sharing and greater resultant fairness. While some sharing of resources does indeed occur, practicalities of transport, availability or timetabling can often limit the potential benefit of such opportunities, however. Although the proposed amendment was withdrawn, the government's 2016 consultation paper repeated the demand that independent schools' charitable status be used for the wider benefit, containing proposals to 'ensure that independent schools are doing more to benefit ordinary families'. The government is 'asking that independent schools spread their expertise through the state system'.[19]

In another bid to ensure retention of charitable status by helping the community more widely, some independent schools have sought, and been encouraged, to increase the number of bursaries that they are able to offer. Prohibitively high fees make private education look less like an act of charity than a privilege of the rich, unless provision is extended; the problem of course for the many private schools that do not enjoy large endowment is that the more fee income they direct towards bursaries, the higher the fees have to be raised to finance the scheme, making the schools themselves even more exclusive.

'Partnerships' between independent and state schools are the latest in a rapid volley of ideas suggested with the goal of fairer outcomes, and the sharing more fairly of the success that independents still disproportionately enjoy. Jon Coles of United Learning, an organisation he describes as the 'leading provider that has brought together independent and state education'[20] has identified a number of − somewhat caricatured − differences of approach between the two systems, which he sees as complementary: state schools are more interested in pedagogy (the method of teaching) and the independents in subjects (the content of teaching); state schools spend discretionary funds on interventions (providing additional assistance to individuals) and independents on co-curricular activity; state schools are more reliant on systems, the independents on ethos, for example.

Over a thousand independent schools (over 96 per cent of ISC schools) are involved in partnerships of one type or another with state schools.[21] A report published in 2017 indicated great variety in such independent–state school partnerships (ISSPs), ranging from low-impact informal projects to others with impact across all areas of school life, involving dedicated staff and shared governance. The report recommended that it would be valuable to ascertain the exact characteristics of such partnerships, and for more detailed research to be carried out to evaluate their impact.[22]

Such partnerships may indeed provide more nuanced understanding and sharing of expertise, a narrowing of these identified ideological gaps and extend educational opportunity as a result. Coles has called for mutual respect, suggesting that each can learn from the other; because the contexts of schools vary so vastly, however, dialogue can have hope of succeeding only if those contexts are taken into account, he argues.[23] Practical partnerships in teacher training, excellence visits where best practice is shared on a two-way street, and increased conferencing are all offered as means of facilitating this sharing.

In due time, it may become apparent that all the anxiety and perplexity over (what *The New Statesman* has described as) Education's Berlin Wall[24] – and how to break it down – may be serving as a distraction from thinking about what a good education actually is. In itself, a focus on managing discrepancy, reducing disparity or eradicating polarity will not necessarily mean that anyone is educated well, unless we know what it is to be well educated.

This book instead offers a new approach, providing an analysis of independent prep school education at its best, from which it creates a theoretical model or construct of good education. The model can be used as a frame of reference, as desired, in both private and state-funded settings.

The prep school ethos and its underlying principles

The outward summative practices of individual pastoral care, within a strong community, and striving towards excellence for all, within and beyond the curriculum, constitute dual characteristics towards which the best prep schools strive. With ethos defined by the *Oxford English Dictionary* as 'the characteristic spirit of a culture, era, or community as manifested in its attitudes and aspirations', this distinctive combination may be regarded as the central 'ethos' of these schools.

Identification of ethos provides a stepping-stone towards the abstraction that we are seeking. Articulating it in this way is the first step towards the goal of being able to see beyond the outward practices of a group of schools operating in specific (and generally privileged) contexts, and move towards identifying some underlying principles that might be more widely applicable. The next question to consider is the nature of those essential, inherent, principles which lie beneath the surface of such an ethos, and on which it depends.

The importance given to caring for every single pupil through both personal pastoral care and wide curricular provision puts the individual child centre-stage in the prep school ethos. Prep schools are typically child-centric. Centuries, if not millennia, of received wisdom, mirrored in our instincts and confirmed by our observations, tell us that every child is a complex being, a multifaceted indivisible mix of heart, mind, body and spirit, with intertwined moral, intellectual, emotional, physical, spiritual and social needs. This holistic view of the child brings implications for education that have been recognised at many points through the centuries. Theodore Roosevelt is quoted as saying, 'To educate a man in mind and not in morals is to educate a menace to society',[25] and the same ideas are reflected in the wording of the English National Curriculum (1988). This states at the outset that the curriculum should promote 'the spiritual, moral, cultural, mental and physical development of pupils at the school and of society'.[26] It is also reflected in the emphasis already noted on the development of character within prep school pastoral care, and on the important place of arts and sport alongside the academic.

The prep school ethos endorses and rests on this holistic principle. A child does not come to school simply as a means of transport for his or her brain, to bring it into the learning environment where it will be exercised in isolation. The prep school ethos recognises and reflects the importance of caring for and supporting the development of the whole child, as an individual, within a community.

This holistic principle takes us to the heart of the matter, but raises a question: while caring for the development of the whole child is necessary and right if a good education is ultimately to be achieved, how should this best be done? It was C.S. Lewis who said that 'Education without values, as useful as it is, seems rather to make man a more clever devil'.[27] To construct an effective model of good education, specific values concerning the child at the heart of the matter must be identified and articulated as the starting point.

Notes

1   A Cambridgeshire Village College replaced this same motto in 2016, with 'Inspiring Minds', provoking a response from Professor Mary Beard: www.the-tls.co.uk/nisi-dominus-frustra-why-ditch-a-motto/, accessed 28 July 2017.

2   The seven associations are: Girls' Schools Association (GSA), HMC (Headmasters' and Headmistresses' Conference, IAPS (Independent Association of Prep Schools), ISA (Independent Schools Associations), The Society of Heads, AGBIS (Association of Governing Bodies of Independent Schools), and ISBA (Independent Schools' Bursars Associations).

3   www.isc.co.uk/about-us/associations/, accessed 28 July 2017.

4   www.hmc.org.uk/about-hmc/membership/full-membership/, accessed 28 July 2017.

5   https://iaps.uk/about, accessed 28 July 2017.

6   www.giggleswick.org.uk/houses, accessed 28 July 2017.

7   From the text of the speech, held in the archives of the IAPS.

8   *Oxford English Dictionary*.

9   www.oxforddictionaries.com/definition/english/old-school-tie, accessed 28 July 2017.

10 http://dictionary.cambridge.org/dictionary/english/the-old-school-tie, accessed 28 July 2017.

11 www.cheltladiescollege.org/about-clc/why-clc/vision-mission-and-values/, accessed 28 July 2017.

12 www.kings-school.co.uk/about/aims-ethos/, accessed 28 July 2017.

13 See for example, Durham University's research comparing academic performance in state and independent schools: www.isc.co.uk/media/3140/16_02_26-cem-durham-university-academic-value-added-research.pdf, accessed 28 July 2017.

14 The Organisation for Economic Co-operation and Development (OECD) first ran its Programme for International Student Assessment (PISA) test in 2000, and it is repeated every three years with fifteen-year-olds.

15 www.suttontrust.com/research-paper/leading-people-2016/, accessed 28 July 2017.

16 Lord Adonis speaking at the 15th Specialist Schools and Academies Trust Annual Lecture, 2011: http://independenthead.blogspot.co.uk/2011/07/lord-adonis-calls-for-new-settlement.html, accessed 28 July 2017.

17 Ofsted is the Office for Standards in Education, Children's Services and Skills.

18 Sir Michael Wilshaw speaking at a summit hosted by the Sutton Trust in 2016: http://schoolsweek.co.uk/wilshaw-remove-independent-schools-tax-breaks-if-they-dont-sponsor-academies/, accessed 28 July 2017.

19 https://consult.education.gov.uk/school-frameworks/schools-that-work-for-everyone/supporting_documents/SCHOOLS%20THAT%20WORK%20FOR%20EVERYONE%20%20FINAL.PDF, page 12, accessed 28 July 2017.

20 www.independent.co.uk/news/education/schools/one-chief-executive-two-different-schools-of-thought-8205974.html, accessed 28 July 2017.

21 https://consult.education.gov.uk/school-frameworks/schools-that-work-for-everyone/supporting_documents/SCHOOLS%20THAT%20WORK%20FOR%20EVERYONE%20%20FINAL.PDF page 13, accessed 28 July 2017.

22 *Independent-State School Partnerships: An initial review of evidence and current practices*, http://etoncollege.com/userfiles/files/Lucas.pdf, accessed 28 July 2017.

23 www.independent.co.uk/news/education/schools/jon-coles-michael-goves-ambition-to-tear-down-berlin-wall-between-independent-and-state-schools-is-9124679.html, accessed 28 July 2017.

24 www.newstatesman.com/2014/01/education-private-schools-berlin-wall, accessed 28 July 2017.

25 August Kerber, *Quotable Quotes on Education* (Detroit, MI: Wayne State University Press 1968), 138.

26 www.legislation.gov.uk/ukpga/1988/40/pdfs/ukpga_19880040_en.pdf, accessed 28 July 2017.

27 The Abolition of Man, 1943.

2

Creating a model of good education

I like work: it fascinates me. I can sit and look at it for hours.

Jerome K. Jerome, *Three Men in a Boat*

3

Foundational values

The essential heart

Education is complicated. Simplifying complex concepts without distorting or caricaturing truth is challenging. But in creating a model of good education that has wide applicability, clarity of thought and economy of expression are important goals. Foundational values concerning the individual child are the starting point for building this model. Establishing as clearly and succinctly as possible a sense of the child at the heart of the matter enables the heart of the model to be created.

A trip to Wells, Somerset

Back in the 1990s, having recently been elected as a parent-governor of my children's Church of England Primary School, I recall on one occasion visiting the tiny medieval city of Wells, which lies deep in the Somerset countryside. The smallest city in England, with just 10,000 inhabitants, and sitting snugly on the southern side of the Mendip hills, Wells is home to a majestic thirteenth-century cathedral – complete with its moated Bishop's Palace – and hence to the Diocesan Board of Education. All new school governors had been invited for a day's training. It turns out that while Wells may be small in stature, it is great in wisdom. The training I received that day has remained with me since, and has influenced my thinking profoundly.

A church school, we were told, should resemble a stick of seaside rock: wherever you break it, the message is the same. Whether in a geography lesson or on the games pitch, in assembly or the art room, in the dining hall or the drama studio, the core values of the school should not only be accepted in principle but should also be evident in practice. Such values are not simply, or even primarily, about what is taught in Religious Studies lessons or celebrated in assembly, but profoundly impact the way we teach every lesson, interact with our peers, speak to other members of the community, behave in general and think about our policies, procedures and practices. They form the bedrock of the ethos which will ultimately determine the topography of our educational provision.

Introducing foundational values

We all have core or 'foundational' values: they are essential and inescapable. Every individual, institution, organisation or business has some sort of basis on which its structures and practices depend, which informs decisions and judgements and which determines goals and outcomes. In some instances these values may be consciously articulated and closely defined, such as those of the largest primary academy trust, REAch2, which describes its 'solid, unshakeable foundation, defined by exceptional teaching experiences and shared Touchstone values of learning, leadership, enjoyment, inclusion, inspiration, responsibility and integrity'.[1] Elsewhere, foundational values may be unconsciously assumed or simply regarded as obvious; they may be rigidly fixed or constantly developing, but they will be there, behind the scenes, in one form or another.

Within education, such underlying values determine principles, priorities and outcomes and they also act as a plumb-line against which ideas are judged, whether consciously or not, and so determine what is promoted and achieved. In short, it is foundational values that determine and create educational ethos. It is perhaps fair to say that the more consciously held and clearly articulated these values are, the more consistently they are likely to be made manifest. The schools of the Diocese of Bath and Wells were encouraged to be explicit in their advocacy of their values, and hence its schools would be expected to have a strongly held ethos clearly evident in every context.

As has been noted, much current educational debate tends to focus on systems and structures, which may be determined variously by political doctrine, educational theory, resource availability or even historical accident. Of course, having good systems and structures is important, but they do not make a satisfactory starting point for describing the essential elements of a good education. I believe that the fundamental place to begin is with a clear articulation of the foundational values associated with the individual girl or boy at the heart of the matter.

A clear view of who a child is provides a firm and explicit foundation on which to construct an educational model. In other words, adopting this approach would be to think first of all not about how to cater for the five hundred children in my school (let alone the eight million across the country, or two billion cross the globe for that matter) but about just one. The model of education described in this book places the individual child at its very heart.

Faith and foundations

As far as education is concerned there is no value more fundamental than the view of the child. A moment's thought reveals that contrary to what might be assumed, however, there is no absolute or objective foundational value concerning the child. Different societies, cultures, ages – and individuals within them – have regarded children very differently. Definitions of childhood, adolescence and adulthood vary with time and place, as do what are considered to be acceptable practices. Attitudes towards gender, child labour, child marriages or the militarisation of children, for example, still vary across the world, and within a society, because of fundamentally different general world-views and, more specifically, views of the child.

What then should be our attitude towards the child now in the early decades of the twenty-first century, and how is that attitude to be determined? Is a child to be regarded primarily as a present statistic (playing their part by making up a specified proportion of the population who do or do not achieve 'five good GCSEs') or as a future employee ('We need more Engineers')? Is the child a piece of clay to be moulded into a predetermined shape in the hands of the educator, or an empty receptacle waiting to be filled with knowledge, or part of a country's 'natural resource', a source of future wealth and prosperity, or an agent of change? Or is the child to be regarded in yet some other way?

The view of the child held is likely to be the result of another larger set of beliefs or ideas, some sort of *Weltanschauung* or overarching world-view. These beliefs may be of a religious or political nature, or they may be the result of community consensus; they may be carefully thought through and articulated or not, but either way in the broadest sense of the word they are effectively a matter of 'faith' – that is, of personal or collective conviction, creed or confidence, rather than of objective 'givens' or scientific proof. The IHEU (International Humanist and Ethical Union), for example, states that 'Humanism . . . affirms that human beings have the right and responsibility to give meaning and shape to their own lives',[2] a statement with which most people would probably agree, but which cannot be objectively or scientifically proven; rather it is a matter of collective conviction.

Any view of the child is, of necessity, a matter of conviction rather than proof. In this sense all schools, at least as far as their view of the child is concerned, have a 'faith' basis which will impact the life and learning of the school, and the education it provides. For what are known as faith schools (that is, schools which have a religious-faith foundation), foundational values are provided, or at least informed, by the particular religion, and are generally explicit as a result. The Swaminarayan School in London quotes on its website The Prince of Wales' description of their community as being 'clearly inspired by the values of Hinduism, the children of which are also brought up and educated within the framework of such values'.[3] The Association of Muslims Schools, AMS UK, states one of its aims as being to 'encourage and promote education and schooling for Muslim children that is rooted in Islamic principles and values . . .'.[4]

Around one-third of all state schools in England are faith schools, approximately 96 per cent of which are Christian, including our stick-of-rock Church of England primary school in Bath. The sentiments expressed by the Oxford Academy, on its website, are therefore echoed in state schools all over the country: 'Our Inclusive Christian values underpin all we do'.[5]

The origins of the IAPS lie in the early 1890s, with a significant number of prep schools being established in the closing decades of the nineteenth century. As might be expected of England at that time, Christian values were widely presumed and explicitly held in the early IAPS schools, many of which had headmasters who were ordained ministers in the Church of England.

Today, over 200 traditional English independent schools still declare themselves to be specifically Church of England,[6] while many others also cite a Christian foundation or ethos. Harrow School, for example, one of the country's oldest and best known independent senior schools, states that 'our four Values [courage, honour, humility and fellowship] link closely to our Christian foundation and the principles of "Godliness and good learning" established by our founder, John Lyon'.[7] Barnard Castle's entry in the Good Schools Guide states, 'The School is a Christian foundation and the chapel stands at the heart of the School in more than just a geographical sense'.[8] The school our children attended as teenagers has a Methodist foundation; its website states that 'The School's Christian ethos lies at the heart of our education philosophy'.[9]

In order to explain such a widespread influence, the significant role of Christianity in English education over the centuries bears a brief examination, before considering the specific view of the child that it suggests, and which thus informs its educational principles.

The influence of Christian values in English education

Christianity had arrived in England in the first century, and the oldest school in England is believed to be King's School Canterbury. It was probably founded by St Augustine around the year 597 AD and was associated with the cathedral as part of its monastic establishment.

Christianity steadily gained acceptance and influence until the time of the Norman Conquest, which firmly cemented the power of the church in England. Grammar schools, such as King's, initially established to teach Latin to English priests, in the following centuries also gradually began to teach the 'liberal arts' including rhetoric, dialectic, music and arithmetic.

In the centuries that followed, the influence of the church contributed extensively to the country's legal, social and cultural development, including education. Further schools began to open, largely for boys from families who paid fees, and which combined grammar school education with the social training of the chivalric system. Such schools, including Winchester College, founded in 1382 by William of Wykeham, Bishop of Winchester and Chancellor to Edward III and Richard II, and Eton College, founded by Henry VI in 1440, developed into the 'Public' (so-called, as opposed to local) schools of today.

It is estimated that by the start of Henry VIII's reign in 1509 there may have been as many as 400 schools in England, and while some of these were closed under his leadership, others were opened, including twelve new re-founded grammar schools as part of his 'new foundation' cathedrals.

Debate about the nature and purpose of education was widespread through the seventeenth century, with the Czech educator, John Amos Comenius, commissioned by the House of Commons to set up an agency for the promotion of learning, and John Locke publishing 'Some Thoughts concerning Education' in 1693, which stressed the importance of broad intellectual training as well as moral development. By this time the grammar schools amounted to a handful of 'leading' schools, serving the aristocracy, mostly boarding and maintaining a traditional classical curriculum; further endowed schools, serving a more local population, and also offering classical education; and a number of schools in larger cities serving families of merchants and tradesmen which offered a developing curriculum including mathematics and the natural sciences. There are also believed to have been around 460 charity schools by the end of the seventeenth century.[10]

For the vast majority of children, however, access even to elementary education was entirely haphazard both in availability and quality, until the Industrial Revolution gathered pace in the final decades of the eighteenth century. Education, like so many other areas of life, was due to experience a period of rapid and far-reaching change.

Robert Raikes, whose monument stands in London's Victoria Embankment Gardens, is celebrated as the pioneer of Sunday Schools. Established in the early 1780s, initially for boys who worked in factories six days a week, these schools provided four or five hours of primary instruction free of charge every Sunday. By 1785, a quarter of a million children (and many additional adults) were attending Sunday Schools in England, with over 5,000 such schools in Manchester alone. Speaking of the scheme, which was Christian and cross-denominational, philosopher and economist Adam Smith said: 'No plan has promised to effect a change of manners with equal ease and simplicity since the days of the Apostles'.[11] By 1831, Sunday Schools were teaching well over a million children.

Raikes' work is seen as the precursor of state education in England, and in 1811, the year in which he died, The National Society for Promoting Religious Education was established to provide schools for poor children. The aim was to found a church school in every parish to provide elementary education for every child in the country. An enormous undertaking, by 1851, still twenty years before the state took any responsibility for education, there were 12,000 National Schools in England and Wales.

The National School legacy means that in England around a million children are still educated in some 4,700 Church of England schools, an estimated fifteen million of the population have received at least some of their education in a church school, and the Cathedrals Group of universities provide initial teacher training for 20 per cent of all primary school teachers in the country.[12]

Alongside what we may think of as traditional church schools with long-established roots, with more than 750 academies, the Church is also the biggest single sponsor of academies in England. A quarter of all primary schools and over 200 secondary schools in England are Church of England schools with explicitly Christian foundational values,[13] making the church the largest single provider of education in England. With over 2,000 schools, and over 800,000 pupils, the Roman Catholic Church is the largest provider of secondary education and the second largest provider of primary education in England.[14]

It is important to note that Church of England schools are self-consciously inclusive, 'not "faith schools" for Christians but Christian schools for all and, as such, are committed to serving the needs of the local community'.[15] Their vision is articulated as being 'deeply Christian, serving the common good',[16] or as Professor David Ford, chair of the group who developed the vision has paraphrased it, 'deeply Christian, healthily plural'. Church of England schools exist to work for the common good of their local communities, recognising their diversity. Similarly, the Roman Catholic Church seeks to bring widespread benefit, placing 'a duty on Catholic schools to care for the poor and educate those who are socially, academically, physically or emotionally disadvantaged'.[17] This is reflected through the pupil populations in Catholic schools, which are over-represented in the most deprived areas at both primary and secondary level. Like Church of England schools, Roman Catholic schools welcome children from a range of faith backgrounds, and have a 'track record of supporting minority religions as they integrate into the local community'.[18] Reports suggest that members of other faith groups also value the respect also afforded to faith within Church of England schools.[19] Private independent schools, including those with a Christian ethos or foundation, also typically welcome all children irrespective of their faith background.

It is the Christian values and principles (including the view of the child) on which these schools are based then, which characterises schools with Christian foundations, rather than any exclusive serving of Christian communities. Such schools typically hold appeal for many non-professing parents as well as those who would describe themselves as Christian or of other faiths. In 2011, around 60 per cent of the population of England and Wales identified themselves as Christian in the census, and a 2009 educational poll revealed that '60 per cent said they thought children benefited from a faith-based education, while 69 per cent of those with school-age children supported a religious ethos at school'.[20]

Not surprisingly, given the Christian heritage of the country, some state schools which are not faith schools as such, nevertheless hold explicitly Christian values, one such primary school stating, for example: 'The Christian Principles that underpin our school provide values and moral direction for children to develop the skills they need to become "well rounded" citizens'.[21]

For those schools that do not hold Christian values explicitly, foundational values may still very often be derived from a deeply rooted ethical code arising at least in part from the country's Christian heritage. Indeed, some schools that are entirely secular appear to have very similar foundational values to Christian schools, arising from a similar ethic, although, of course, not all will necessarily.

Much publicity has been given to the duty of all British schools 'to actively promote the fundamental British values of democracy, the rule of law, individual liberty and mutual respect and tolerance of those with different faiths and beliefs'.[22] It is not difficult to see how these British values can form a subset of broader whole-school values. Their origins, however, are political rather than educational, and they have been articulated in order to address a perceived need at a particular time; therefore, while valuable for their own purposes, they do not form a complete set of foundational values on which an entire educational ethos may be established, although we would expect them to fit comfortably within, or arise from, such a set of values. In particular, they do not articulate a view of the child from which can be built a comprehensive educational philosophy.

The purpose of this book is to see how foundational values concerning the child can be used as the starting point for forming a generalised and widely applicable educational model. Despite the increasing secularisation of society, the cultural and historic influence of Christianity in England means that Christian foundational values still underpin more of our schools than any other single, articulated set of values. They are explicitly held by many schools, tacitly held in others and are likely to be relatively widely accepted and acceptable in further English schools due to the country's heritage and history. It is therefore justifiable to use them as a starting point.

Importantly, however, although the model has its origin in the historical Christian world-view of traditional prep school education and rests on that rationale – as most English education still generally does – the model can be used with or without reference to its Christian origins. Similarly, it can be used with or without reference to its prep school origins. Going back to 'first principles' in this way simply offers a transparent account of the foundation on which this model of good education is built, making explicit its rationale.

For these reasons, the model itself, once constructed, can cut free of its origins and be equally relevant in an entirely secular context or within a Christian, or other faith, framework. It can equally be referenced in an independent or state school context, both within the UK and further afield.

The Christian 'story' and its implications for the view of the child

Before jumping to what we may think of as Christian values, it is worth briefly considering the Christian 'story' that gives rise to them, and without which they could appear to be somewhat arbitrary. In very simple terms, the Christian narrative starts with a Universe created by an all-powerful and all-loving God. People were created 'in the image of God'[23] with the capability of goodness, creativity, love and responsibility. However, the human condition is also deeply flawed, both humanity and the world having become subject to negative and destructive forces which alienate them from the perfect God and damage these capabilities. The central tenet of the Christian faith is that in an act of love for the world, God sent his Son, Jesus Christ, to live as a man on earth and to die in order that forgiveness and reconciliation with God and one another might be made possible. Jesus was raised to life and returned to heaven, and through his Spirit God remains at work in the world and in individuals bringing about his good purposes of restoration, love, mercy and justice, which will one day come to completion.

Even this very basic and limited description of the Christian story demonstrates the key points held within a Christian world-view which give rise to foundational values. First, and generally, there is something bigger than ourselves as a result of which life has meaning; supremely governed by love, we inhabit a moral world in which we are called to discern right and wrong, in which actions have consequences, in which people matter individually, as does community and in which there is an example to follow. Such foundational values are widely (but not universally) held and accepted within, but also beyond, Christian education by people of no religious faith, or other faiths, as well as those of Christian faith.

These moral values are endorsed within the UK government's guidelines for schools on 'Improving the spiritual, moral, social and cultural (SMSC) development of pupils',[24] which state the importance of enabling all pupils to 'distinguish right from wrong' and 'accept responsibility for their behaviour'. This essential starting point, that we live in an inherently moral world in which people have both freedom and responsibility, validates a values-based approach to education.

Second, this world-view has implications for the way in which people are regarded, and specifically, the child is perceived. The four-dimensional model presented in this book starts with the identification of four distinct attributes of every child (indeed of every person); and these four attributes constitute the foundational values which form the heart of this educational model.

Four foundational values at the centre of four-dimensional education

Four attributes of the child are derived from the Christian world-view described above, and these are regarded as the foundational values on which the model is built. They concern, in turn, the nature of the *worth*, *identity*, *interaction* and *development* of the child. These four are central and foundational, and from them the rest of the model stems.

Using a diagrammatic representation, the child at the centre of the four-dimensional model is represented by a square, divided into four sections, each of which represents a foundational value concerning every individual child (Figure 3.1).

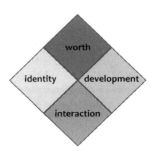

FIGURE 3.1 Four foundational values concerning the child

Each of these four values is described and explained briefly, and some educational implications outlined.

Value one: worth – inherently precious

First, imbued with a spark of the divine, every child is seen as having intrinsic individual worth. This immeasurable, incalculable, inherent worth is represented here in the phrase 'inherently precious' (Figure 3.2) and it applies equally to every child whether girl or boy, rich or poor, weak or strong.

In the Christian world-view this perception of individual worth arises from a belief in the creation by God of people 'in his image'. However, the conviction that all human life is precious is deeply embedded in Western society's cultural values and beyond. Comenius, writing around 1630, described children as being 'dearer and more precious . . . than gold and silver, than pearls and gems'.[25] It would surely be regarded as the norm to assume this across all our schools in England, whatever their faith position, even if it is not articulated in precisely these words. The individual worth of every single child is inestimable, beyond measure; not surprisingly, this profoundly impacts how children should be educated.

This is not the same as a 'child-centred' philosophy of education, if such is defined as seeing the child's needs and wishes as paramount,[26] but rather it means that the inherent worth and significance of each child determine the way in which they should be regarded.

While many implications of such ideas have become very deep-seated in our thinking and enshrined in our laws, this is perhaps all the greater reason to linger on what might otherwise so easily and perilously be overlooked. Re-examining and re-articulating these foundations helps ensure that we build well on them.

First, if every child is inherently precious, a good education will cherish the individual and aspire to the very best for each one. This view of the child means that people matter more than anything else, and specifically, for educators, children matter more than anything else. If children matter they need to be both valued and protected. They are not there as a means to an end, but are of worth in their own right. Every individual child matters in his or her own right, not

FIGURE 3.2 The inherent worth of each child

just as a member of a cohort or as a statistical contribution. The individual child matters more than examination results, than league tables, than reputations, than economic contributions. No one should be neglected, misused or overlooked. Each one matters. Each one counts.

Value two: identity – uniquely gifted

Second, in the Christian world-view, every child is seen as unique with his or her own distinctive identity, individually known by God, including an individual combination of strengths, gifts and creativity (Figure 3.3). This arises from the central idea of being created as creative beings, with a positive purpose to find and fulfil.

We probably all remember learning as children that every snowflake is unique, that every leaf on every tree has its own identity; so too, we were told, no two sets of fingerprints are the same – every person is a one-off, an irreplaceable individual, an inimitable being. Today's knowledge of genetics and the unique structure of each individual's DNA provide a scientific basis for this foundational value of the uniqueness of each child. Interpreting this as unique gifting rather than simply regarding everyone as being different carries significant positive implications for education.

First, every single child has a *unique* identity, as personal to them as those fingerprints. Alongside personality, individuality, idiosyncrasies and cultural and genetic factors, a child's identity includes their individual learning profile. This will include a pattern within and across subject areas of things that they find easier or harder, the varying pace with which concepts are grasped or skills learnt, and different levels of enjoyment and interest for different topics and subjects. It will include instinctively different approaches and perspectives, and different pathways of learning, creating a rich variety of learning journey, not fixed or predictable. Far from being predetermined or assumed, in all areas there is every opportunity for individual growth, maturation and change. All of this is enriching for the community, and is liberating for pupils, especially when it is remembered that as well as being tremendously diverse, they are all of equal worth. Not only is this normal and to be expected, it is positively to be encouraged and celebrated.

Second, within this diversity, a key Christian perspective is that every pupil is *gifted*. With a unique identity comprising all that we have been given to work

FIGURE 3.3 The unique identity of each child

with, each has a distinctive combination of strengths, aptitudes, interests and pattern of creativity that they and they alone can develop in order to flourish as an individual, but also to contribute to the community for the greater good of society. That is their two-fold gift – in that it is a gift that they have received and also a gift that they can contribute or share with others.

While the drive to identify a fixed proportion of pupils as 'gifted and talented' was a well-intended attempt to ensure that children's strengths were recognised and catered for, it is not a helpful approach to supporting the principle of unique gifting for all, if it leaves the vast majority under the impression that they are not among the gifted. This is completely contrary to a world-view which sees everyone as having a unique contribution to make.

Again, however, the concept of unique gifting is only of value when it is held alongside the first principle that all pupils are of equal worth no matter what their giftings are. The implication of this is that one of the purposes of education is to help children to recognise their individuality and help them to see their giftedness – and to celebrate these together. How this is to be done in practice will be considered in the later chapters, but it is worth mentioning here that this requires educators knowing individual children well, honouring their identity, taking an active interest in them, offering breadth of opportunity and seeking to build up the important characteristics of confidence and service.

Value three: interaction – mutually dependent

Third, children are viewed as relational beings, created for relationship with God, and personal relationships in which we interact with others, in communities within which we have a part to play, societies to which we are connected and an environment towards which we have responsibility. We are mutually dependent and mutually supportive – that is, each needs the other in order to flourish fully (Figure 3.4).

We know instinctively that as humans we are not made for isolation: people enjoy and need each other's company and more is achieved together than apart. The snowballing of social media is testimony that the twenty-first century recognises our need for each other every bit as much as earlier generations did, even if our means of communicating may be rather less instinctive.

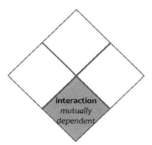

FIGURE 3.4 The interdependency of each child

The foundational value that children are relational beings must impact our educational provision and practice.

This model of good education has a deep appreciation of community, based on the understanding that I need my neighbour and my neighbour needs me. We are not beings made for isolation, but are social creatures. The outworkings of this are numerous.

First, the sense that everyone in a community needs each other implies that the whole is greater than the sum of its parts: together we are stronger and richer than we would be alone. This is not surprising if we believe in the unique contribution that everyone has to make – clearly every member of the community is enriched by the uniqueness of all those around. It also means that the community has worth in itself, in addition to the worth of the individuals within it. The importance of community will be recognised, valued, promoted and supported.

If my community has intrinsic worth, and I have a unique contribution to make to my community, then I need to exercise that by taking responsibility for making my contribution. A good education will encourage every pupil to develop as a strong and effective contributor to their community and wider society, albeit each in their own inimitable way as befits those who are uniquely gifted.

Furthermore, a good education will encourage a sense of wider connectedness, a sense of each of us being members of and contributors to the global community. Gaining a global perspective is important in cultivating informed and responsible attitudes towards creation, the environment and all the inhabitants of our planet. As one Canadian aboriginal speaker has put it, 'Learning is holistic and we need to focus on connectedness and relationships to oneself, family, community, language, culture and the natural world'.[27]

Value four: development – continually learning

Fourth, the Christian world-view envisages a true and moral universe, in which no one is perfect (in wisdom or deed) but in which all have the opportunity and freedom to change, progress and grow, and in which all need the opportunity for forgiveness, restoration and fresh starts. Each of us is a 'work in progress', a pilgrim on a journey of development, continually learning (Figure 3.5).

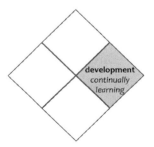

FIGURE 3.5 The ongoing development of each child

It is not a smooth and predictable path on which we run. In fact, life's race, and even that through the years of formal education, is perhaps most akin to a marathon cross-country run with unpredictable obstacles *en route*. For in the midst of the celebration of uniqueness, joy of giftedness and gratitude for community, any values-based education has to be realistic about the damaged world in which we live and the imperfect nature of humankind inhabiting it.

Our self-knowledge, the pages of our history books or an honest appraisal of our closest relationships can all remind us starkly of our weakness, vulnerability and effortless ability to make the wrong choices, intellectually and morally. This model is realistic about the imperfect nature of all individuals and their consequent needs. Because we all make mistakes, we all – repeatedly – need a fresh start: grace, mercy and forgiveness. In the words of John Stott,[28] 'grace is love that cares and stoops and rescues'. Mercy shows compassion and clemency rather than harm or punishment. Forgiveness wipes the slate clean, keeping no record of misdemeanour, rather like a debt being cancelled.

This is all good news, because it allows room and creates freedom for personal growth and development. Because all children are continually learning, perfection is never a prerequisite, and error never a calamity, but rather opportunities and encouragement are continually sought to keep learning, moving forward, advancing, maturing, growing and changing for the better. The educational model with these values at its heart is both realistic and optimistic, recognising that learning is continual, echoing what Matthew Syed has described as 'a capacity to leverage these failures in the dynamic process of change'.[29]

Each of these four values at the core of the educational model to be constructed – concerning the worth, identity, interaction and development of children – can be seen to stem from the Christian world-view described above which is the basis of the prep school educational ethos. However, for the purposes of seeking a much more broadly applicable model, it is reassuring that they also resonate strongly with widely held values arising from other faith, or secular, positions, and found across the world's cultures. Others may arrive at similar or compatible conclusions from a different religious or non-religious starting point, although the concepts themselves and the rationale underlying them may be expressed differently. The United Kingdom is a country with diversity of faith and origin, and the commonality of these values is both a reassurance and endorsement, resonating with Professor David Ford's reminder of the importance of 'wise faith . . . fuller understanding, better education and a commitment to the flourishing of our whole planet'.[30]

This approach plays its part in working together, as The Prince of Wales has commended, 'to create a world in which the fruits of faith – understanding, tolerance and compassion – enrich and safeguard the world of our children, and our children's children'.[31]

While there may be a degree of consensus about these values, however, they should never be taken for granted or ignored. Many know from scarring personal

TABLE 3.1 The four foundational values

FOUR FOUNDATIONAL VALUES CONCERNING THE CHILD

Worth	*Every child is inherently precious*
Identity	*Every child is uniquely gifted*
Interaction	*Every child is mutually dependent*
Development	*Every child is continually learning*

experience or their reading of *Hard Times* or *Tom Brown's Schooldays* the damage that can be done when good values are neglected, forgotten or corrupted within education.

Summary of foundational values

These four foundational values form the first layer of the four-dimensional model of education. The values define children as being inherently precious, uniquely gifted, mutually dependent, and continually learning (Table 3.1).

Viewing every child in this way is the essential, central, foundational starting point in the construction of the four-dimensional model of education. These four values act like four cornerstones, markers which will determine the shape of the ensuing structure and ensure that nothing is thrown out of kilter. It is precisely because they are of such great impact that it is necessary to make explicit their origins and rationale.

Of course, the challenge for each successive generation is to interpret these or other such foundational values as well as possible for the good of the children in its care, to determine their educational implications and to establish relevant implementation for its own contemporary context. How do these values impact what should be taught, and how it should be taught? Where do we start when confronted with a class or school of inherently precious, uniquely gifted, mutually dependent and continually learning children or young people? It is the challenge of this question that the next layer in the four-dimensional model must address.

Notes

1 http://reach2.org/, accessed 28 July 2017.
2 http://iheu.org/humanism/what-is-humanism/, accessed 28 July 2017.
3 http://londonmandir.baps.org/about/the-swaminarayan-school-london/, accessed 28 July 2017.
4 http://ams-uk.org/about-us/ams-vision-aims/, accessed 28 July 2017.
5 www.theoxfordacademy.org.uk/Aims-Ethos-and-Values, accessed 28 July 2017.
6 www.churchofengland.org/education/church-schools-academies.aspx, accessed 28 July 2017.
7 www.harrowschool.org.uk/Our-Values, accessed 28 July 2017.

8   *Independent Schools' Year Book 2012–13*, p. 26.
9   www.theleys.net/426/academic/academic-overview accessed 28 July 2017.
10 For further information on education in England pre-1800, see www.educationengland.org. uk/history/chapter01.html, accessed 28 July 2017.
11 *The Life of Adam Smith* by John Rae, Cosimo Classics, New York. The reference to the Apostles is to the first-century church leaders.
12 www.churchofengland.org/media/2532839/2016-church-of-england-vision-for-education-web-final.pdf, accessed 28 July 2017.
13 www.churchofengland.org/education/church-schools-academies/church-schools-and-academies-information.aspx, accessed 28 July 2017.
14 www.catholiceducation.org.uk/about-us/faqs, accessed 28 July 2017.
15 www.churchofengland.org/education/church-schools-academies.aspx, accessed 28 July 2017.
16 www.churchofengland.org/media/2532839/2016-church-of-england-vision-for-education-web-final.pdf, accessed 28 July 2017.
17 www.catholiceducation.org.uk/about-us/faqs, accessed 28 July 2017.
18 *Ibid.*
19 www.telegraph.co.uk/education/2017/02/20/muslim-parents-send-children-christian-schools-toprepare-life/, accessed 28 July 2017.
20 www.theguardian.com/politics/2009/mar/02/education-standards-poll, accessed 28 July 2017.
21 www.lhpa.co.uk/
22 www.gov.uk/government/news/guidance-on-promoting-british-values-in-schools-published, accessed 28 July 2017.
23 *The Bible*, Genesis chapter 1 verse 27.
24 www.gov.uk/government/publications/improving-the-smsc-development-of-pupils-in-independent-schools, accessed 28 July 2017.
25 *School of Infancy*, Claims of Children 5:12, https://archive.org/stream/schoolofinfancye00 comeiala/schoolofinfancye00comeiala_djvu.txt, accessed 28 July 2017.
26 *The Cambridge Dictionary* defines child-centred as 'used to refer to ways of teaching and treating children in which the child's needs and wishes are the most important thing'.
27 *Aboriginal Worldviews and Perspectives in the Classroom: Moving Forward*, p. 15, www2.gov.bc.ca/ assets/gov/education/administration/kindergarten-to-grade-12/aboriginal-education/awp_ moving_forward.pdf, accessed 28 July 2017.
28 Revd John Stott (1921–2011) of All Souls Church, Langham Place, London, was ranked by *Time Magazine* in 2005 as being among the most 100 influential people in the world.
29 www.wired.co.uk/article/preventing-medical-error-deaths, accessed 28 July 2017.
30 Quoted on the Cambridge Interfaith Programme website, www.interfaith.cam.ac.uk/, accessed 28 July 2017.
31 *Ibid.*

4

Character traits

Living it out

With mastery of understatement, Tolkien's fictional hero, Gandalf, explains to the humble hobbit Frodo that 'all we have to decide is what to do with the time that is given to us'.[1] The foundational values lying at the heart of the four-dimensional model, concerning the individual child, suggest that the first thing to de done is to determine how to live in the light of those values. Specific character traits are to be promoted and encouraged individually and communally within a good holistic education.

What makes the best of our education so good?

Not long ago, I heard the account of a prospective parent visiting a school: she was most impressed by a particular incident. She described seeing an eco-racing car that had been built from a kit by the pupils, as part of a nationwide schools' initiative, them having first secured sponsorship from a local company for the project. They had subsequently installed a Raspberry Pi computer to give feedback on performance data so that the car could be modified to improve efficiency. They had then raced the car in a national competition. Clearly the project had been hugely successful, and the pupils learnt an enormous amount along the way. Moreover, they were just nine years of age.

None of this, however, was what had impressed her the most. Rather, it was the fact that the pupil showing her round and telling her about this had not actually taken part in the project herself, and yet she took such evident pleasure and pride in the achievements and success of those of her friends who had. It was the generosity of spirit and evident sense of community, alongside the academic and practical achievement, that had impressed most.

In this analysis of good education, the child lies at the heart, and the foundational values concerning the child – worth, identity, interaction and development – form the first layer of the model. The second layer within it is made up of specific character traits that arise directly from those four founda-tional values and which should be evident in a good education. These character traits will not only be cultivated in the child, but lived out in practice in the community.

Cultivating character traits

The view of the child already described implies that in considering the worth of the child, it is the whole person that is of value, not just the intellect or some other subsidiary part. The Judeo–Christian tradition speaks of loving God 'with all your heart and with all your soul and with all your strength and with all your mind'.[2] This ancient articulation of the multifaceted yet fully integrated nature of individuals is respected and reflected in the holistic approach to education already briefly described. The result is provision for the education and development of the whole person.

Holistic education aims to help develop the emotional (heart), spiritual (soul), physical (strength) and intellectual (mind) elements of the child. It sees the child as a unified whole that cannot be subdivided: the whole child is to be cared for. Attempting to care for only one 'part' of the child is to deny the totality and the reality of who a child is, and is therefore effectively to diminish their worth, as well as short-change them educationally.

Alongside this holistic view of the individual, the notion of community, our mutual dependence and complementarity, is also central to the heritage from which the model's foundational values stem. 'You shall love your neighbour as yourself', the speaker goes on to say in the passage quoted above.[3]

As described in the University of Birmingham Jubilee Centre's *A Framework for Character Education*, the cultivation of virtues of character, or aiding students in 'knowing the good, loving the good and doing the good',[4] touches on every aspect of the whole person. 'In a wide sense, character education permeates all subjects, wider school activities and general school ethos; it cultivates the virtues of character associated with common morality and develops students' understanding of what is excellent in diverse spheres of human endeavour'.[5] This has been part of schooling for millennia: 'Our examination is not to know what virtue is, but to become good', said Aristotle.[6]

Despite many centuries of being central in education, the importance of 'character education' within the mainstream of education waxes and wanes, at times taking pre-eminence and at times being more marginalised or even dismissed altogether. Following some post-war decades in the doldrums (reflected in the more or less absence of character education in the schools I attended as a pupil), in more recent times its value has been reasserted. President Clinton hosted no less than five conferences on character education during his presidency, for example, and it certainly seems to be in the ascendency again in the United Kingdom given statements made by politicians across the parties.[7]

More recently opened schools, including those with a secular foundation, once again seem to place considerable importance on holistic education, including that of character. The University of Cambridge Primary School, for example, which was opened in 2015, states that its 'curriculum intends to provide an holistic learning experience, informed by strong values which emphasise equality, compassion, courage and community in which everyone's voice is welcome and valued'.[8]

My contrasting experiences as a pupil and teacher in respect of character education have convinced me that a good education is one which provides as fully as possible for the development of the whole person, with the development of good character permeating all. Character development is therefore not just the preserve of a few enthusiasts, like some sort of minority sport, but is essential for all. But neither will 'character development' be listed as a subject on the timetable or allocated an hour a week: it will not just get an airing in the assembly hall on a Monday morning, or be used as filler in a Friday afternoon PSHE[9] lesson. Rather, it is integral to the whole educational endeavour, taught through every lesson and lived through every hour.

Character development is neither directly measurable − belonging to the world of standardised scores and percentile rankings − nor does it simply occur automatically by being in the right place at the right time as if by osmosis. On the contrary, the development of character is the core, intentional business of a good education. It is an inherent part of education, a part of the intrinsic whole that cannot be ignored, wished away or compartmentalised. The development of character runs through an individual's education, just as the values of the school run through its fibre and fabric − the lettering through that stick of rock, again.

With resurgence in support for intentional, integrated character education, it might be assumed that there is a fairly broad consensus in concept and content as to what character education actually means. After all, it has a long and established history on which we now build. However, an increasing trend in the conversation about character education seems to be to reduce 'character' to somehow being solely about inner, personal, 'performance' virtues such as grit, resilience, determination, and similarly individualistic 'intellectual' virtues such as creativity, critical thinking and so on. I believe such a narrowing should be resisted.

Such traits are necessary but not sufficient, missing out on those aspects of personality which impact our interactions with others. To those performance and intellectual virtues listed above need to be added moral virtues (such as compassion) and what may be described as civic virtues (such as service), since 'character development involves caring for and respecting others as well as caring for and respecting oneself'.[10]

Nonetheless, even if it were possible, it is probably not desirable to try and create a definitive list of virtues which is uniformly and equally applicable in every situation, social circumstance and context. What is more helpful is to elucidate some broad categories of virtues (which may be inclusive of other traits) which encompass performance, intellectual, moral and civic virtues, while also reflecting the characteristics of the whole child as already described. Such broad categories may be interpreted and applied readily in a variety of contexts, an important aim of the model.

The next layer in the model is thus comprised of important elements of character formulated as pairs of traits. Each pair arises from one of the four foundational values concerning the worth, identity, interaction and development of the child already described; one of each pair is primarily inward-looking (personal) and the other corresponding characteristic is primarily outward-facing (communal). Thus while these are not exhaustive, they incorporate all the various areas of character already mentioned without being overly complex.

These four pairs of character traits, which arise from the foundational values concerning the child, form the second layer in our model of good education.

Integrity and respect

The worth of a child: An education which views each child as being inherently precious will encourage integrity of character (inward-looking) and promote respect for others in the community (outward-facing).

In this model, the first and most important foundational value underlying a good education is that every member of the educational community is believed to be inherently precious: every individual child is of incalculable, incomparable worth.

The personal inward-looking characteristic that is nurtured if every member of the community is viewed as being of inherent worth is *integrity of character*. If I am of value, then it matters how I develop. It matters that I am honest, reliable and sincere, meaning what I say and saying what I mean; the values I have run through me like letters through rock too. Particularly important in a world of so-called 'fake news' and falsehood, children need to learn that integrity incorporates truthfulness – not being deceitful or disingenuous. Integrity takes responsibility. It creates transparency. It generates trust.

Integrity means making the right choice even when it is the hard thing to do, or when no one is looking. As one of our broad virtue categories, integrity therefore also encompasses the desire and willingness to put my own needs, comfort and safety to one side in order to do the right thing. Fairness, bravery and fortitude result. It is integrity that puts the common good before selfishness. Integrity is characterised by dignity.

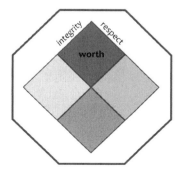

FIGURE 4.1 Endorsing individual worth encourages integrity and promotes respect

Such an essential characteristic grows out of self-respect which itself follows a sense of self-worth, in turn grounded in a foundational belief in the inherent value of every person. I should be able to respect myself, believing myself to be what I am – inherently precious, and therefore to be regarded and treated as such by myself. An education based on these foundations emphasises the development of individual integrity, self-respect and personal responsibility.

If all children (and indeed all people) are inherently precious, then every member of the community is equally of worth. This has very great practical implications for educational provision, in what is recognised and rewarded, and in what is deemed to be important. If this principle is believed and put into practice, there is no room for favouritism, but justice must prevail: all must be treated fairly. No favouritism means that we provide equal opportunities, ensuring equitable access to facilities, resources and teachers. It means that the concept of justice is not only endorsed in word but in practice.

SUMMARY BOX 4.1: The components of integrity

Integrity:
honesty + reliability + sincerity + truthfulness
+ transparency + braveness + fortitude + dignity + justice

It also follows that the weakest are to be very carefully looked after. The divine spark is to be nurtured, encouraged, supported and at all times protected: the vulnerable are to be especially cared for, and the stronger expected to support those who may seem to be weaker. Those who might be at greatest risk of being overlooked, those struggling at any given point, those whose work is backstage rather than in the limelight, will be respected every bit as much as anyone else. Within this ideal, pupils are not valued primarily for what they contribute, but for who they are. The brightest pupil academically is not of any more value to the school than the pupil who struggles. Honour, time and attention will be given to all, and perhaps especially where there is specific need.

The outward-facing character trait which pairs up with integrity is thus *mutual respect*: if integrity is cultivated inwardly, then respect is cultivated outwardly (Figure 4.1).

An education based on the value that all people are equally, inherently precious promotes respect. In fact, there is no place for disrespect at all, but instead all people must be shown equal honour and justice. This works both ways: I show respect to all and am shown respect by all. Children are treated with respect and expected to show respect, to all peers and to all adults. In a school community which values all people equally, for example, infants, juniors, seniors, teachers, assistants, librarians, cooks and cleaners are all shown equal respect and consideration.

This broad characteristic includes those virtues by which we show respect: listening to others when they speak – and hearing what they are saying; an attempt to understand all, including those whose customs, speech or background may be different from ours; tolerance towards those whose views, manner or experiences may be at variance with our own; gratitude towards others for who they are and what they do. Respect welcomes and accepts someone new into the group; it is the starting point for reconciliation when disharmony threatens. Such characteristics are intensely important for individual human flourishing and society as a whole.

SUMMARY BOX 4.2: The components of respect

Respect:
listening + understanding + tolerance
+ gratitude + welcome + acceptance + reconciliation

In an education based on these values, respect is not earned by certain people because they are good at what they do, or presumed because particular individuals share ideals, or effected because the law demands it. Respect is afforded to all in recognition of the inherently precious nature of every individual.

My experiences over the years as a pupil, teacher, parent and governor confirm my belief that the best education rests on the bedrock of cultivating good character, and that the two most significant elements of character, namely integrity and respect, arise from a solid appreciation of the intrinsic and incalculable worth of every single human being. Without genuine promotion and cultivation of integrity and respect, education is in danger of being merely an insubstantial and unstable facade.

Distinction and positivity

The identity of the child: an education which views each child as being uniquely gifted will encourage individual distinction (inward-looking) in a community characterised by shared positivity (outward-facing).

The second foundational value on which to build a good education is the assertion that every member of the school community is uniquely gifted, that is to say, that every single person has their own contribution that they and they alone can make. No two children are alike – and experience bears this out – even though they are of equal worth. Two broad character traits emerge here too.

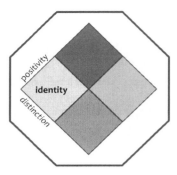

FIGURE 4.2 Recognising unique identity encourages distinction and promotes positivity

If the principle is held that every child is uniquely gifted then there is a rationale to developing the individual to the full, in order that everyone might thrive by developing their own potential and be able to contribute fully to the community in which they find themselves. A gift, by definition, is something precious, to be both cherished and cultivated. As a result, children will be encouraged to develop the inward-facing character trait of *individual distinction* (Figure 4.2). The encouragement of distinction means that pupils are urged to reach high, to fulfil their potential, to do as well as they possibly can, to be their best selves.

Explaining the Quaker educational philosophy, Graham Ralph makes the same point: 'As individuals and as a community, we are committed to helping everyone strive towards and if possible reach their potential. Working towards realising the measure of talent we have might also uncover other surprising attributes. Our philosophy should be one of hopeful expectancy in the potential of all members of the community'.[11]

Such hopeful expectancy establishes aspiration, encouraging children to reach up to make the most of their individual gifts and talents. 'Just do your best', I was repeatedly told as I grew up, a message both comforting and daunting in equal measure: no one could ask more of me than my best efforts, but neither should I settle for less. Each of us as a unique individual has our own unique best to aspire to.

Thus encouraging individual distinction is not about fostering a competitive environment in which children try to outdo each other. Neither is it to encourage the cultivation of excellence solely in those areas in which they or others perceive themselves to be especially strong. Rather it is about encouraging an expectation of excellence across the board, adhering to the old adage that 'if a job's worth doing, it's worth doing well'. In a good education, excellence is encouraged, valued and celebrated in every area, because individuals, with their unique giftings, are valued.

Once again this is a broad characteristic which incorporates many performance virtues, such as industry, creativity and intellectual virtues such as curiosity and critical thinking. Without these, there can be no individual distinction. It is through such virtues that children fully engage with their studies, grapple with problems and forge deep and secure roots of learning.

The understanding of uniqueness guards against adopting a one-size-fits-all approach to education. It also provides an antidote to hot-housing, since children are not to be forced like identical sticks of rhubarb, but rather a more natural cultivation will be encouraged which allows each child to develop to the best of his or her own ability without comparison with peers. A good education must be one which brings out the best in everyone, recognising that every individual is unique, rather than trying to make everyone conform to a norm.

SUMMARY BOX 4.3: The components of distinction

Distinction:
aspiration + excellence + industry
+ creativity + curiosity + critical thinking + engagement

If individuals from an early age understand that they have a unique contribution to make to the community, which they can and should exercise to the best of their ability for the common good, then within that community a *shared positivity* will emerge (Figure 4.2).

A community of individual distinction is a community that believes its members to be capable of achievement and expects the very best of them. It is a community that spurs one another on to greater things and that has a confident and aspirational sense of self-belief.

Positivity extends to attainment in the academic, sporting and artistic realms, but also to behaviour where high expectations apply equally to conduct, attitudes, manners and morals. A good education is one in which each child is expected to do well, that is, to do the very best they can in every sphere of their activity.

But positivity extends beyond individual and corporate achievement, generating a widespread sense of gratitude and appreciation across the community. A spirit of optimism prevails in a positive environment in which difference is seen as strength and is therefore appreciated and valued. Children are believed in and championed. Humour, joy and faith are all by-products of a positive spirit which values the talents and gifts of individuals, fans them into the flame of personal distinction and joyfully celebrates them together.

I recall the words of an inspirational head teacher I once heard speaking at a conference. He was introduced as having been given a year to step in to a school deemed to be failing and to turn it around, if it were to be saved from closure. In describing the way this had been achieved, he mentioned the rule he had for his staff, despite the difficulties and challenges they faced: relentless positivity at all times. The broad trait of positivity is mother to many virtues, and is powerful in effect.

SUMMARY BOX 4.4: The components of positivity

Positivity:
optimism + expectation + appreciation
+ confidence + humour + joy + faith + celebration

How important it is for a school to retain positivity, focusing on what is good, rejoicing in what is achieved and believing in its young people. As one ancient writer commended his readers: 'whatsoever things are true, whatsoever things are honest, whatsoever things are just, whatsoever things are pure, whatsoever things are lovely, whatsoever things are of good report; if there be any virtue, and if there be any praise, think on these things',[12] words which I would read every day as a pupil, as I passed through my school assembly hall, where they were inscribed on a mural.

Building on a foundation of every child being uniquely gifted – with a responsibility to use those gifts for the greater good – promotes shared positivity and encourages individual distinction. Within such an education there exists a rationale and motivation for wanting to see every pupil achieve. The positive expectation of excellence for all within the community – albeit in varied guises – provides protection against unhealthy competition, rivalry or factions, but rather fosters a sense of mutual appreciation and communal success.

Initiative and service

The interaction of the child: An education which views children as being mutually dependent will encourage personal initiative (inward-looking) and within the community will promote an attitude of service (outward-facing).

In order to make their unique contribution and use their gifts for the benefit of others, pupils need to develop confidence, a spirit of enterprise and personal endeavour. A good education actively creates opportunities to encourage the development of such personal characteristics. Building on the core value of mutual dependency, a good education thus encourages the broad trait of *personal initiative* (Figure 4.3). Taking the initiative involves assuming responsibility, working hard, thinking for oneself, exercising common sense, making judgements and displaying wisdom.

Children need to be given the opportunity and encouragement to develop initiative within the boundaries of service, however. The model of good education

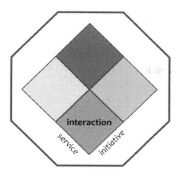

FIGURE 4.3 Confirming mutual dependency encourages initiative and promotes service

described here has as one of its foundational principles the fact that we need each other and we need to look out for each other. This model of education does not promote a self-serving or self-seeking attitude, but encourages selflessness and generosity as being the ideals for which we should strive and the example which we should follow.

SUMMARY BOX 4.5: The components of initiative

Initiative:
responsibility + contributing + enterprise
+ endeavour + judgement + wisdom + selflessness + generosity

While the idea of service may sound old-fashioned, in fact service is central to the way our individual lives and those of our communities run. From the civil service to the emergency services, the National Health Service and what we describe as the service industries, our country is run by its servants. Since the word minister means the same as servant, our Prime Minister together with all those who are in administration are servants – of each other and the wider community.

A good education promotes an *attitude of service* (Figure 4.3), and prizes helpfulness highly. Such an education expects and encourages people to do things for each other rather than themselves: it is the antidote to selfishness. This creates a harmonious environment where individuals pull together for the common good.

An education built on this value promotes team spirit, teaching and modelling how to get along together, how to work collaboratively, how to cooperate rather than be isolated or negatively independent. Building on the value of individual giftedness, it asserts that each person has something unique and very special to contribute to the community, without which the community will be diminished. 'No man is an island entire of itself', famously wrote John Donne, but 'every man is a piece of the continent, a part of the main'.[13] We are only complete when we recognise, celebrate and exercise our mutual dependency.

Thus the inward trait of initiative and the outward-facing trait of service are closely intertwined. If my neighbour needs me, if I am an indispensable part of the community, then I need to take my role seriously, not waiting for someone to tell me what to do, but taking the initiative, knowing that I am there to support the whole community not to act in my own interests. It is estimated that each of us will influence an average of ten thousand people in the course of our lives.[14] A good education will enable that influence to be for the maximum benefit.

Robert K. Greenleaf, founder of the modern Servant Leadership movement, said 'Good leaders must first become good servants', an idea echoed by Theodore Roosevelt when he advised that 'No one cares how much you know until they know how much you care'. Leadership skills encompass thinking *for myself* and thinking *of others*. Taking responsibility, influencing others for good and speaking words that build others up are all developed in community and for the good of the whole; they cannot be developed in isolation. A good education recognises this and deliberately provides opportunities for the active encouragement and development of such altruistic traits.

A mutual dependency means that there is no room for arrogance because any one person's success will have been the result of the input of many. Rather we learn about our own need and how others can meet it. Something I may have can be of value to my neighbour and work for the common good, but by the same token, such an attitude will result in a healthy humility: I need my neighbour, just as my neighbour needs me.

SUMMARY BOX 4.6: The components of service

Service:
helpfulness + support + harmony + team spirit
+ cooperation + altruism + leadership + humility

No one has all the answers, no one has a monopoly on the truth, no one can go it alone – neither myself nor my fellows. A good education encourages personal initiative and promotes an attitude of service.

Perseverance and compassion

The development of the child: An education which views children as being continually learning will encourage determined perseverance (inward-looking) and within the community will promote a widespread spirit of compassion (outward-facing).

The journey of education, let alone life itself, is a varied and exotic mix of adventures and successes, challenges and pitfalls. One of the requirements of a good education is that children and young people are fully equipped to respond to both types of experience, having the necessary knowledge and strength of character to respond appropriately either way.

Much has been written of the need to encourage in our children tenacity, resilience, stickability, what in some circles is perhaps described as 'grit'. In other words, we need to encourage in our young people the trait of *determined perseverance* (Figure 4.4). To persevere is to keep going for a long time, whatever the odds. It recognises that times can be hard, for all sorts of reasons, and those are the times when we need to keep going and not give up. Gain is not always in the short term. Perseverance in itself generates resilience and inner strength and helps to develop robustness. It cultivates hope, but also grows out of hope. The positivity already described as a result of understanding uniqueness within the community comes into play here too, as children and young people have a 'can-do' attitude towards problems and challenges. It encourages us to remember that it is often the most worthwhile things that are the hardest. In fact much good learning takes place in the most challenging of situations and without these experiences slower and more limited progress would be made in the long run.

Perseverance also encourages us to pick ourselves up after experience of setbacks, failure and disappointment. Each of us falls short of perfection by a considerable margin, but this in itself need not be problematic if there is recognition that we are all continually learning. Self-awareness and self-acceptance enable each of us not merely to recover from setbacks of our own or others'

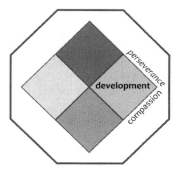

FIGURE 4.4 Acknowledging continual development encourages perseverance and promotes compassion

makings, but to learn from them, as we continue on our journey. A good education encourages each individual pupil to keep going. It prizes perseverance.

SUMMARY BOX 4.7: The components of perseverance

Perseverance:
tenacity + resilience + robustness
+ hope + self-awareness + self-acceptance

But if the inward-looking trait is perseverance, such personal toughness is complemented by an outward-facing *spirit of compassion* (Figure 4.4). In noting the ongoing nature of learning, we recognise that everyone faces setbacks from without and disappointments from within. A good education encourages a spirit of generosity, of forgiveness, of compassion within the community. For a whole host of different reasons, for some people, life is very hard all of the time; for all people, life is very hard some of the time: everyone needs compassion.

Everyone makes mistakes; everyone fails their own or others' standards whether academically, intellectually, morally or emotionally. As Cranmer put it in his *Book of Common Prayer*, 'we have left undone those things which we ought to have done, and we have done those things which we ought not to have done'. A good education recognises this, cultivating an attitude of compassion which is supportive and caring. A good education teaches young people to be kind. It teaches that there is forgiveness, a fresh start: none of us needs to be bogged down by our inevitable mistakes and failings but there is a way to move beyond them.

A good education helps children in situations where they have fallen short intellectually or morally, enabling understanding of their error and then helping them to correct it and move forwards.

Sometimes correction is needed, and sometimes forgiveness, but always compassion. The character trait of compassion encompasses other virtues too. A school which fosters compassion will demonstrate and encourage patience within its community. A good education has a gentleness, humility, kindness and humaneness which provide a perfect counterbalance to the robustness, toughness and resilience of grit. Compassion for all fosters empathy and sympathy. It leads to selfless concern for the well-being of others, love in action and a desire for justice.

Compassion is not passive but is evident in active, unconditional love, which is selfless and kind. 'I expect to pass through this world but once', wrote William Penn. 'Any good therefore that I can do, or any kindness that I can show to any fellow creature, let me do it now. Let me not defer or neglect it, for I shall not pass this way again'. John Wesley said something similar: 'Do all the good you can. By all the means you can. In all the ways you can. In all the places you can. At all the times you can. To all the people you can. As long as ever you can'.

SUMMARY BOX 4.8: The components of compassion

Compassion:
generosity + forgiveness + supportiveness + kindness + patience
+ gentleness + humility + humaneness + empathy + sympathy + love

---

No one knows everything. We are all learning. It is unlikely that anyone would take issue with either of these statements, but acknowledging and articulating this is important. Children need to learn resilience: if something is hard going, we do not give up. If we make a mistake, get something wrong or have a bad day, we persevere, knowing that things will improve, even if only slowly. If our neighbour finds something hard going, makes a mistake, gets something wrong or has a bad day, we exercise a spirit of compassion, knowing that in our common humanity we all need each other's support.

The message that we are all learning, continually, gives freedom for children to grow. They may have to take responsibility for grappling and struggling with something they find hard, they may have to try several times before success is achieved, they may have to exercise and receive patience, but the sense of achievement – together with a healthy sense of humility – is of inestimable value as an essential survival skill in later life.

A good education encourages individual perseverance and fosters a spirit of compassion.

Foundational values and character traits: a summary

Resting at the heart of education is the view of the child – determined by a faith position or some other underlying set of beliefs or assumptions. The view of the child creates the foundational values of an education. The foundational values determine the way in which the child is treated and taught. They also determine the extent to which character traits are encouraged and nurtured and the types of qualities promoted.

The four foundational values on which the four-dimensional model of education rests have been described as these: children are inherently precious, uniquely gifted, mutually dependent and continually learning. A good education is one which consciously cares for and supports the development of each individual child as a whole person and as a precious and unique member of the community.

TABLE 4.1 Four foundational values and four pairs of character traits

FOUR DUAL CHARACTER TRAITS ARISING FROM THE FOUNDATIONAL VALUES

VALUES	PERSONAL TRAITS	COMMUNITY TRAITS
Worth	*Integrity of character*	Mutual respect
Identity	*Individual distinction*	Shared positivity
Interaction	*Personal initiative*	Attitude of service
Development	*Determined perseverance*	Compassionate spirit

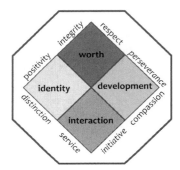

FIGURE 4.5 Four foundational values and four pairs of character traits

An education based on these values fosters a community of respect made up of individuals of integrity. There is a strong sense of positivity within the community as personal distinction is celebrated. Initiative and perseverance are encouraged in the context of service within a compassionate community (Table 4.1 and Figure 4.5). I believe that these ideals lie at the theoretical heart of a good education and, in real practical terms, are the heartbeat that pulses through every part of the life of a good education.

In a good education, such traits of character will be both taught (explicitly) and caught (by example); they will be both learnt and lived. How this is done in practice will be considered in due course, but of immediate importance next is to reflect on how these core values and their consequent character traits also map directly onto some essential educational principles.

Notes

1   *The Fellowship of the Ring*, by J.R.R. Tolkien.
2   *The Bible*, Luke chapter 10 verse 27, and similar in Deuteronomy chapter 6 verse 5 and Matthew chapter 22 verse 27.
3   *Ibid.*

4   https://futureprepared.org.uk/sites/default/files/University-of-Birmingham-Framework-for-Character-Education.pdf, accessed 28 July 2017.

5   *Ibid.*

6   *Nicomachean Ethics*, 1103b 28–9.

7   The Secretary of State for Education announced a new fund to place England as a 'global leader' in teaching character, resilience and grit in December 2014.

8   www.universityprimaryschool.org.uk/wp-content/uploads/2014/09/Prospectus.pdf, accessed 28 July 2017.

9   PHSE (personal, health, social and economic education) has been part of the National Curriculum in the UK since 2000, its goal being to equip young people to live healthily, safely, productively and responsibly.

10 https://futureprepared.org.uk/sites/default/files/University-of-Birmingham-Framework-for-Character-Education.pdf, accessed 28 July 2017.

11 *Faith and Practice at a Quaker School* by Graham Ralph, published by Quacks Books, York, 2014.

12 *The Bible*, St Paul's letter to the Philippians chapter 4 verse 8.

13 MEDITATION XVII, Devotions upon Emergent Occasions.

14 Cited, for example by John Maxwell: www.johnmaxwell.com/cms/images/uploads/ads/Leading_a_Life_of_Intentional_Influence.pdf, accessed 28 July 2017.

5

Educational principles

Distinguishing practices

The foundational values regarding the child give rise to character traits to be fostered, but also to four clear educational principles which form the most distinguishing features of the four-dimensional model. Height, breadth, depth and length spread out in four directions like the guiding points of a compass. They indicate the lie of the land and direct us where to cast our gaze to ensure that nothing is missed.

Ionic columns, oxbow lakes and mountaineers

My own memory of the things I learnt at school, especially in the early pre-public examination years, is of a weird and wonderful eclectic mix of information, facts and knowledge. It can perhaps best be described as resembling a handful of pages torn at random from an *Encyclopaedia Britannica* and now blowing about loosely in the wind.

I recall, for example, learning that there were three types of ancient Greek column: Doric, Ionic and Corinthian, and I can picture them still. I remember thinking at the time that there must be an important reason why I had been taught about these and asked to produce careful sketches of them, and waiting to find out what it was. I am still waiting. Did I miss something or was that it? Doric, Ionic and Corinthian . . . full stop: the beginning and end of Greek columns. It was certainly interesting and informative, but whether there was any further reason why I learnt that specifically rather than anything else about the Greeks eludes me still. On another occasion I remember learning about oxbow lakes. Not that to the best of my knowledge I have ever seen one, but the lesson stays with me, and I will certainly know one if and when I do encounter it. I recall learning my multiplication tables (by rote) and remember learning how to spell *woollen* and *mountaineer*, perhaps because I got them wrong in the subsequent spelling tests. I remember learning how to carry a pair of scissors safely.

But amidst these fragmentary memories shines out an unforgettable, exhilarating moment. I must have been six years old and I was with my classmates, all of us to a person champing at the bit, expectant and enthralled at the prospect of what was to come. The gun fired. We ran, helter-skelter, limbs flailing lankily, pony-tails streaming behind, our plimsolls punishing the grass beneath our feet, as we made our ungainly way as quickly as we knew how down the length of the field between the white painted lines towards the tape at the finishing line. In the greatest sporting triumph of my life, I reached the finish and realised to my utter delight that I had come in a triumphant second – and as a result, won sixpence. What joy!

How do the fine aspirations of seeing each child as inherently precious, uniquely gifted, mutually dependent and continually learning – with all the resultant character traits that we so wish to cultivate – inform what and how we teach, whether or not we include Corinthian columns and oxbow lakes, spelling tests and competitive sport? What will a good education look like in practice?

Four educational principles

The attributes of the child already considered in detail directly lead to four educational principles which form the next layer of this framework of a good education. Each of the four foundational values (concerning worth, identity, interaction and development) is shown to generate and map onto a distinct educational principle concerning, respectively, excellence, attainment, engagement and endeavour (Table 5.1). These are described as *the four dimensions* of learning, because the defining principles are *heights* of excellence, *breadth* of attainment, *depth* of engagement and *length* of endeavour. It is these four 'dimensions' that result in the phrase 'four-dimensional education'. This description sums up this model because it speaks eloquently of its holistic, rounded nature which itself reflects the perceived nature of the child which lies at its heart.

These four principles form the key components of the four-dimensional model of education, and so each will be considered in detail in turn.

Heights of excellence

A good education is characterised by the vital pursuit of excellence.

TABLE 5.1 Four educational principles emerge

FOUR EDUCATIONAL PRINCIPLES ARISING FROM THE FOUNDATIONAL VALUES

VALUES	DIMENSION OF LEARNING
Worth	*Heights of excellence*
Identity	*Breadth of attainment*
Interaction	*Depth of engagement*
Development	*Length of endeavour*

If a child is perceived to be of inestimable worth, then everything that he or she does has value. It is not a difficult logical step to take to say that those things should therefore be as good as possible, both in recognition of their value and to maximise their value: in other words, a good education will be characterised by *heights of excellence* (Figure 5.1).

It is worth noting that this model of education values the child first and therefore what the child does becomes of value. This avoids the all-too-easy pitfall of valuing children because of their achievements.

Excellence can mean two different things. First, striving for 'heights of excellence' implies setting ambitious goals and demanding levels of stretch. Second, excellence is to do with the standard of work produced, being demonstrated in a high quality of product. These two elements of excellence may seem to be in conflict one with the other: if work is too difficult, the end product will not be good; if the output is of exceptionally high quality, might the work have been too easy, not providing sufficient challenge? I think that both are valid, important and complementary components of what we mean by the educational principle of height. It should not be a case of choosing between them, but of embracing and ensuring both.

Ambition in learning: appropriate difficulty

In a good education, every opportunity must be provided for children to reach up as high as possible in their learning. Teachers (and parents) often talk about children being stretched, which can sound quite uncomfortable, painful even. But for children to reach up as high as they can, as it were to pluck the fruit of

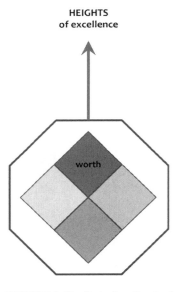

FIGURE 5.1 The first educational principle: height

challenging and demanding knowledge, understanding and skill, is exhilarating. Excellence in this sense implies reach, appropriate levels of difficulty, and fitting but challenging demands being made on the mind, body and spirit. It suggests going as far as possible, as fast as possible, as well as possible.

I recall on one occasion working with a group of children on a project for two hours a day for a week. Their task during this time was to build a scale model of the solar system. There were several criteria: the model had to include the sun, the earth and all the planets in the solar system; every planet had to be big enough to handle; the sun, the earth and the other planets had to be built to scale and made of durable materials; and the sun, the earth and the other planets had to be placed at the correct distances apart.

First, the children had to research the sizes of the planets (and the sun), and the distances between them. Then they had to work out a useable scale so as to work within the parameters. Next they had to calculate the diameters of the sun and planet models and the distances between them, before deciding on the materials to use to make them and the locations in which they would eventually be placed. All these tasks had to be divided up between the group of twelve or so children who ranged in age from nine to twelve, and they had to work extremely quickly to complete the work in the time. At the end of the week, they had created a model sun with a one-metre diameter, made out of chicken wire and plaster of Paris, and all the planets had been made. On the Friday afternoon, the sun was positioned outside the headmaster's office; Mercury found its home in the school gym; Jupiter made its way to the grounds of another, local school; Neptune was in the porch of a country parish church out of the city; and Pluto (which back in those days was still a planet) was ceremoniously couriered by school minibus to be placed in the window of a village post office some 12 km hence. It was the size of a small dried pea.

As this example shows, within such intellectual pursuits, we find that reaching high has several characteristics. Knowledge, understanding, application, analysis, creativity and evaluation, familiar from Bloom's taxonomy,[1] are all required for there to be real stretch. I would add to these appreciation, enjoyment and enthusiasm for learning, all of which are vital ingredients in cultivating the other dimensions of learning, described below.

As well as this however, this challenge itself was, frankly, difficult. The children were not simply following a recipe, but were devising a solution to a problem, being genuinely creative in doing so. They had to think, research, decide and communicate for themselves, for real. There was nothing mechanical about it at all.

Examples can similarly be provided from other areas of the curriculum. Sports day races quickly progress from the sack race to the hurdles, and elsewhere in athletics the bar literally gets higher. Within the arts, pupils can be encouraged to undertake really challenging tasks, whether that means taking a high-grade performance exam or putting on a Shakespeare play. Excellence is about appropriate stretch.

Achieving quality: successful results

The second aspect of excellence, however, is the notion of producing a high-quality product: the output should be really good. Perhaps music exams provide a useful example here. If the ambition in learning is encouraging a pupil to enter their grade V music exam, the other side of the coin is the aspiration to do that grade V exam with the best possible quality – to aim to achieve as high a mark as possible, perhaps even gaining a distinction.

This helps us to see that excellence does not and cannot look the same for every child. An ambitious goal for one pupil will be to sit their grade V exam, but for another it will be to go for grade VIII, and for another grade I. Yet within this, all can aim for the highest possible standard of performance, each at his or her own level.

Individuality means that no two children will produce excellent work in exactly the same way or at an identical level. Six-year-old Doris can produce excellent work, but it will not be the same as that of fourteen-year-old Maurice. Equally, not all six-year-olds will be able to produce excellent work of the same level of difficulty as that of Doris, nor all fourteen-year-olds as that of Maurice. The teacher needs to ascertain that a task provides the particular children doing it with the opportunity and means to demonstrate excellence.

We have already considered how the inherent worth of a child means that the characteristics of integrity and respect will be fostered individually and within the community. These characteristics of course play their part in the pursuit of excellence. An individual's integrity – their deep-seated responsibility, reliability, trustworthiness – is such an important element in grasping the notion of excellence, of doing something really *well*, in the fullest, richest sense of the word. Within the community, the fostering of respect extends to an appreciation of the worth of each other's work as well as their person.

SUMMARY BOX 5.1: The components of height

Heights of excellence: ambition + quality

Striving for heights of excellence is central to the culture of a good education, and so is not confined to the classroom or attitudes within it. The practical implications and outworkings of these principles will be considered later, but it is important here to stress that excellence in the exercise book is a reflection of excellence in the wider educational environment and community, including sports and the arts, but also other elements of school life, from the maintenance of the buildings to the manners of the children. It is easier to advocate excellence when it is evident all around, and in a good education excellence is in the air;

it is evident in all aspects and areas of life, including the way in which members of the community regard themselves, each other and their environment.

Breadth of attainment

A good education provides wide-ranging opportunities and encourages breadth of attainment.

If the ultimate worth of every child causes us to value all that they do (rather than the other way around) and pursue excellence, then the uniqueness of every child quickly reminds us that they will not all experience or demonstrate excellence in the same way. And the holistic view of education reminds us that it is not just the mind which is to be cultivated in a good education, but the development of the whole person.

These two ideas therefore combine in the provision within good education of opportunities to attain in all sorts of different ways and areas. This is a key characteristic of what is regarded as traditional English education: an education which is rounded, or broad, and which provides for opportunities to excel in different areas. And so the second educational principle which makes up this model of a good education is *breadth of attainment* (Figure 5.2).

Academic breadth

Self-evidently, an academic education enables the development of the mind and thus attainment in the intellectual area.

We have already considered how the pursuit of excellence (for example, in building the scale model of the solar system) enabled academic or intellectual attainment. It is helpful here to note how that particular task required the application and development of knowledge of science (the solar system), maths (scale and proportion), art and design (design and construction of models), geography (map work to determine suitable locations for the planets) and English (written descriptions of planets to accompany each model).

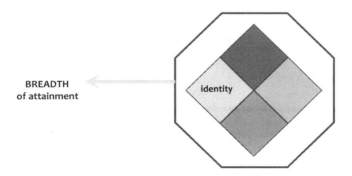

FIGURE 5.2 The second educational principle: breadth

Within the academic arena itself therefore, there is a breadth in types of attainment. The traditional academic subjects, such as maths and history for example, encourage different types of attainment and draw on different types of expertise. While both are intellectual, maths draws on quantitative, spatial and logical awareness and history on linguistic, interpretative and analytical skills. Of course there is a degree of overlap but nonetheless there are also distinctive features of each: they are not identical. It follows that children, differing as they do one from another, may engage and perform with differing degrees of readiness in any particular subject area.

Sports, the arts and personal development

Breadth of attainment does not just occur within the academic sphere however, but so much more richly beyond. A good education is one which promotes the development of body, soul and spirit as well as mind.

Whether or not Wellington claimed that the battle of Waterloo was won on the playing fields of Eton (which historians advise us is less than likely), perhaps once upon a time sport was a key element in all English education, including state-funded primary schools like mine. Certainly, my triumphant silver-medal race was run on a field which, as far as my memory serves me, was a great and glorious savannah of grassland, stretching away to distant trees, although I suspect the reality was somewhat more limited and prosaic.

On attending my secondary school, we trooped off down the road to playing fields where we ran around in studded boots, come wind or rain, wielding fearsome-looking lacrosse sticks and lashing out devoid (in my case) of anything resembling skill or finesse, but armed with enthusiasm alone, with not so much as a shake of the head in the direction of health and safety: no gum-shields had crossed the horizon of the early 1970s. But soon the playing field itself was nothing but a memory, the fields having been sold for building land. Sport became a trip to the leisure centre in a bus, where my friend and I whiled away an hour each week sitting, unseen, on the floor of a squash court, chatting.

In some schools sport has historically mattered greatly and remains a key component, a huge amount of space being created for it, both literally in some cases, or on the timetable, in others. In such schools, the more seriously it is taken, the more joyous and exuberant its significance seems to be in daily life. Traditionally seen as building character, sport of course does this and so much more. Sport keeps pupils fit and healthy. It encourages team spirit and loyalty, sportsmanship and fair play. Competitive sport energises its participants, giving a goal to strive towards, and children – by and large – enjoy it, especially if an element of choice can gradually be included. It is of course also excellent for those pupils who would far rather be running around than sitting still; and most of us have some sympathy with those for whom that is the case.

In terms of attainment, sport, by which I include both Games (competitive team sports) and Physical Education (which incorporates skills and fitness), creates opportunities for pupils to experience success (and indeed excellence) in a sphere beyond the academic, and indeed to learn through play. Some children attain more readily academically, and some more readily within the sporting arena – and there are some who seem to be particularly proficient in both. The provision of sport in developing the whole person and in enabling a greater breadth of attainment is invaluable.

But in addition to these two great areas, a third should be added: the arts. Here I include both the visual arts (painting, drawing, design, sculpture and so on) and the performing arts (music, drama and dance, and arguably gymnastics and so on). It is perhaps within these areas that we see the element of spirit being most particularly developed: empathy, sympathy, aesthetic appreciation. A pupil who learns to make music and to share that experience with others is in touch with the truth that there is more to life than the purely material. A pupil who plays a part in a piece of drama or mime learns about how personality expresses itself, how actions have consequences, how a gesture, expression or single word can either heal or kill.

It is of course true that the academic subjects, sports and the arts can all be seen to contribute to the whole person: each can be considered from an academic perspective, each can be taught in such a way as to develop spiritual awareness and to promote physical development. The point here is that all of these areas are significant in a rounded education.

A good education needs to encompass the opportunity to attain in all these areas. Pupils' strengths will vary, each having their own unique identity with its combination of gifts and creative strengths, but this is all the more reason to provide opportunity for these areas to be experienced and explored. They are of value in their own right, of value in providing breadth of opportunity to achieve, and of value in helping young people to mature as rounded and grounded individuals.

Here too we see how the characteristics promoted in the individual and community through an appreciation of the uniqueness of every child – distinction and positivity – are of essential importance in achieving breadth of attainment. Pupils are encouraged to achieve in their areas of strength and gain distinction in them. Within the whole community, there is a heightened sense of expectation as shared positivity believes high attainment to be possible, whether on the sports field, in the classroom or on stage.

A good education not only promotes excellence, it provides for breadth of attainment across the academic, sporting and artistic spheres, in addition to providing opportunities for building up the character traits explored in Chapter 4.

SUMMARY BOX 5.2: The components of breadth

Breadth of attainment:
academic + sports + arts + personal development

Depth of engagement

A good education encourages learners to dig deep and forge strong roots of learning.

The third dimension to be considered is that of depth. A good education values and promotes rigorous roots of learning, strong academic foundations on which a structure of understanding can be built. A good education is an antidote to superficiality, glibness, lazy thinking and 'dumbing down'. A good education is one in which pupils deeply engage with their learning (Figure 5.3).

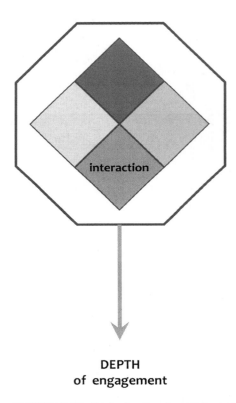

DEPTH
of engagement

FIGURE 5.3 The third educational principle: depth

Like many foundations, or roots, the characteristics of this third dimension tend to be the hidden, unseen elements of learning, and so need searching out in order not to be overlooked: they may not seem to be as glamorous or obvious as some other elements of education, but are nevertheless of vital importance – perhaps of greatest importance.

To help consider *depth of engagement*, we can think of four distinct, but interlinked, elements: the nurturing of collaboration, curiosity, creativity and rigour.

Collaboration

The third educational principle, depth, links with the third foundational value: the interactive nature of children, and indeed of humankind. We have already noted that as social creatures, we have a mutual dependency that informs those character traits which we encourage within an educational (and wider) community. As learners, however, it is also true that we are not isolated but are part of a learning community which stretches far beyond the confines of our classroom or even our generation. As learners we all famously stand with Sir Isaac Newton (or sit with Bernard of Chartres) on the 'shoulders of giants', enabling us sometimes to see a little further as a result.

An education does not take place in isolation, but encourages its students to learn both from and with others. The ancient tradition of 'manuduction' perceives the teacher as leading the student by the hand, guiding and introducing them to shared wisdom and a deepening of their intellectual habit. Good education builds carefully on the wisdom and learning of past generations to ensure that received understanding is passed on. This does not mean that there is a blind acceptance of all that has gone before, but that there is an appreciation and understanding of how ideas grow, develop and are sometimes challenged. Science provides a good example: pupils will be taught what previous (and contemporary) generations of scientists have discovered about the universe in which we find ourselves, but will also understand that this body of knowledge is continually developing and maturing, and is always incomplete. In order for this to be facilitated there needs of course to be a shared language of communication, with agreed grammar, vocabulary and syntax, in order that ideas are understood and passed on to successive generations with as little ambiguity of understanding as possible. Grasping this is key to putting down good strong roots of learning.

A good education encourages pupils not only to benefit from the learning of others across generations and continents, but also from working with their immediate peers. A collaborative approach allows pupils to work together on experiments and projects and engage together in debate, discussion and research. Grappling together over a difficult problem, whether it be a moral or mathematical question, enables ideas and approaches to be considered and evaluated. Group work enables projects to be undertaken which would simply be impossible if tackled by the lone learner – far more material can be covered, the end result demonstrating the whole to be greater than the sum of the parts, our solar system project being a case in point.

Technology enables collaboration with those not immediately present, but in partnership schools whether in neighbouring towns or on the other side of the globe, enriching learning and developing an essential local and global perspective, as a result.

Working together in such ways, pupils come to see themselves as potential contributors to the world's ever-growing body of knowledge and understanding.

The introduction of a school pond, for example, provides the perfect opportunity for pupils to do some real long-term research on how species populate a new area; in doing so they gain the thrill of realising what genuine research feels like – being the first in the world to find something out, and so contributing to the ever-expanding reservoir of understanding.

We all need to learn with and from each other, and acknowledging the importance of collaborative learning means that pupils develop a healthy humility. No one has a monopoly on the truth; each of us will sometimes be wrong; each of us needs to listen to and learn from those around us and those who have gone before us.

Curiosity

Depth of engagement is all about how children learn, and how we can ensure that they learn as well as possible. Children are natural learners, and a good education capitalises upon the instinctive curiosity which is part of children's nature, harnessing it and encouraging it to grow rather than dwindle.

One of the ways in which natural curiosity is encouraged is through careful content choice, matching what children learn to their particular interests, to areas which they will instinctively feel drawn to find out about. There are certain essentials in learning, but some of the content of education is rather more arbitrary. Children need to learn to read, for example, but there is considerable choice about exactly what they might read. History and geography are essential to gaining a sense of perspective on the world and understanding our place in it, but there is no way in which any pupil going through school can learn about every part of history or every element of the world's geography. There is room for choice.

Opportunities can also be created to allow children and young people the chance to do some real research into things they have a genuine interest in. A Year 8 Science fair I know of provides every pupil with the opportunity to devise their own scientific experiment in order to try and answer an original scientific question they have formulated. Topics explored have ranged from finding out how much water certain fruits contain to whether listening to music affects heart rate. Allowing 13-year-old pupils this kind of choice and enabling them to put their scientific knowledge into practice builds on their natural curiosity, but also encourages it to grow.

In another example, children take part in the construction of a time-line, called Great Eights. Working in groups, children research eight examples on a particular theme: battles, poets, inventions, monarchs and so on, and include a specific date for each, such as the start of a battle, the birth of a poet, patenting of an invention or coronation of a monarch. On completion of all eight fact-file entries for all groups, a large-scale time-line is compiled. The key point here is that groups are arranged and topics allocated on the basis of the children's interests, capitalising on their curiosity and encouraging it to grow.

Curiosity is not only fostered through the choice of subject matter, but also the way in which it is presented. Presenting a piece of English text as a detective puzzle to be explored, or a maths task as a code to crack, can capitalise on natural curiosity and foster its growth.

Creativity

Good education is not sterile, dry, dusty, repetitive and dull, but shines, sparkles and sings. One of the ways in which this is achieved is through encouraging individuals to exercise and hone their creative skills. Children are inherently creative, and in turn, creativity is inherent across the whole range of subjects in school. It is also an essential life-skill.

Perhaps most obviously we think of the arts when it comes to creativity: dramatic interpretation, musical composition, a sculpture in clay or a pencil sketch all allow scope for individual expression and the creation of something entirely novel. But this is also true for computer programming, devising a new scientific experiment, or finding a way through a mathematical investigation, as well as in the more obvious writing of poetry or stories. On the sports field, creativity may be the additional magic ingredient which combines with skill and commitment to make real champions. In fact, almost every pursuit within a good education can be seen to have a creative element within it.

Whether a child goes on to become an engineer, carer, teacher, chef or gardener, creativity is essential for success in the chosen career. At a more fundamental level, the ability to respond effectively to the changing circumstances of life and an unpredictable future requires creativity. We are adaptable creatures (as well as creatures of habit), and the ability to come up with a creative response is essential for success. Creativity requires knowledge, understanding, skills, application, imagination – and courage. It is not hard to see why the ability and confidence to be creative are such important factors in developing strong roots of learning and why fostering creativity is such an important element of a good education.

Valuing creativity also reflects the value placed on the individual at the heart of education, since creativity is a reflection of individuality and unique gifting: it is precisely because each individual is unique that creativity is possible. It is because of each individual's worth that it is so highly prized.

Rigour

A fourth and final contributing component to depth of engagement is rigour. By this I mean particularly laying foundations which are strong and trustworthy – making sure that as each layer of understanding and knowledge is laid down it is done so with care, precision and accuracy so as to ensure that it is perfectly stable, reliable and solid for the next layer to be built on it with confidence.

Certain knowledge and skills are self-evidently foundational since other subject areas depend upon them: reading, writing and maths are obvious examples, as are communication and presentation skills more generally, and the ability to reason and be logical, for example. It matters that these foundational skills are acquired with the greatest possible levels of accuracy and reliability. Teachers need to get things right in our teaching and in children's learning, and rigour stems from an attitude that says it matters that foundational work is correct, done to a high standard, with as few errors, blemishes or omissions as possible.

When our son was in his first year at school, aged five, one of his friends asked his teacher how he should indicate that someone was speaking in the story he was writing; he had perhaps noticed, or had pointed out to him, speech marks in a book he had been reading. The teacher had a choice: she could explain the tricky rules of punctuating direct speech to a five-year-old (widely regarded as completely age-inappropriate due to its complexity), or she could tell him that it didn't matter for now, that he would learn later.

She chose the former option, exerting her professional judgement in deciding that this particular child was ready to learn this particular skill, difficult as it was, and that he was better off getting his work right from the outset than having to relearn later. In doing this, she was choosing rigour.

An appreciation of the importance of rigour is a defining principle of a good education; that boy on that occasion was being well educated. He was learning to get things right and do things well from the very outset.

This culture of wanting work to be correct, accurate, precise, flawless even, is very much part of cultivating excellence. It is closely associated with paying attention to detail. Often the difference between simply doing a task and doing it well is a matter of paying attention to detail. This is a hugely important principle for children to grasp in their learning.

If we take maths as an example, we quickly and easily can see why detail matters so much. Maths is either right or wrong: two and two always equal exactly four, not more or less, not sometimes or usually, but always exactly. If we consider the long-multiplication sum 267×29, the way I was taught at school, there are no fewer than fourteen operations required to arrive at the answer. At any point an error can be made, but even if one such error is made, the whole calculation is incorrect: one error and the mark awarded is a round zero. 'Details matter' is an attitude and approach to be cultivated as a key to the pursuit of rigour.

Interestingly, this is not universally regarded as being important. I recall on one occasion a parent speaking to me of a school their child had previously attended: 'I don't think much attention was paid to detail there', the father said, 'it just wasn't considered to be very important'. If we want education to be good, detail matters, because rigour is an essential element of excellence.

This needs to be held in balance with the provision of appropriate levels of challenge already discussed. Rigour is not about work being so easy that it is always right: it is about appreciating the importance of work being correct, even (or especially) when this is most difficult to achieve. It is also important to guard against the pursuit of rigour stifling creativity in a misplaced perfectionism; rather, rigour should be seen to ensure that the foundational skills are reliable so that creativity can not only occur but find expression and flourish fully.

Of course, it must be remembered that there is not always necessarily a right or correct answer – sometimes a whole range of approaches or responses can be chosen from, which is problematic in its own right for some learners. Sensitivity on the part of the teacher and knowledge of individual pupils is essential here.

Once again it is clear how the characteristics fostered within the community facilitate and encourage this sort of learning. To engage deeply with their learning, pupils have to take personal responsibility: they need to draw on their reserves of initiative. The onus must be on pupils to develop for themselves a personal engagement with their learning. And yet as members of a learning community they will serve their fellow learners through collaboration and teamwork. There may sometimes be healthy competition, but there is no room for selfishness or isolation when we regard pupils as being mutually dependent. They will give and receive in their learning.

SUMMARY BOX 5.3: The components of depth

Depth of engagement:
collaboration + curiosity + creativity + rigour

Through fostering collaboration, creativity, curiosity and rigour, pupils engage with their learning at a profound rather than superficial level. They become immersed in their learning, absorbed by it, both individually and collectively. Such depth of engagement leads naturally to the fourth education principle: length of endeavour.

Length of endeavour

A good education leads to a personal commitment to learn.

The fourth dimension of learning is length. This is perhaps the easiest dimension to overlook, as it takes us beyond the immediate, but a consideration of the fourth foundational value – development – reminds us that children (and adults) are works in progress, continually learning, always changing. A good education recognises and reflects this, and taking the long-term view, values and fosters length of endeavour (Figure 5.4). Developing a personal commitment to learn, pupils will persevere with their studies in each lesson, each year, across each stage of school and beyond the formal years of full-time education into the long-term future.

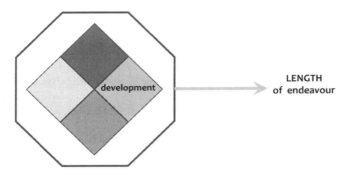

FIGURE 5.4 The fourth educational principle: length

Length of endeavour can helpfully be considered in two ways: the short term, the time-frame of a lesson or topic and the long term, which is ongoing over a period of months and years. Although linked, they have distinguishing elements.

SUMMARY BOX 5.4: The components of length

Length of endeavour:
short-term longevity + long-term longevity

Short-term longevity of learning

First, in the short term, a good education is one which enables pupils to grapple and battle in order to learn, not giving up when learning is difficult or a problem is tricky, but to keep going until a solution is reached. This 'short-term' longevity requires at least three things.

Diligence

Diligence is a hard-working attitude. It is an essential characteristic of a good education that a pupil works hard. Being thorough, attentive, conscientious and careful all play their part in diligence. Pupils who are diligent take responsibility for their learning and take their work seriously.

Not everything about learning is necessarily enjoyable, and sometimes we have to demonstrate an unswerving ability to see something through against the odds. We can see this in music practice where a scale may have to be practised over and over and over again until perfection is reached. And then it needs to be practised over and over and over again until perfection is automatic. A willingness to do this stems from an attitude that values working hard and has developed the self-discipline to do so.

Diligence is not just about repetition, rote learning and lengthy exercises, however. The ability – and willingness – to take the initiative and think for oneself is essential too. This comes through grappling with difficult problems, digging deep into one's own resources, and being confident to step out in a new direction to come up with a novel idea or unique solution. Independent thought is an essential ingredient for longevity of learning and an indication of hard work in action.

Tenacity

Tenacity is allied to diligence. Tenacity is the ability to hold on and not let go. Like a puppy with a toy clamped between its teeth, tenacity enables us to hold on tight and push forwards to reach a solution despite difficulty – even when we feel like giving up, perhaps because something more enticing is on offer, or because work seems routine and unappealing, or because a problem requires huge mental effort to be solved.

It is helpful to remind children that everyone finds something difficult in their learning, at some point. It may seem obvious, but if they find something difficult this is a reason to work harder at it and not less hard. The example I sometimes use is my own: swimming. I found learning to swim horribly difficult. Used to splashing in and out of the sea from the earliest age on holiday, it should not have been a problem, but faced with an early-morning, outdoor, unheated, chlorinated swimming pool, which was where my school swimming lessons took place, I felt utterly at sea (ironically enough). I can recall the swimming teacher walking a few paces ahead of me, holding out into the water a net on the end of a pole that I had to try and reach out for stroke by stroke. It was an utterly miserable experience, but is a good metaphor for tenacity. We have to keep stretching forward to try and grasp something just out of our reach until we make it through and have it in our hand. A good education enables that to develop, hard as it is. It is all about keeping going.

Resilience

Resilience is the ability to pick up and carry on after disappointment, and is another critical ingredient for developing this short-term longevity of learning. Resilience is the ability to go back out and bat in cricket despite having been out first ball last time. It is the attitude that is willing to learn from mistakes rather than be defeated by them. A good education encourages resilience across the subject areas, learning what needs to be done to make an essay more effective, appreciating how a performance in drama could have been better, not feeling crushed by a disappointing test result in maths, but looking at it square on and determining to do better next time.

Much is said about the need for children to develop 'grit', which although hard to define, I think certainly has these elements: diligence, tenacity and resilience. A pupil with grit will persist with their work however hard it is, however long it takes or however disappointed they feel. There is some debate as to how it is best learnt – taught about or experienced. While I am convinced that children need to learn to acquire 'grit', I am not persuaded that they will acquire it through 'Grit lessons', as such. Rather, if the temptations to over-help children, spoon-feed to get instant results or make work too easy are resisted, pupils will experience for themselves what is sometimes called the 'trough of difficulty'. As E.M. Forster said, 'Spoon-feeding in the long run teaches us nothing but the shape of the spoon';[2] by contrast, the responses and reactions of teachers when learning is hard going can encourage grit to develop. Rewarding diligence, praising tenacity and applauding resilience in practice are more effective than teaching a lesson on any one of these qualities.

This may all feel a little negative, but these are essential qualities for a good education to develop because neither life nor learning is necessarily easy. In fact, it is possibly precisely when these characteristics are most sharply being developed that the most learning takes place. And if they do sound a little negative, then we can take comfort from the fact that their longer-term counterparts certainly sound a little more positive.

SUMMARY BOX 5.5: The components of short-term longevity

Short-term longevity (grit):
diligence + tenacity + resilience

Long-term longevity of learning

Looking at the long term, a good education is one that outlives the input, which creates sufficiently strong habits of learning that learning itself becomes a lifelong endeavour. This 'long-term' longevity of learning also requires at least three things.

Openness

The characteristic of openness is essential for lifelong learning. Openness is about making oneself available to gain new knowledge, to acquire new skills, to think in new ways. It is the opposite of having a fixed, closed mindset and again reflects the humility noted as a key element in collaborative learning, admitting that I need to learn more, and in different ways.

Dr Carol Dweck's much-publicised research on growth mindsets[3] bears out the importance of openness to learning in achieving the best and most successful educational outcomes. Similarly, the Learning without Limits[4] research project provides a reminder of how important it is for the learning community to be optimistic about children's capacity to learn, always adopting a positive attitude, rather than assuming a fixed or limited educability.

Having an open mind for learning also suggests having a positive, proactive desire to keep on learning. We only need to take up a new interest, visit a new place or read a book on a topic new to us to discover another whole world about which we know nothing. But an open mind will want to grow in knowledge and understanding. Having an openness to learn means that we want to gain knowledge even though an infinite body of knowledge and understanding will continue to lie beyond our grasp. A good education is one which will foster long-term openness of mind.

Adaptability

The most enormous changes have taken place during my working life as I have lived through the Information Revolution. When I started teaching, working online was unheard of: it has now become the bedrock of working life. When my father retired, computers were considered the preserve of the younger generation. Yet now in his 90s, he happily uses his PC to shop, research and write, and communicates using email as readily as the best of the young generation. Human beings seem to be remarkably adaptable. In the last thirty years we have all learnt to communicate in ways which the previous generation would have found utterly inconceivable.

We cannot predict the future, except to say that it is unpredictable. To survive, humankind has to adapt; to flourish as individuals and communities, we have to be able to adapt readily and confidently. A successful working life requires us to be able to keep learning, building on what we already know, but not relying upon current knowledge or skill sets as sufficient. A good education fosters adaptability, and the positive embracing of change and challenge, recognising that it is simply laying a foundation on which lifelong learning will have to build. A good education is one which encourages and enables this characteristic of adaptability.

Commitment

Creating the right conditions for lifelong learning is an essential characteristic of a good education. If someone has been educated well, they will want to keep on learning. They will have found joy in learning and will be keen to continue to learn, not wanting to stagnate or entrench, but be willing and able to move forward and grow in mind, body, soul and strength – intellectually, physically, emotionally and spiritually. They will be committed to learning, and this in turn is essential for a flourishing life. This commitment to learning in the longer term is encouraged and fostered by a good education.

Just as we regarded the short-term characteristics of length of endeavour to be summed up in the word grit, so I think that this long-term openness, adaptability and commitment to learn can perhaps be summed up by the word 'drive'. This suggests a forward momentum in our learning, a recognition that we are never static.

A good education creates lifelong learners. It does this through a wide-ranging, inspiring, engaging curriculum which will be enjoyable for pupils and encourage them to see learning as a wholly positive and worthwhile activity. While from time to time work may be hard, tedious or discouraging, the development of grit – the determination to keep going – ensures that learning will be achieved.

This learning in turn brings with it a joy and satisfaction which encourage the pursuit to continue in the long term. The drive to continue to learn throughout life requires openness, adaptability and commitment, but is a hall-mark of a good education.

The characteristics fostered within the individual and learning community arising from seeing the pupils as being continually developing are of key import-ance here: perseverance and compassion. It is essential that pupils have developed the personal characteristic of perseverance in order to exercise grit, to be able to work hard, and keep going, no matter the setbacks *en route*. This matters equally in the longer term, where perseverance will enable openness, adaptability and commitment to bear fruit. Equally important, however, is the trait of compassion, because within the community, perfection will never be attained in any of these areas. Inevitably, pupils will tire, learners will flounder, mistakes will be made. Compassion encourages those who are faltering, assists those who are struggling and brings a warmth and generosity of spirit to enable the fresh starts which are essential if learning is to continue throughout life.

SUMMARY BOX 5.6: The components of long-term longevity

Long-term longevity (drive):
openness + adaptability + commitment

Put together, the four educational principles of excellence, attainment, engagement and endeavour thus fan out in four directions to create a high-quality, balanced and effective education (Figure 5.5).

It is perhaps surprising to be this far through a consideration of what we mean by a good education and yet not know what we are actually likely to see in practice. Should we not be discussing *results*? It is of course tempting to say that a good education is one which produces the results that we want to see and so then to use the results as a starting point in defining and describing a good

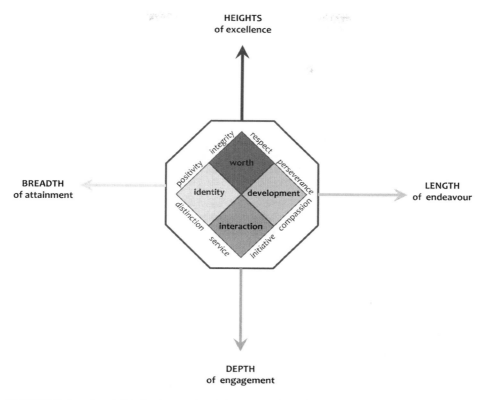

FIGURE 5.5 Four foundational values, pairs of character traits and educational principles

education. This book has tried to come from the other point of view, by asking what the values are that underpin education and what the principles are on which education should be built.

However, of course the outcomes are of supreme importance, and it is to these that we now turn as we look at the final element of the four-dimensional model of education: practical outcomes.

Notes

1   *Bloom's Taxonomy* was created in 1956 under the leadership of educational psychologist Dr Benjamin Bloom in order to promote higher orders of thinking in education.
2   Published in *The Observer* on 7 October 1951 under 'Sayings of the Week'.
3   See for example, www.childstudysystem.org/uploads/6/1/9/1/6191025/mindset_book_study.pdf
4   https://learningwithoutlimits.educ.cam.ac.uk/downloads/creatinglwl_forumarticle.pdf, accessed 28 July 2017.

Practical outcomes

End results

The final layer in the four-dimensional model is made up of the distinctive outcomes we would expect to see from a good education. These 'end results' are just that – not a good education in themselves but, rather, the evidence that a good education is in place.

Reading, reading, reading

As a young child I was fortunate enough to have a caravan holiday each summer in north Wales. Many memories stand out in my mind from those times, but two are particularly relevant for these purposes. First, was the regular sense of pleasure at waking up and hearing the steady tapping of raindrops on the caravan roof: I did not have to get up, but instead, could lie in bed and read. Second, I clearly recall the more clement days on which we would all stride purposefully out to conquer one or other of Snowdonia's magnificent peaks. As the youngest of the family, I had not only the shortest legs but also the shortest time-frame against which to measure the passage of time, as a result of which these walks always seemed to me to be interminable. Hours spent on steep grass slopes were interleaved only with painful scrambles through brambles, wading through sodden swampy flushes and frustrating back-sliding down scree-covered slopes. Nearly there now, I was told encouragingly, as one false-summit after another came and went. It will be worth it when we see the view, I was repeatedly told. Of course it was always worth it on reaching the summit, as I would once again retrieve my book from my pocket, find a sheltered spot and sit and read, swept away to whatever childhood storyland was my particular favourite that year.

I learnt to read with the famous *Janet and John*, our children with Biff and Chip, equally well known as inhabitants of the *Oxford Reading Tree*. But of course it is not who we learn to read with and by what method that matters in the long run, but whether we want to carry on reading when no one is telling us to.

My comic mountain-top scenario offers an illustration of the practical outcomes that we want to see from a good education – a desire and ability to be an independent learner. Not, of course, that well-educated people will necessarily prefer reading to enjoying a view from the top of a mountain – I realise now that both can be enjoyed, although best not concurrently – but nevertheless a good education will be evident far beyond the classroom walls and years of schooling: that is its point. What that looks like in practice is where attention is finally turned in the four-dimensional model.

Practical outcomes

The fourth and final layer in the four-dimensional model of education is made up of the *practical outcomes* that will be evident. Each of the four educational principles discussed leads to its own specific distinctive outcome, these being, in turn: the experience of success, achievement in diverse ways and areas, good habits of study and the love of learning. The precise ways in which these will be in evidence will vary for every child and in every context, but these are general descriptors, each a hallmark of a good education, which leads to and supports the others (Table 6.1).

Before considering each of these outcomes in turn, however, it is pertinent to note the increasing emphasis placed on publicly assessing the outcomes of education through examination results, and comparative performance. School performance tables, providing information by listing examination results or test scores, were first published in the UK in 1992, and were rapidly used by the media to create so-called school league tables, ranking schools by attainment within these parameters. As already noted, in 2000, the first PISA survey took place aiming to 'evaluate education systems worldwide by testing the skills and knowledge of 15-year-old students'. A triennial event, over half a million students took part in the 2015 survey, representing 72 countries and economies.[1]

Such performance indicators are useful for their own purposes, but they do not, however, contribute in a particularly effective way to creating a model of good education. When effectiveness of education is measured through the analysis of performance against a national or international norm, the focus shifts away from the achievements of an individual pupil or student towards the statistics for a cohort. Such a measure therefore addresses a different question from whether an individual pupil is being well provided for educationally and achieving a level of personal excellence. A further unavoidable drawback of any

TABLE 6.1 Four practical outcomes result

FOUR PRACTICAL OUTCOMES ARISING FROM THE EDUCATIONAL PRINCIPLES

PRINCIPLE	OUTCOMES
Excellence	*Experience of success*
Attainment	*Variety of achievement*
Engagement	*Habits of study*
Endeavour	*Love of learning*

such scheme is that anything 'below average' can often be perceived as being poor, although in reality the nature of statistics dictates that half of all results will be below average by definition, however good the education.

Such measures are also necessarily limited in scope, and cannot attempt to consider the breadth of attainment considered here to be essential within a good education. Typically, nothing other than core academic prowess, such as the wider curriculum, sports and the arts, is addressed by performance tables, let alone those intangible character traits which a good education fosters individually and in the community. Thus performance tables do not really measure height of achievement for all pupils, and nor are they a measure breadth of attainment. Neither do they purport to consider the depth of educational engagement or length of endeavour.

The four practical outcomes identified within the four-dimensional model of education are not quantitative, but rather qualitative. They are a reminder that, as Einstein allegedly said, 'Not everything that counts can be counted, and not everything that can be counted counts'. Each will be described in turn.

Experience of success

Success is defined by the *Oxford English Dictionary* as the 'accomplishment of an aim or purpose'. Excellence leads to success, and it is not hard to see why. In order for success to be achieved, a goal has to be set and a standard reached. This model of education has the cultivation of excellence as one of its four key educational principles. Central to a good education is working with integrity. Doing things well, striving for and achieving as high a standard as possible through the cultivation of ambition and quality, are key. Supported by a firm and secure base of knowledge, understanding and skill, success is an inevitable outcome (Figure 6.1).

Experiencing success results in a great surge of confidence. Whether it is the passing of a maths exam, scoring a try in rugby or playing a scale without a mistake, success makes children feel good about themselves. In turn this encourages pupils to branch out and push themselves further and harder, believing themselves to be capable of achieving – because success builds confidence. It is also true that confidence builds success: the two form into a virtuous circle. The greater the success, the more confidence builds. The greater the confidence, the more will be attempted and achieved. Self-belief grows out of confidence and a 'can-do' attitude develops.

Experiencing success in one area can also lead to confidence in another. Recognising and celebrating success on the sporting field can help the child who feels less confident in maths, just as the child who grasps maths more readily can find her confidence grow in the arena of sport where she may feel instinctively less certain.

It is important to note that success is not necessarily about coming first or winning prizes. Success is more subtle than that, incorporating a sense of pride in having achieved a personal goal, worked successfully in a team or influenced

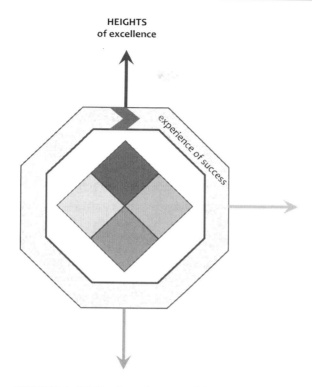

HEIGHTS
of excellence

experience of success

FIGURE 6.1 Heights of excellence result in success

others for the better. It incorporates feeling genuinely pleased with one's own efforts and the outcomes, irrespective of how they compare with others. Success in this sense is richer and fuller than an accolade; it grows from self-knowledge and self-respect, an acceptance of and joy in one's own inherent value, and gratitude for one's identity and what can be achieved through it. Experience of success is the complete opposite of feeling a failure.

Variety of achievement

In a good educational environment, where there is breath of opportunity in which to attain, pupils do well across a range of endeavours: there will be variety in the types of achievements (Figure 6.2). Within a broad education, this success is spread across the disciplines – academically, in music, art, drama or on the sporting field. It will also be evident in acts of service to other members of the community, and in producing a happy and supportive environment.

The sort of education that has been described results in a wide variety of achievement, and a school's aim should be that every pupil gains a sense of particular achievement in one or more areas. Every pupil has unique gifts, creativities and talents to be fostered; each deserves to have those gifts recognised and

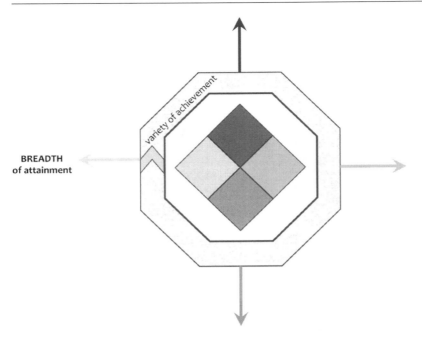

FIGURE 6.2 Broad attainment leads to varied achievement

encouraged, and their understanding in those areas to be developed as fully as possible. As appropriate opportunities are provided, they see their gifts come to fruition in some form of tangible and successful outcome.

With every child being uniquely gifted, with their own spread of strengths, interests and creativities, if a broad range of opportunity for attainment is provided, each child's pattern of distinction will be different. They will gradually develop areas of more significant interest and eventually wish to make choices in their learning. Within the learning community such variety of achievement and interest will be welcomed and celebrated.

In the pre-public examination years, before choices are to be made, however, an aim will also be for all pupils to have the opportunity to develop as well as they can across all spheres. Pupils should aim to do their very best across the disciplines: academically, in music, art, drama and on the sporting field, as well as in acts of service.

So in addition to varied attainment across the learning community, variety of attainment will also be evident for each member of it personally. The four-dimensional view of the child is holistic, acknowledging the need for everyone to develop intellectually, physically, emotionally, morally, culturally, aesthetically and spiritually, albeit each in his or her own unique way. A four-dimensional education therefore provides opportunities for each child to develop in their own way in each of these areas, and to know a rich mix of achievement as a result.

From a rich curriculum of opportunity, and a culture of positivity, should emerge children who can appreciate and participate confidently across the range of endeavours, while also enjoying particular individual distinction in some special area. They will be academically assured and culturally knowledgeable; aesthetically engaged and enjoying their sport; and they will contribute positively and generously to the learning community. All this should characterise the well-educated child, and these are also characteristics which will stand them in good stead in the years beyond formal education.

Habits of study

Third, this model of education results in good strong habits of study (Figure 6.3). Children who have a good education should work hard, with thought, care and commitment. They should take responsibility for their individual learning, but also be good collaborators and communicators, grasping the importance of the learning community and the part that they play in it. While taking the initiative in their own learning, they will also see their responsibility to contribute to the life and learning of others. Critically, they will be in the *habit* of working in this way – it will become the norm, the default, the expected way of working. As we would expect, a well-educated child can and does work well, and has developed all the skills necessary to do so.

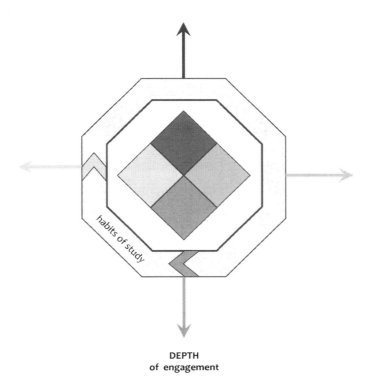

DEPTH
of engagement

FIGURE 6.3 Deep engagement cultivates good habits of study

Habits of study include a range of attitudes and behaviours which make a positive contribution to the present learning environment and set the pattern for a life of learning. What Professor Deborah Eyre describes as 'high performance learning' includes the 'right attitudes and approaches – curiosity, persistence and hard work'. These approaches, she suggests need to be supported at home and in school.[2] Such habits are not only contributors to a good education, but are the results of a good education, and contributors to its long-term benefit.

Love of learning

Finally, the fourth practical outcome of a good education is love of learning (Figure 6.4). We should not be satisfied with an education which simply has our children working hard and doing well, vitally important as these are. There should also be the element of passion: enthusiasm, enjoyment, delight and a sense of wonder at the world we live in, of all that has been discovered and created, of all that has been accomplished and achieved. Pupils educated in this way develop a deep appreciation of the world in all its richness, complexity and beauty, and a profound respect for it and for the endeavour of learning about it.

They will have learnt the value of persevering and experienced a compassionate response in the more challenging times, which will spur them on. A well-educated child will want to learn, and go on learning, having been enthused, engaged and encouraged.

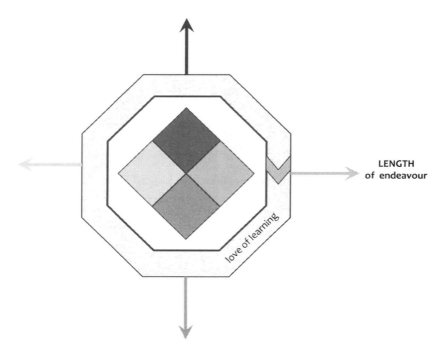

FIGURE 6.4 Length of endeavour fosters a love of learning

An unbroken cycle of learning

These practical outcomes of learning are inextricably linked and it is very difficult to talk about one without mentioning another. But as the final part of our model falls into place, it is good to see how these four practical outcomes lead to and support each other.

A love of learning leads to pupils wanting to study. In this way, good habits are further developed. As good habits of study develop across the disciplines, so achievement will be evident in diverse ways. Allowing for pupils to achieve in different ways enables all to experience success in one form or another. Success leads to enjoyment, enthusiasm and a greater love of learning. As knowledge, understanding, skills and appreciation meld together, enabling excellent attainment through engaged endeavour, they contribute to these practical outcomes, each of which supports, enriches and encourages the next, producing a positive virtuous circle of good educational outcomes (Figure 6.5).

The upshot of this is that a good education is characterised by pupils with good habits of study, achieving across a range of disciplines, experiencing success as a result and developing a lifelong love of learning. This virtuous circle of learning helps contribute to a flourishing life for the learner and the learning community.

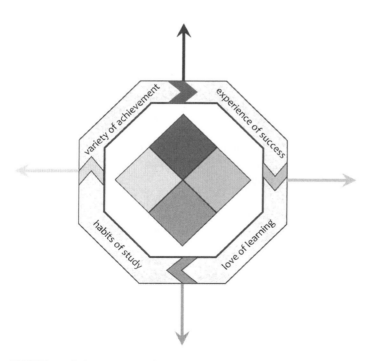

FIGURE 6.5 A virtuous circle of learning

Summary: the four-dimensional model of education

To recap and summarise, the four-dimensional model of education now constructed, initiated from a consideration of values we might associate with the
individual child.

Four essential foundational values

- As all human life is precious, every child is of inestimable worth.

- With an inimitable and distinctive identity, every child is unique.

- We cannot function independently, but are mutually reliant.

- No matter our stage or age, we are all continually learning.

These four foundational values concerning the worth, identity, interaction and
development of the child form the starting point and core of the model of good
education which is proposed.

Four pairs of character traits

If these values are taken seriously, there will be important consequences for
the ethical or moral elements of education – what we might think of as the
development of character both individually and within the learning community.

- Individually: integrity, distinction, initiative and perseverance.

- Communally: respect, positivity, service and compassion.

Four educational principles

Beyond and in addition to any such character implications, the foundational values
also give rise to some explicit and ambitious educational principles, which will
be evidenced in distinguishing practices.

- Excellence is to be expected, because each child is inherently precious, so it
  matters that they develop and contribute in the best possible way.

- Achievement will be broad, because each child is multifaceted and has a
  unique pattern of gifts, interests and creativities.

- Deep roots of learning are to be established because we are interdependent
  and learning requires the efforts, wisdom and support of others.

- Lengthy endeavour is going to be necessary, because every person is a lifelong
  learner, so we are in for a long haul.

Four practical outcomes

The upshot, if this is successfully recognised and promoted, is distinctive practical outcomes among learners who will be seen to:

- experience success
- achieve widely
- study well
- love to learn.

All these are characteristic hallmarks of a good education.

These foundational values and consequent character traits, together with the educational principles and consequent practical outcomes, form the 'four-dimensional' model of education. The title derives from the four educational principles: heights of excellence, breadth of attainment, depth of engagement and length of endeavour (Table 6.2 and Figure 6. 6). Taken together, all the elements of the model act to form a practical and coherent framework for describing and ensuring a good education. This model is a distillation and encapsulation of all that a good education means.

TABLE 6.2 All the elements of the four-dimensional model

THE FOUR-DIMENSIONAL MODEL OF EDUCATION

FOUNDATIONAL VALUES CONCERNING THE CHILD	DUAL CHARACTER TRAITS		EDUCATIONAL PRINCIPLES	PRACTICAL OUTCOMES
	PERSONAL	**COMMUNITY**		
Worth: **Inherently precious**	*Integrity of character*	Mutual respect	HEIGHTS of excellence	**Experience of success**
Identity: **Uniquely gifted**	*Individual distinction*	Shared positivity	BREADTH of attainment	**Variety of achievement**
Interaction: **Mutually dependent**	*Personal initiative*	Attitude of service	DEPTH of engagement	**Habits of study**
Development: **Continually learning**	*Determined perseverance*	Compassionate spirit	LENGTH of endeavour	**Love of learning**

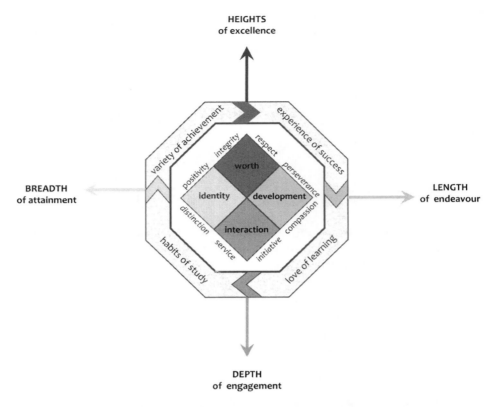

FIGURE 6.6 All the elements of the four-dimensional model of education: four foundational values, four pairs of character traits, four educational principles and four practical outcomes

Notes

1   www.oecd.org/pisa/aboutpisa/, accessed 28 July 2017.
2   www.theguardian.com/education/2017/jul/25/no-such-thing-as-a-gifted-child-einstein-iq, accessed 28 July 2017.

3

Applications, implications and implementation of the four-dimensional model

And so for a time it looked as though all the adventures were coming to an end; but that was not to be.[1]

C.S. Lewis, *The Lion, the Witch and the Wardrobe*

CHAPTER

7

The four-dimensional school

Values and principles in practice

The four-dimensional model of education is a framework that has potential to be applied in any educational context. Its constituent parts are not particularly complex, and there are no structural or resourcing prerequisites for its application, because the principles can be applied in widely differing ways. To begin with, it can be applied to whole-school policy and practice, bearing in mind that the contexts in which schools sit can indeed be very diverse.

North Harrow, Bath and Cambridge

I suppose that it is to be expected that a school will reflect the character of the village, town or city in which it is situated – both for better and worse. My schooldays were located in Betjeman's Metro-Land, poignantly remembered in his poem 'Harrow-on-the-Hill':

When melancholy Autumn comes to Wembley
And electric trains are lighted after tea
The poplars near the stadium are trembly
With their tap and tap and whispering to me,
Like the sound of little breakers
Spreading out along the surf-line
When the estuary's filling
With the sea.[2]

Like countless others of my generation, I walked to my primary school (and walked back home for lunch before making the return trip in the afternoon) and took Betjeman's 'electric train' to secondary school, passing the row upon row of semi-detached 1930s three-up-three-downs which filled the outskirts of north-west London as far as the eye could see.

Unlike the homely 'Tudorbeathen' semis, my junior school was housed in a typically modernist block built in 1934, apparently its claim to fame being that it was the first school designed by Curtis (the county architect) and Burchett (the assistant architect to the education committee) to feature concrete slab floors supported by pillars. I found it rather foreboding, but it served its purpose, housing some four hundred pupils then as it still does today. The wonderful grassy plane of my infant-school running triumph stood adjacent to it.

By contrast, by the time our own children were at primary school, 'the school run' had become a phenomenon. Living in Bath, this involved driving up a precipitous, ear-popping hill, followed by a daily search – in competition with several hundred other parents – for a parking place, and then walking past what was proudly believed to be the longest Georgian terrace in Europe. The 1840s school founded by the local Anglican church for 'the poor and manufacturing classes of Beacon Hill' had a small grassy 'field' on which – among other things – the annual school fun-run took place. This was particularly good fun for the parental spectators, not least since being on the side of an inordinately steep hill meant that there were two level sides of the fun-run (top and bottom), one somersaultingly steep downhill side on the right and one gruellingly steep uphill side on the left, where the fun-run became a fun-walk. This field also leant a considerable home-team advantage in football matches.

These two very different contexts, of place and time, resulted in widely differing educational experiences and, consequently, memories. And when it comes to considering how the four-dimensional model might apply practically in a school situation, context has to be borne in mind. The Greater London primary needed to guard against the impersonal and monotonous; the Bath primary enjoyed a supportive proactive parental group: the two contexts were very different, bringing their own sets of unique opportunities, strengths and challenges, as will be the case for every school. Inevitably, my current context – living and teaching in a thriving university city which is characterised by high academic ambition and successful entrepreneurship – colours my current experiences and attitudes; these are also reflected in the city's schools, all of which seem to like to pride themselves on their sharing of the city's strong academic traditions and confident future focus.

Although settings vary however, whatever the educational context (indeed sometimes despite the context), if a good education is to be provided all the elements of the model, as described in Part 2, should ideally be in evidence. This does not mean a formulaic approach should be adopted to achieve this; if anything the opposite should be the case, celebrating the unique context of each school as we do the individual pupils within it, and catering for the needs of that unique community using local personal knowledge and understanding.

The four-dimensional model has its origins in work with seven- to thirteen-year-olds. Its most direct applicability is therefore to the junior and lower secondary years of schooling and, in the application of the model that follows, examples are drawn from these years. It need not be confined to these, however, and it is not difficult to see how its four-fold elements speak with relevance to all stages of education.

The four-dimensional model of education is a construct or scaffold which consists of a distillation of the essentials. It is more akin to a map which shows the key features of the landscape, rather than to a set of directions dictating a specific route. Like any map, it should be of use in helping to ascertain the lie of the land, identifying the starting point of the journey, locating the desired destination and assisting in planning the most effective and scenic route.

In order for the model to be applied practically in schools, it is helpful first to consider briefly some essential factors for the success of any organisation. These will necessarily be in place if the four-dimensional model is to be of any use in practice.

Clarity, commitment and culture

It may be that the hardest part of any ambitious enterprise is capturing absolute clarity of thought about it. In an educational context, this may be especially true when the immediate demands of a busy school life take up so much time and energy. The four-dimensional model in essence is simple enough, but as Steve Jobs, co-founder of Apple, is quoted as saying, 'Simple can be harder than complex: you have to work hard to get your thinking clean to make it simple. But it's worth it in the end, because once you get there, you can move mountains'.[3] Or as Winnie-the-Pooh said, 'It is more fun to talk with someone who doesn't use long, difficult words but rather short, easy words like, "What about lunch?" '[4]

The most important, perhaps the only, prerequisite for implementing good education is commitment to its values and principles – an embracing of the culture it promotes. The governors and staff of a school, and above all its head teacher, need to believe in these values, want to see them implemented and be willing to devote themselves to their realisation.

Schools and teachers are indeed in the business of moving mountains – even if they do so in tiny incremental steps. But to have impact on a mountain-moving scale, the clarity of vision once identified must be matched by an equal and wholehearted commitment to the culture and its implementation.

Consensus, consideration, consistency and communication

Aesop's 'Four oxen and the Lion' may have been one of the earliest articulations of the often-repeated phrase 'united we stand', but the truth contained in it has stood the test of time. All organisations, including schools, find strength in consensus. If a school is to implement a good education, once the culture to which it aspires has been simply and clearly articulated, and commitment to it agreed upon, that understanding needs to be shared.

Within the last few decades, mission statements have become popular for organisations of all sorts. Although typically limited in scope and detail (for a while, Walt Disney's was 'We make people happy'), they have the virtue of reminding participants of the importance of pulling in the same direction, and having shared goals. The participants in a school community include not only the leaders, teachers and pupils, but also non-teaching staff, governors, parents and the neighbourhood, including the residential, commercial and academic communities; the more that these groups are able to work together, the stronger the enterprise can be.

Schools need to have a particularly sharp, shared focus in what they are doing because every pupil only has their chance once: once to go through an academic year, or unit of work, or individual lesson, or specific question. How clearly I recall a mark in a specific Latin exam forty years ago (47 per cent – nothing to be proud of) or can visualise my maths teacher's tiny, tidy, green-ink handwriting in my book. In education, the experiences gained by pupils come in very small parcels: a word from a teacher, an incident at play-time, a specific mark in a test, and yet the totality also matters, the long-term progress, the end results, the lifelong journey. The tiny cell-like experiences build incrementally into the whole organic structure, patiently forging annual growth-rings as they go like some mighty redwood: and each part matters because the whole matters.

The pressure is therefore on, to make each particular experience as good a part of the educational whole as possible. For all leaders and teachers within schools this means that careful consideration must be given to every element, from big-picture thinking about curriculum change down to establishing the specific goals for an individual lesson. In busy school environments, consideration, deliberation and reflection are easier said than done, however; often the urgent takes precedence over the important, and it requires conscious effort to take time to step aside or stand back to gain the bigger perspective or take a long-term view. Across a school, teachers and leaders need to protect their thinking time to consider what to do and how to do it well; in this respect the long holidays can provide helpful periods for reflection.

Even if there is strong consensus of vision and careful consideration of means to support it, a new initiative or emphasis will only bear real fruit if its implementation is consistent. Inconsistency makes for a flaky, unreliable structure, whereas consistency creates strength. This requires commitment from individual teachers but also buy-in from all involved – perhaps including parents, other staff, governors or pupils.

This in turn means that channels of communication need to be excellent. Everyone involved in the educational community needs to hear and understand the same message. Schools variously use weekly newsletters, targeted emails or social media to try and communicate clearly, but ironically the more we try to communicate, the less effective communication tends to become. The crowded street-sign syndrome needs to be avoided if we are to communicate effectively rather than create information overload. Counterintuitively, in some schools, communication has been found to be improved by having one morning per week without email: people meet face to face and speak in person. Good communication is essential within the learning community, but sometimes a great deal of imagination has to be exercised to find good communication solutions.

With consensus from stakeholders regarding vision, a priority placed on protecting time for thoughtful consideration of ideas, consistency in their implementation and clear systems of communication, the conditions are right for a good education to flourish. Attention can turn to what this entails in practice.

The first of the four dimensions which should be evident in any school providing a good education is a commitment to heights of excellence. This is most effectively achieved through a judicious embrace of traditional values and innovative development.

Heights of excellence across the school

At a whole-school level, if good education is to be provided, quality has to be valued. A high-quality education characterised by heights of excellence does not just happen, in any context, no matter how richly endowed or highly privileged. High-quality education occurs because excellence is first understood, then valued and finally actively promoted. It rests on a sense that the educational enterprise is thoroughly worthwhile and therefore worth doing as well as possible (which in turn arises from believing in the worth of the individuals being educated). Recognising the worth of each individual, and encouraging personal integrity and respect for all, leads to heights of excellence and the experience of success (Figure 7.1).

This being the case, within a good education, excellence is sought for its own sake, a goal in its own right, rather than as a means to an end. No place then for a curate's egg version of education, good in parts; rather, excellence will be evident everywhere. From the signage outside the school to the tidiness inside a cupboard, from the detail of how a pencil is gripped to the structure of an argument in an essay, from the precision with which a word is enunciated in a school play to the precise measuring of a variable in a science experiment, from keeping the playground free of litter to taking down out-of-date posters, within a good educational environment, excellence is in evidence. Excellence is about attention to detail found in the work and habits of teachers, cleaners, secretaries and pupils. There is nothing that does not matter.

The individual and community character traits arising from the worth of the pupil help to support this principle: if every member of the community works with real integrity – teachers, support staff and pupils – excellence will be achieved. Mutual respect, too, goes a long way towards ensuring quality is maintained: teachers who respect their pupils and colleagues will aim to teach as well as possible; pupils who respect their teachers and peers will aim to learn as well as possible. Putting values at the heart supports excellence across the community.

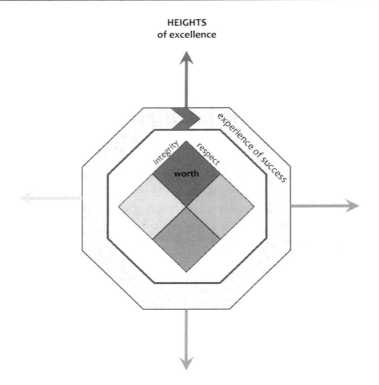

HEIGHTS
of excellence

FIGURE 7.1 Valuing individual worth results in a successful community

The attitude of mutual respect across the community is essential in its own right and should be proactively promoted through assemblies, services or other such community activity. Systems and structures which support respectful attitudes have to be maintained, and at the whole-school level, not only do these attitudes need to be actively endorsed but sanctions have to be in place in case they are flouted. An essential part of (lifelong) education is the understanding that every human being is worthy of respect *per se*, not because in our eyes they have earned our respect, but because they are a human of intrinsic worth. We may not like what others do, and we need not agree with their views or actions, but acting with a respectful attitude is an essential discipline to civilised living. Such things must be taught, and lived, at the whole-school level. Personal integrity is the other side of the coin and also needs to be taught: I am worthy of respect and should act responsibly as a result; I need to take responsibility for my own actions, should be able to distinguish right from wrong, should have the moral fibre to choose what is right and the humility and honesty to admit when I fail to do so.

Every school will have its own system to support its moral code, however that may have been formulated, and this will vary depending on the ages of the children and the local and historical context. Our school teaches the children to 'be their best selves', remembering the three Rs: respect of myself, respect for others, responsibility for all my actions. Expanding these simple ideals, in the first of nine carefully explained characteristics, the children are reminded that 'We try to be fair, so that we treat other people as we would ourselves expect to be treated, and learn about justice'. Integrity, patience, altruism, tolerance, perseverance, mercy, fortitude and trust complete our list of qualities promoted.

Excellence cannot be advocated in one area of school life unless it is advocated in all, and excellence of behaviour is of paramount importance to a good education, not only creating the best climate for learning but also reflecting the intrinsic worth of the activity and its participants.

The manner in which specific rules are spelled out, and the extent to which this happens in order to create a safe, happy, considerate and pleasant environment, will vary from school to school. To some extent this reflects the personalities of those leading the school: some people instinctively like rules, while others prefer the community to live by guiding principles. While a rules-approach may not be appealing, at the very least it is essential that pupils are given clear explanations and examples of what it means to show respect and take responsibility, so that a strong tradition of good behaviour is established.

Heights of excellence: the place of tradition

Many schools have built up traditions of strong and effective practice over the years that promote excellence in different ways. These may include formal occasions such as speech day, prizegiving or inter-house competitions, which promote and celebrate excellence of performance in one way or another; these standing items in the calendar are to be valued, treasured and jealously guarded. Similarly, other manifestations of tradition reinforce attitudes of excellence, such as (in some cases) school uniform, already considered in Chapter 2. Such traditions, and numerous others besides, do not in themselves either prove or create excellence, but they may well signal that excellence is valued, and they may also assist in celebrating excellence.

In a more general sense, the traditions of a school may be regarded as any habitual practices which ensure that things are done well. From customary manners such as standing when a visitor enters a classroom, to consistent practice such as pupils writing in blue ink which flows from a fountain pen, these traditions and conventions uphold standards. If such things help to maintain excellence, they should become traditions if they are not already; and if we have traditions which do not uphold excellence, then they should cease to be traditions.

For the fact that a school is a community, means that it has the characteristics of anything organic: responsivity, growth, change, development and maturation are all inevitable and invaluable. Excellence needs to be understood, valued and promoted, but to do so at any time, there will always be some things that need to change.

Within a school, something may have been done well in a certain way for years, and indeed this is often how traditions can emerge which are valuable and valid. Change, however, is essential for growth and survival. Schools must be responsive to the changing needs of their pupils, and the changes which take place in the wider society. They cannot be held hostage by tradition.

Technology provides a ready and obvious example of external advances impacting school practice and provision. Curricula have had to be adapted and methods of teaching, learning and working have all been modified in response to the Information Revolution. If excellence is measured in some way as things being done as well as possible in any given context, it stands to reason that if the context changes, such as through technological advance, excellence will only be retained if there is a commensurate commitment to responsiveness on the part of the school.

Heights of excellence: the place of innovation

Just as there is no merit in tradition *per se* unless it is supporting excellence, however, the same is true of change: every school has to avoid novelty for its own sake, and be judicious in the changes that are introduced and the way in which this is done. One of the reasons that change has to be so carefully managed at whole-school level is that, obviously, each pupil only has one bite at the cherry when it comes to education. If I decide to rearrange the timetable, for example, it will impact the entire school for the following year. Pupils cannot have that year again; they have had their one chance at it. Far from this being a reason to stagnate thinking and fossilise practice, however, rather this means that innovation is introduced with due diligence having been carried out first.

There are at least six stages to introducing major (whole-school) change, and how significant the change is will determine how long each takes. First there needs to be a period of preliminary thinking on the part of the leadership or management team; second there needs to be consultation among interested and affected parties; third there needs to be a careful planning stage (taking consultation into account and consulting further if needed); only fourth comes implementation; fifth, there should be a feedback and review period; and sixth, refinement.

In planning changes to the structure of our teaching week, stages one to three took a full year; the implementation and review period took a further year, and refinement was implemented the following year. By contrast, at one stage we considered introducing a leavers' 'baccalaureate' or some such end-of-school certificate for our thirteen-year-old leavers. Preliminary thinking took several months; consultation took a period of several more months. And the idea was pursued no further: consultation had revealed that it was not the right time to introduce change of that sort. It was essential that the process had been followed carefully rather than plunging in headlong, imposing a bright idea on everybody only for it to fail at the first hurdle or limp on listlessly.

TABLE 7.1 Innovation planning grid

	PRELIMINARY THINKING	CONSULTATION	PLANNING	IMPLEMENTATION	FEEDBACK AND REVIEW	REFINEMENT
New subject	✓	✓	✓	✓	✓	✓
Rewards system	✓	✓	✓	✓	✓	
Duty rota	✓	✓	✓	✓		
New committee	✓	✓	✓			
School grounds	✓	✓				
Activities programme	✓					

At any given time, in managing change it can be helpful to have a spread across the stages of innovation. There might be six different initiatives on the go, each of which could be at a different stage (Table 7.1): a new subject might have been introduced into the curriculum, now being fine-tuned; feedback might be being gathered on a newly implemented rewards system; a new duty rota system might be being introduced; a committee structure for heads of departments might be at the planning stage; consultation on how the school grounds could be used better for teaching purposes might be under way; and thinking might be starting on the provision of after-school activities.

Across a school, ensuring that good traditions are retained and good changes made requires a long-term vision and good short- and medium-term planning. Organic school improvement plans that are regularly referred to, reviewed and implemented are valuable tools. Clear, succinct and relevant policy documents that define practices and protocols which a school has established to be good are invaluable as frames of reference: good policies do not generate good schools, but good schools generate good policies.

Excellence establishes good traditions. Innovation replaces good traditions with something even better. The two are complementary: both are needed and each keeps the other in check in the pursuit of excellence.

SUMMARY BOX 7.1: The components of whole-school excellence

Whole-school heights of excellence:
tradition + innovation

Breadth of attainment across the school

In order that every pupil is able to flourish personally and contribute meaningfully to their community as they enter adulthood, good standards of speaking, reading, writing, maths and (we should now add) computing are evidently essential, as is an understanding of the world in which we live. Schools have an evident obligation to equip their pupils for future learning and ensure the strongest possible qualifications for further study and work. For this they need to be held to account.

For some years, primary school effectiveness has been assessed by the government in England by measuring pupils' performance in written tests in English and maths. Securing the highest possible success in these subjects is clearly of great importance in laying the foundations for study at secondary level, but such tests neither aim nor claim to measure the totality of learning, or even provide for any attempt at assessing breadth of experience. I recall speaking with one primary school teacher who had a child in his class who did not speak at school. At least, she did not speak at the start of the school year. By the summer term, after a lot of patient support and encouragement from the teacher, she was speaking in class. By any measure, this is a wonderful success story for that pupil. The only problem is that there was no recognised measure for recording her remarkable progress. While this need not necessarily be a problem in itself, it does make the point that there is very much more to learning than was being measured.

Secondary school effectiveness has been measured most recently in terms of the proportion of pupils achieving five GCSEs at grades A★ to C. Such a scheme acted as a notional safety net, but since it was a minimum standard, in itself it could not act as a means of cultivating ambition for schools or individual pupils; on the contrary its purpose was to indicate a level below which a school should try not to fall. Progress 8[5] is notably broader than the 'five good GCSEs' measure it replaced, and recognises that maximising pupils' individual *progress* is important as well as their absolute attainment. Encouraging greater breadth of academic achievement in this way is important and valuable.

Ambitious goals must be set by individual schools, including in the pre–public examination years, however, if we are to serve our young people well. So, important as high achievement in maths and English is at eleven (and GCSEs are at sixteen), it may be helpful to think of these as essential and important *starting points*. Ambitious goals should incorporate breadth of attainment within and beyond the academic sphere, because of the unique and complex make-up of every individual learner.

Breadth of attainment: cultivating ambition

It would be interesting to note how our teaching ambitions might change if we were all charged with the responsibility of taking every pupil as far as they could possibly go in our subject in that one year of teaching, as if we imagined that it was the last chance they would ever have to learn. Teachers appointed from eleven-plus secondary or senior schools to schools which keep pupils to thirteen, often comment on how ambitious the academic programme is for the Year 7 and 8 pupils, the youngest years of a typical secondary school. If they are at the top of the school, the school is likely to try and take them as far as possible before they leave. In an eleven-plus school, where they would be the youngest, the emphasis can sometimes appear to be on using the early years to ensure that everyone is ready to start their Year 10 GCSE courses, a very different goal, and not necessarily an ambitious one. At every stage of schooling, academic goals must be genuinely ambitious across the subjects, and any temptation to tread water academically must be avoided.

Ambitious goals include those which have readily quantifiable targets, such as test and exam results, across a range of subjects including English and maths, sciences, humanities, languages and technologies. They can also include competitions, challenges and award schemes with various levels of attainment. Examples include the Duke of Edinburgh's Award (which includes elements of volunteering, physical activities, development of skills and expeditions), the Arts Award (which encourages connection and participation in the wider arts world) and CREST Awards (encouraging investigation in the STEM subjects). All these encourage children and young people to aspire to high standards across a wider range of activities.

Pupils can be set ambitious goals which are measurable and yet value breadth. Such specific measurable goals are helpful, but ambition has more to do with mindset than measure, and it comes back to a spirit of positivity which believes in taking children and young people as far and fast as possible – whatever that may mean for each individual. Truly ambitious goals will lie well beyond that which is measurable by examination or award scheme alone.

The four-dimensional model values the gifting and strengths of every individual child, recognising that their combination of strengths is unique to them, that each has a vital contribution which they and they alone can make to the learning community and more widely. Encouraging personal distinction, one of the roles of school is to foster every pupil's talents in whatever areas they may lie in a spirit of shared positivity and belief (Figure 7.2). These may be many and varied and schools need to have the confidence to value, promote and celebrate achievements beyond those by which they will be judged externally.

If a school has a positive culture of expectation – doing things well – and of valuing every member of the community for all they have to offer, then ambition will reach high in academic areas and beyond, into sports, the arts and further afield.

Within the arena of sport, one school's ambitious goal will be to ensure that some sporting fixtures start to be arranged, where for another school, an ambitious goal will be to provide each pupil with an opportunity to represent their school once each term in a fixture; for still another school, its ambitious

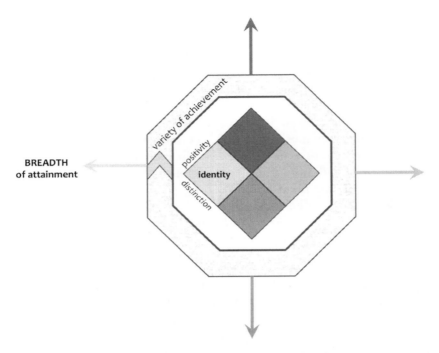

FIGURE 7.2 Valuing unique identity results in an achieving community

goal will be to win a county cup or national championship. Yet another school may provide an opportunity for pupils to take up a new sport or activity – yoga has proved to be a popular innovation in some schools with no sporting tradition, for example. In schools where sport is a huge part of the weekly life and results are very good, ambitious goals might include expansion of opportunity for those in lower teams, so that they can start to enjoy opportunities often reserved for only the most able. For the secondary school I attended as a pupil, the goal should have been to check that all pupils were actually participating in their sport at the leisure centre, and not just sitting chatting. The point is that ambitious goals in sports need to be set by all schools in all areas according to their own context, and they will vary considerably.

A similar story is true in the arts. An ambitious goal may be to put on a school play once a year, or for each house to put on a concert each term. It might be to encourage more pupils to learn a musical instrument or to provide opportunities for pupils to recite poetry in front of their peers. Can my school put on an art exhibition in a local cafe or introduce a half-term photographic competition? Each school needs to know what its ambitious goals are, and to strive to meet them across the disciplines.

Ambitious goals can extend beyond the academic, arts and sports into the wider development of character and citizenship. Time, energy and resource need to be committed to promote the ambitious development of character traits. These will be both caught and taught, and in both ways will be valued and promoted. Goals in terms of character formation, ethos and atmosphere are unlikely to be quantifiable, but may be nonetheless ambitious for that. In fact, some of the most ambitious goals in a school may revolve around character formation. One primary school head teacher told me about his three-word goals for his pupils: show me courage, show me kindness, show me integrity. In the classroom his pupils were encouraged to 'serve your classmates by speaking confidently'. Such goals are ambitious.

From the UK Maths challenge and Foyle Young Poets of the Year Award to swimming badges, music exams, black belts in judo and certificates for citizenship, there are plenty of opportunities for breadth of attainment. Schools need to make such opportunities available, giving every pupil the maximum chance of achieving a real sense of success as they go through school, and maximum variety of achievement.

Within the independent sector, the whole breadth of a school's attainment is scrutinised in 'educational quality' inspections, which report on two main outcomes for pupils: achievement and personal development. Those areas of a school's life, including opportunities provided within co-curricular activities for example, which may be where an individual pupil is able to develop significantly, achieve personally and gain distinction, are considered to be of sufficient value to be inspected. This would seem to be an appropriate assessment of what is important.

Breadth of attainment: keeping track

Much effort has lately been put into tracking pupils' academic attainment, and this has proved to be most valuable in raising standards. The sophistication with which data can be analysed enables schools to monitor progress and provide intervention where it is most needed.

It is equally valuable to keep a record of pupils' broader areas of strengths, not least so as to ensure that by the time pupils leave school at least one such area has been identified for each one. For some pupils an outstanding gifting is obvious; for others giftings are multiple; but for some, a lot of time, effort and patience needs to be dedicated in order to ascertain what it is that they can uniquely, positively contribute. Nevertheless, it is firmly within the remit of a good education that this should be done for every pupil.

A useful distinction here is for pupils to be identified on a three tier-level for any area of strength, indicating whether they are outstanding at national level (N), at school level (S) or at a personal level (P). For example, an N-level maths pupil would be one who qualified for the national Olympiad; an S-level pupil might have come top of the year in a recent maths test; whereas for a P-level pupil, maths might be their best subject area even if they are not at the top of the year, or even top of their class. Keeping simple records of areas of strength like this enables a school to see who is in danger of being overloaded or, alternatively, overlooked. Sometimes special opportunities need to be given selectively to those who do not yet have 'N, S or P' beside their name for anything in order to find something special for them, an area in which they can taste success.

Breadth of attainment: celebrating success

If schools set ambitious goals, academically, across the arts and sport, and in terms of standards of citizenship and personal development, then it is equally important that attainment in these areas is celebrated. In common with many schools when I started teaching, Colours could be awarded for outstanding participation in Sports. A boy might have his first team Colours for rugby, half-Colours for athletics or second team Colours for hockey and so on. It was a complicated system, with all sorts of different badges signifying different achievements, fully understood only by the cognoscenti. A very sporting pupil could end up looking like a military general such was the array of badges on the lapel.

Of course the problem was that the non-sporting child was not recognised at all by this system, no equivalent being available for musicians, actors, linguists or anyone else for that matter. Within the last fifteen years all that has changed. Colours are now awarded across a range of four categories: academic, the arts, sports and service, so that equal recognition can be given to those who have achieved or contributed across a broad range of areas. Achievement is celebrated not only through pupils being nominated for Colours but through ceremonially handing out the Colours certificates and badges in front of the whole school. These accolades are available only in the top years, but the system gives all pupils something to aspire to and work towards.

Across all year groups, opportunities for success to be recognised and rewarded need to be in place, reflecting and cultivating positivity across the school. This may be through commendation certificates, praise postcards or by some other means. Schools need to be careful that they reward what they consider to be important. Hard work and effort need to be recognised across the whole school as well as attainment, and it can be effective to have a whole-school system in place to publicly recognise and reward those who work the hardest, have the best developed learning habits, whose effort improves the most or who are exemplary in their service of the community. It is also important that those pupils rewarded in any sphere are also those who have developed positive character traits which support the harmony of the school and help to create a happy and studious environment.

In schools which award prizes it is important that the range of prizes given reflects accurately the emphasis placed on breadth of attainment. Awarding the same number of prizes or certificates for maths, sport and music emphasises that pupils' attainment in each area is equally valued.

The four-dimensional model suggests that breadth of attainment is to be cultivated within the pupil body so that everyone knows they have a unique contribution to make to the community, tastes success and feels valued; achievement is to be recognised and celebrated in a spirit of positivity at every stage and at every level as much as possible.

SUMMARY BOX 7.2: The components of whole-school attainment

Whole-school breadth of attainment:
cultivating ambition + keeping track + celebrating success

Depth of engagement across the school

One of our most popular innovations among pupils over the past few years has been the appointment of a new four-legged member of staff: Bonnie, the Learning Support dog, patiently listens to struggling readers, never rushes anyone, never criticises, never compares. Sometimes she thumps her tail, closes her eyes and falls asleep in the middle of a session but no one minds. A good education encourages and enables engagement of all its learners at appropriate levels – with or without the help of a dog.

Whatever their needs may be, a good education makes appropriate provision for every individual pupil, all along the ability spectrum including at the extreme ends and in the middle ground. The range of ability within schools varies enormously, some schools being highly selective academically and others very much less so or not selective at all, but whatever the range, every school is made up of unique individuals who need to be regarded and catered for as such. Engagement of each and every pupil in his or her learning has to be the goal.

Academically, nothing is more important than reading and every school has a duty to ensure that its pupils are able to get to grips with reading as early and fluently as possible. In order to pick up and support those who are struggling in this or any other area of their learning, teachers need to know their pupils well and there need to be robust processes in place for ensuring that they can be referred for in-house support or assessment and provided with precisely the help they need.

Depth of engagement: caring and catering for the entirety of the ability range

Recent developments enable schools to do far more in-house diagnostic testing for those who may be finding their learning difficult than was previously the case, and appropriate interventions can be put in place in order to ensure that engagement and progress are maximised for every pupil. The world of special educational need is highly complex and requires specialist professionals; the work which they are able to do is invaluable both in-house and in putting pupils in touch with outside agencies when needed. Supporting children who have barriers to learning increasingly includes helping those with social, communication, emotional or behavioural difficulties. This is highly specialised and often demanding; every school needs to ensure that their Learning Support Department[6] is well resourced and well respected.

A relatively small number of children require a substantial amount of intervention; a substantial number of children require a small amount of intervention. Careful tracking and regular review of progress are needed to ensure that resources are directed appropriately and swiftly according to need.

Of course the majority of children in a school will fall into the category of possibly needing a little additional one-on-one help at some point in some area of their study. Whether or not this is the case for a particular child, every school should know their 'middle' cohort, who make up the majority, really well. No pupil should ever be overlooked. Each pupil is equally valuable and worthy of respect, and school strategies and practices should reflect this. For every single pupil in every single subject, a school should know the areas of strength and the areas that need to be worked on next. Teachers should be able to see whether progress is trailing or tailing off, and be able to make a professional judgement as to when to intervene. Pupils' progress is not linear, and often attainment zig-zags somewhat in a general upward direction with plateaus and even sometimes troughs. Teachers need to gauge whether a problem is emerging or not, and this is only possible if each pupil is known as an individual.

Pupils should be encouraged to be reflective learners, and take responsibility for their own learning from a young age: taking the initiative with their learning and setting their own ambitious goals are part of developing their depth of engagement. Schools can encourage this responsibility in different ways. Subject surgeries run by teachers at lunchtimes, for example, provide opportunities for self-selecting pupils who would like to seek a little help or clarification on a subject, to drop in for some extra tuition.

While some pupils may need specific support with their learning, either from time to time or continually, all pupils need to be provided with stimulating and challenging work to take them as far as they can go and to ensure maximum stretch. Ambitious opportunities to challenge pupils academically may include both examined and non-examined elements. GCSEs may be taken earlier or in greater number, for example, but there will be other elements such as access to talks, cultural visits, opportunities for curiosity-led research, participation in local and national competitions, and the use of in-house expertise to extend horizons, and develop higher-order thinking skills which all help to provide fitting opportunities for engagement. There is certainly more to catering for very able children than acceleration, although this may sometimes be appropriate.

Schools have to find their own ways of ensuring that pupils are catered for at the appropriate level, but sometimes they can be wary of offering opportunities only to some pupils. This does indeed become problematic if special opportunities are only ever given to the same, small minority of pupils. This, however, should not be the case if recognition of breadth is taken seriously, since pupils will be known to have aptitudes in widely varying areas. One approach which can be valuable in helping to select pupils for a given limited-opportunity activity is to take into account the degree of effort that they have been putting into their work in that area. Assessing and grading effort according to a number of specific criteria, including readiness for lessons, punctuality, participation and so on, indicates those who have shown that they are committed to learning and who will benefit most from additional opportunities.

Depth of engagement: recognising everyone's contribution

A school needs to have some means of ensuring within the community that individual engagement and personal ambition in study are recognised, supported and valued. There are many ways in which this can be done, from merit schemes to the award of effort grades or house-points. Online learning platforms enable virtual art galleries to be created, poems to be published and contributions made to online discussion groups. The principle is that as a school, engagement in studies is endorsed, hard work is encouraged and it is expected that pupils will take responsibility for their learning. Opportunities to showcase work, applaud creativity and endorse collaborative effort all need to be created imaginatively and used consistently.

Within the learning community, everybody needs to play their part. Recognising that we all need each other is the other side of the coin to regarding everyone as being uniquely gifted. There is a complementarity of gifts within the community such that if any one member cannot or does not contribute their gift fully, the community as a whole as well the individual suffers.

The school orchestra provides a metaphor for the wider school community. Not all musicians in school are at the same stage of musical development or even equally talented musically; they do not all play the same instruments; they do not all find it equally easy. But the orchestra can only function if each individual plays their part, and the music can only be created if each contributes their gift at their level of expertise. The collaborative whole is greater than the sum of the parts: the community is stronger, musically, sportingly, dramatically and academically than the individuals who make it up. Each has a unique and important part to play, and each must be encouraged and supported in being able to play their part to the full.

This of course includes areas of service beyond the classroom. One pupil may be a gifted peace-maker, able to sooth troubled friendships; another may be an excellent support to a younger child who is finding play time hard; another may contribute with helpful suggestions on school council or on the school's eco committee. In every example, the school community is the stronger for these gifts of service being exercised, recognised and celebrated.

At whole-school level, depth of engagement entails commitment – to personal learning, to the rest of the class, to the whole school. It takes effort, hard work, personal encouragement and support. It requires pupils to be known, trusted and helped. The bar is set high and so are the stakes. Engagement needs to be ensured for all, fostering strong habits of study as every pupil plays their part as a member of the learning community (Figure 7.3).

The experience of one school in Portsmouth is salutary. It believes in the engagement of all its pupils and puts it like this: 'Work Hard, Be Nice and No Excuses. We mean this, we follow it and we refer to it every day because we believe in it. Every student matters. Every student can achieve. Every lesson counts. We make no excuses and we expect none, from students or staff'.[7] From being described as the third worst school in the country in 2008, by 2010 it achieved a 22 per cent rate of five good GCSEs; by 2014 it was described as being the most improved school in the country, with its GCSE results indicating 83 per cent of students achieving five good GCSEs.

The striking factor is the attention paid to every individual student as a means of ensuring a good education. The measurable results reflect this good practice, and would seem to flow from it. Attention being paid to every pupil within the community and opportunity being given for every pupil to achieve at their level

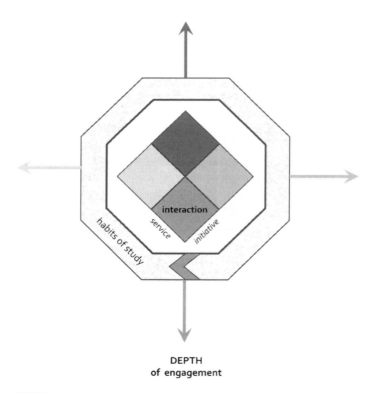

DEPTH
of engagement

FIGURE 7.3 Valuing interaction results in a studious community

of excellence clearly enable real engagement with learning which pays dividends, not least in terms of tangible academic results.

Shared vision, effective systems, good communication and strong teamwork are means to the end of every single pupil becoming a confident and valuable contributor to the learning environment that is the school: work hard, be nice, no excuses.

SUMMARY BOX 7.3: The components of whole-school engagement

Whole-school depth of engagement:
catering for all + recognising all

Length of endeavour across the school

I recall one day in my early years of teaching coming across a boy who seemed to be in some discomfort. I asked him if he was alright to which he replied that his neck hurt. On enquiring further as to what had happened, he cheerfully replied, 'Someone trod on it'.

A good education stretches ahead into a future of lifelong learning. A school therefore needs to provide the right conditions for every child to flourish as a learner, demonstrating resilience and grit, developing drive and determination, and somehow or other, enjoying the endeavour – unfazed by the odd trodden-on neck, as it were.

Length of endeavour: happiness and learning

As a parent, the thing I want more than anything else is for my children to be happy. My instincts as a parent tell me that they need to be happy in order to flourish. They also, of course, need to flourish in order to be happy. In school we see that children need to be happy in order to be able to learn, but equally they need to be learning in order to be happy. How can this be achieved?

The four-dimensional model rests on the premise of the child being regarded as a whole and unique person within the learning community. We cannot really separate out a child's pastoral needs from their academic needs since the two are inextricably linked within the whole person. If a pupil is having difficulty at home, suffering from a family trauma, sickness, bereavement or instability, their learning will be affected: we are whole people. If a friendship issue has erupted during play-time, as likely as not, performance will be affected during the next lesson. Equally, if learning is not going well, a child's happiness and sense of well-being will be affected.

At whole-school level this means that whatever systems of teaching and pastoral care are in place, the teachers involved need to communicate very well with each other. In a traditional primary school, where children have one teacher for all, or almost all, of their lessons this is very much easier than in a large secondary school where a head of year or house with pastoral responsibility for a large number of children may not necessarily even teach all the pupils in his or her care. Such problems are not insurmountable, but they need to be recognised and addressed, the maximum amount of real communication about every pupil (not just those with problems at any given time) being encouraged and enabled. In some schools, concerns and reflections about pupils are shared in weekly meetings.

In almost all cases, however, one teacher, often known as the tutor, needs to act as a central point of contact for each child, even if others are needed in supporting roles, when difficulties do arise. The tutor is the primary carer, defender, supporter and nurturer of the tutees, who in all likelihood will also meet together in their 'tutor group'. Tutor groups can, but need not, coincide with teaching groups and may be gathered into horizontal year groups or vertical houses which may provide further levels of shared community life and opportunities for service, but also provide additional pastoral support as needed.

In common with many other areas of school life, online assessment can now provide most valuable insights into children's attitudes to school and self, enabling a bigger picture and understanding to be gained as to how children are feeling about school life. Such information is a useful addition to that gained in other ways, although thankfully nothing will ever replace personal contact and teachers knowing their pupils really well on a personal, individual level and caring for them tenaciously.

Length of endeavour: home and school

Wherever possible, schools need to try and work as closely as possible with parents. Ideally, learning is a partnership supported by both home and school, and certainly not just the preserve of the latter. Good two-way communication with home is very important, parents letting schools know anything of relevance to their child's learning and well-being, and schools alerting parents swiftly to any concerns that they might have. This kind of communication is based on a relationship of trust which works both ways.

It is also, of course, important that communication is not confined to concerns, but celebrates successes too. I know of one teacher who phoned the mother of a pupil in his class because her daughter had contributed a particularly pertinent and insightful comment in a class discussion. The mother cried on hearing the news, saying it was the first time anyone had said anything positive about her daughter; a phone call would normally be the school wanting her daughter to be removed. One piece of praise can be the start of things turning around.

In some schools, more parental involvement would be welcome progress, and needs to be actively fostered. Numerous initiatives such as breakfast and homework clubs, after-school and holiday care can help to break down the barriers between home and school. Some schools hold regular family learning sessions, parents being invited into the school to listen, and learn, as their children are taught, for example, the beginnings of writing – posture, pencil grip and so on – so that parents can support at home. One school where this happens has worked so hard at its relationships with parents that they enjoy a 100 per cent attendance rate, despite being in an area with considerable social need. Many schools work hard to foster strong community links, recognising that the school can provide a valuable focal point in a community and contribute to the wider well-being of its residents.

Schools can achieve the most when parents are engaged and supportive, and so this relationship needs to be prioritised and promoted through good communication and genuine care. In all schools there needs to be a relationship of trust, parents trusting schools to let them know if there is a problem and be happy to assume that no news is good news; the urge to want daily or weekly updates on 'progress', as difficult to provide as a daily update on physical growth would be, must be resisted, not least to protect teachers' time so that they can focus on teaching. Progress can only be seen over time, sometimes considerable periods of time, and parents need to be reassured that the age-long dual process of children being taught well and working hard, always, somehow, seems miraculously to result in children learning, even if the process by which this happens retains some elements of mystery.

By and large, parents who care about their children's education want to know if their child is happy, is well behaved, is working hard and is making good progress. Teachers should know their pupils well enough be able to answer those questions at any given time, and in addition be able to identify specific strengths and the next steps necessary in the child's learning. How often and in what form this information is communicated will vary from school to school, but it needs to be communicated as clearly and precisely as possible, recognising that using fewer words may actually assist in this; when we reduced our report word limit from a verbose 250 per subject to a succinct 60 per subject we found that quality of communication improved considerably.

Length of endeavour: cultivating love of learning

As children change and mature, or go through periods of suffering or success, they need an environment which is encouraging, compassionate and personal. The kind and dedicated interest of one member of staff, often made available through the way in which pastoral care is provided, can be the difference between keeping going and giving up. Sometimes children need rules, but always they need love.

A happy school environment is created not because everything is necessarily going well, but when everyone in the team feels valued – both for who they

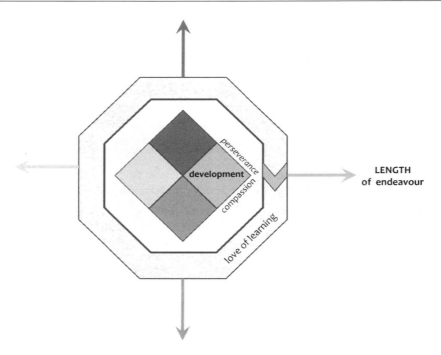

FIGURE 7.4 Valuing personal development results in a learning community

are and for what they do. This includes children but it also includes the leadership, and the teaching and support staff. An atmosphere of respect, care, appreciation and mutual support is firmly set by the leadership in the school. A positive atmosphere, such as this in which learners are loved as individuals within a community, is most likely to create in them a long-term love of learning (Figure 7.4).

SUMMARY BOX 7.4: The components of whole-school endeavour

Whole-school length of endeavour:
happiness + home and school + loving learning

The other ingredient of course contributing to developing a love of learning is actually the content and quality of what is being learnt. A broad, engaging, stimulating and thoroughly enjoyable course of study is what we would expect to see as part of a good education – what might be described as a four-dimensional curriculum.

Notes

1   *The Lion, the Witch and the Wardrobe*, by CS Lewis © copyright C.S. Lewis Pte Ltd., 1950.
2   https://archive.org/stream/sir_john_betjeman_2004_9/sir_john_betjeman_2004_9_djvu.txt number 21, accessed 28 July 2017.
3   Interview with *Business Week*, 1998.
4   *Winnie-the-Pooh* by A.A. Milne, Methuen & Co. Ltd.
5   www.gov.uk/government/uploads/system/uploads/attachment_data/file/583857/Progress_8_school_performance_measure_Jan_17.pdf, accessed 28 July 2017.
6   Or Special Educational Needs (SEN) Department.
7   http://charteracademy.org.uk/vision-and-values, accessed 28 July 2017.

8

The four-dimensional curriculum

Breadth of attainment at the academic core

Having applied the four-dimensional model to determine some characteristics at a whole-school level, it can now be applied to determining the elements that might be included in what is taught. What are the characteristics of a four-dimensional curriculum?

The vital importance of the Bunsen burner

The first teaching job I had involved teaching science to what would now be called Years 3, 4 and 5 (that is seven- to ten-year-olds), alongside helping individual children who were feeling uncertain with their reading or maths. Working as we did just a few hundred yards from a university botanic garden was perfect, and if the sun obligingly came out when a science lesson was due, we would take ourselves off down the road to look at trees and plants, ponds and insects, without so much as a by-your-leave. These were the heady pre-risk assessment days when the phrases *health and safety* and *parental consent form* were yet to pass anyone's lips; if the sun shone, off we went. Apparently, the only thing the children had to have learnt by the end of the three years was how to use a Bunsen burner safely – flame tests would probably be a good thing to do with them. Otherwise, what I taught was entirely up to me. In those days, a head appointed a teacher on the assumption that they knew how to teach and knew what to teach and did not need to be told by anyone else: we were all professionals.

The following year, when I started teaching a Year 5 class as a general-subjects teacher, I was free to teach whatever I liked, whenever I liked – apart from the two afternoons a week when the boys disappeared off for Games. Fortunately, I had some wonderful colleagues who shared their experience and wisdom – and resources – with me. Not that we all did the same: I never rose to the dizzy heights of cooking a pancake for each child in the classroom over a camping gas stove, which one of my colleagues memorably did every Shrove Tuesday.

When I went back into teaching, after what would now be called a career break, things could not have been more different. I was truly bewildered to be given a 'lesson plan' to teach from, which not only told me what I should be teaching, but actually gave me a detailed time-line through the lesson, a word-for-word script, with specific information and instructions to give the children, and questions to ask them *verbatim*. It was a whole new world. The National Curriculum had arrived.

The National Curriculum

The first National Curriculum was introduced under the 1988 Education Reform Act.[1] The Act stated its aims that a maintained school was to have a 'balanced and broadly based curriculum which (a) promotes the spiritual, moral, cultural, mental and physical development of pupils at the school and of society; and (b) prepares such pupils for the opportunities, responsibilities and experiences of adult life'. It was to be made up of the National Curriculum of 'core' and additional 'foundation' subjects, and Religious Education, and it introduced the idea of Key Stages. Onto the Secretary of State for Education was conferred the right to specify the attainment targets, programmes of study and assessment arrangements 'as he considers appropriate' for each subject. Core subjects were defined as English, maths and science, and in Welsh-speaking Welsh schools, Welsh; further foundation subjects were history, geography, technology, music, art and physical education (and for Key Stages 3 and 4, a modern foreign language) – and in non-Welsh-speaking Welsh schools, Welsh.

What turned out to be a highly prescriptive National Curriculum was introduced shortly before I took my break from teaching, and did not apply to independent schools. By the time I returned to the profession post-millennium, the new orthodoxy had sufficient traction that even parts of the independent sector were teaching at the behest of someone else removed from the immediate environment, who was telling me, the teacher, what questions to ask the children I was teaching in my lesson, even though this anonymous figure had never met them and knew nothing of their context.

A Report for the House of Commons published in 2009 described the original version of the National Curriculum as 'overloaded', stating, 'We take the view that the main purpose of a National Curriculum is to set out clearly and simply a minimum entitlement for every child. In its current form the National Curriculum essentially accounts for all the available teaching time. We would like to see this changed and a cap placed on the proportion of the curriculum that is prescribed centrally'.[2]

The coalition government of 2011 promised an overhaul of the curriculum. Its consultation document stated the aims of proposed changes to be 'to ensure that the new National Curriculum embodies rigour and high standards and creates coherence in what is taught in schools' and 'to ensure that all children are taught the essential knowledge in the key subject disciplines'.[3] Beyond that core, the aim was 'to allow teachers greater freedom to use their professionalism and expertise to help all children realise their potential'. The document also spoke of rigour, ambition and comparison with other countries.

A further recent iteration of the National Curriculum was published in 2014. Its aims are virtually the same as the 1988 curriculum, but it gives teachers the greatest freedom that they have had since pre–National Curriculum days.

> The National Curriculum provides pupils with an introduction to the essential knowledge that they need to be educated citizens. It introduces pupils to the best that has been thought and said; and helps engender an appreciation of human creativity and achievement. The National Curriculum is just one element in the education of every child. There is time and space in the school day and in each week, term and year to range beyond the National Curriculum specifications. The National Curriculum provides an outline of core knowledge around which teachers can develop exciting and stimulating lessons to promote the development of pupils' knowledge, understanding and skills as part of the wider school curriculum.[4]

Like private independent schools, academy status schools have complete freedom over their curriculum (although there is an expectation that they will be guided by the National Curriculum). Even the non–academy status schools now have to make choices as to what they should include in their curriculum, in terms both of specific topics and subjects. Once again the onus is on teachers and school leadership to determine what should be taught, and how it should be taught.

Perhaps because of the, at least notionally, greater freedom now enjoyed by all schools in determining their own curricula, there has been a noticeable increase in the advice being given to schools by lobby groups and other interested parties as to what should now be included. Lessons have been urged in resilience, mindfulness, even happiness. Emergent or re-emergent subjects such as computer science and engineering are vying with philosophy and craft for space on the time-table, like never before. And schools are responding with widely varying curricula. The RSA[5] schools, which follow the Open Minds curriculum, emphasise 'twenty competences covering five broad domains of knowledge and skills: managing information, citizenship, learning, managing solutions and relating to people'.[6] Other schools follow a more traditional subject-based or even a knowledge-based curriculum, such as that developed by the think tank Civitas.[7] The 2009 Independent Review of the Primary Curriculum recommended six areas of learning, grouping, for example, 'understanding English, communication and languages' as one and 'understanding the arts' as another.[8] Similarly, the Elements in a New Primary Curriculum as proposed by the Cambridge Primary Review included eight domains of learning, such as 'arts and creativity' and 'citizenship and ethics', carefully listed alphabetically to avoid any sense of hierarchy.[9]

How does the four-dimensional model of education help in making these important choices, now that they are firmly back in the hands of schools, generally, and particularly in the years preceding public examination?

Four-dimensional principles

To return to our model is to be reminded that the curriculum will be informed by our view of the individual child: the view of the child lies at the heart. This is not to be confused with 'child-centred learning', a philosophy which rose to popularity as part of the mid-twentieth-century progressive movement in teaching, and in which the teacher's purpose is to create an environment designed to facilitate child–led discovery.

Rather, within this model, each pupil is regarded as a unique member of a learning community, who should be in receipt of a curriculum that reflects their inherent worth, unique identity, interdependence and ongoing development. Provision for learning needs to be made in such a way as to ensure heights of excellence, breadth of attainment, depth of engagement and length of endeavour.

Every part of an education impacts each of these four dimensions to a greater or lesser degree. Within the taught curriculum, the achievement of heights of excellence largely depends upon the way in which individual subjects are planned and presented, a topic considered in detail in Chapter 10; depth of engagement is typically fostered in individual lessons, as described in Chapter 11.

The organisation of the curriculum, however, is the single factor that most significantly and directly impacts breadth of attainment. According to our model, within a good education, the curriculum will be organised in such a way as to support development of the whole person, reflecting a holistic approach which promotes to the full the development of mind, body, spirit and character.

The National Curriculum aims – for schools to provide a balanced and broadly based curriculum which promotes the spiritual, moral, cultural, mental and physical development of pupils (and of society), and prepares them for the opportunities, responsibilities and experiences of later life[10] – are thus entirely in accord with the four-dimensional approach; they adhere to the holistic approach which has traditionally formed the backbone of English education, and which continues to be advocated by reviews of education nationally.

In addition to promoting development of the whole child, a good education recognises and provides for the unique and distinctive profile of strengths and creativities each pupil has. This means that the curriculum will be organised in such a way as to value and actively foster these gifts in whatever sphere they may occur, and there will be a positive anticipation of distinction across the board (see Figure 8.1). In the four-dimensional model of education, the principle of breadth means provision of a curriculum which facilitates attainment for every child, with variety of achievement evident as a result.

Attempting to cater for the educational development of the whole child, this study considers in turn the areas of learning which particularly develop the mind

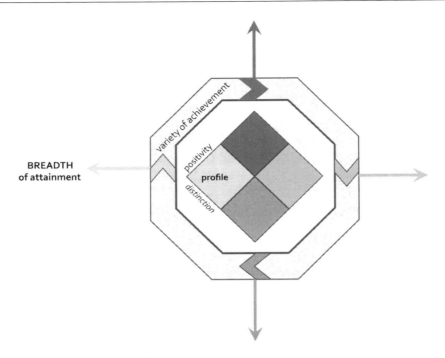

FIGURE 8.1 The principle of breadth and its elements

(academic), spirit (the arts), body (sports) and heart, or character (pastoral elements), breadth of attainment being determined by the inclusion one way or another of all these elements.

These four broad areas (academic, the arts, sports and pastoral elements) are considered through being broken down into their traditional constituent subject areas. The traditional divisions provide helpful points of demarcation in our thinking, helping to determine how each subject might uniquely contribute to developing the different facets of the whole person, and also cater for the broad range of learning profiles and giftings to be found in a school population.

There is some debate as to whether the traditional subject delineations are still useful. One school of thought suggests that 'reading, writing and arithmetic should be de-emphasised, and replaced with comprehending, communicating and computing',[11] for example. To some extent this is a false dichotomy since to read well is to read with comprehension; writing remains a significant form of communication, necessary as much for online communication as more traditional modes; and to be able to compute requires at least some level or understanding of arithmetic: we do not have to choose between these pairs, and in fact each needs the other. This important part of the debate is addressed more fully when considering the four-dimensional lesson and the relative weight given to knowledge and skills, in Chapter 11.

It is important to note, however, that the model does not dictate that the school week should necessarily be strictly divided from an early age into discrete subject areas along the lines of a senior school timetable: the educational principle of the four-dimensional model is that breadth of attainment is to be pursued and ensured, rather than directing precisely how that should be done. No doubt the curriculum could be divided in some other way, and certainly subjects might be grouped, or a timetable organised, along different lines.

The division of knowledge into traditional areas, however, reflects the organic growth of human understanding. It therefore helps to ensure due attention is given to received wisdom, culture and understanding, while remaining sufficiently flexible to be responsive to development and emerging need.

Developing the mind: the centrality of academic study

By their nature, academic subjects develop the mind. They are built on a bank of knowledge and understanding established over generations, taking personal hold of which is essential to a good education. Academic subjects promote rigour and depth of engagement, and establish strong and deep roots of learning.

Beyond what might be regarded as foundational academic expertise (reading and computation, for example), and alongside the deeper study of English and maths, the broader academic arena also includes the sciences (including physics, chemistry and biology), the humanities (including history, geography and religious studies), languages (both modern and classical) and technologies (such as computing and engineering). These subjects are not exhaustive: from architecture to zoology it is possible to consider many academic areas of knowledge to supplement those listed above. However, those given are the most fundamental in that other academic subjects tend to depend on and grow out from them. Of course every area of learning has an academic component, because the mind is involved in all learning, and so other subjects, such as music, will also make an academic contribution.

While to some extent subject boundaries between the academic subjects have an element of the arbitrary about them, within the great sea of knowledge and human understanding, one benefit of retaining and employing them is that by doing so we can ensure that a variety of different facets of academic learning is addressed. For while there is an inevitable and rich overlap between subject areas (both in knowledge and skills), each also has a unique contribution to make to the sum of learning: each has its own distinctive characteristics of excellence, enabling genuine breadth of attainment; each makes a specific, distinct contribution to the roots of learning which, when put down deep, ensure a strong and firm base on which to build a life-time of learning.

For each subject in turn, therefore, it is worth articulating the constituent elements, unique characteristics and specific contribution made to the four dimensions of learning which, when considered as a whole, particularly ensure breadth.

Developing expression, appreciation, independence: English

The effective use and understanding of written and spoken English (or the mother tongue of any country) is crucial to successful learning in all subjects, and to successful life in the modern world. At the most foundational level, all children need to be proficient in the use of the written and spoken word. In a good education aspiring to maximum excellence, attainment, engagement and endeavour, it must be an absolute priority to ensure that this is achieved as early and as securely as possible.

Typically, speaking comes first, generally learnt at home through listening. The ability to speak in turn precedes the ability to read, which in turn generally precedes the ability to write: that is to say, that usually children can understand words before they can speak them, and can speak them before they can read them; they can read more complex texts than they are able to write: speaking first, then reading, then writing.

Children need to develop confidence to express themselves, whether in speaking or writing, best cultivated through praise and encouragement. Every effort must be made to allow children to learn through the stimulus of success, encouraging and enabling them to form and communicate their opinions effectively through speaking and writing with accuracy and clarity. Every pupil should be encouraged to aspire to his or her best and be supported in being adventurous, imaginative and creative in the expression of ideas. These are important and grand ideals because on them rests a pupil's future success, academically and beyond: a good education will not short-change any pupil in their ability to comprehend and communicate with confidence, competence and flair.

In addition, curriculum English also has the aim of engendering both enjoyment and expertise in the use of the English language for its own sake. English lessons should not only enthuse children in their own creative expression but also in that of others, helping them to access and appreciate their rich literary heritage. The development of a strong and healthy reading habit needs to be planned for and taught systematically, with each year building upon the previous year in a carefully structured process. At the appropriate stage and in an appropriate way for them to be understood, enjoyed and appreciated, pupils will be introduced to great novelists such as Austen and Dickens, great poets such as Keats and Yeats, and great playwrights such as Shakespeare and Wilde. They will meet humour and tragedy, satire and allegory; they will read works by men and works by women; they will read works written in English – at home and abroad – and works in translation, works from their own and from previous decades and centuries. In doing so, they will also inevitably encounter and ponder the big questions about life and death, goodness and evil, love and ambition: literature has a moral and spiritual dimension, and is never simply academic.

The goal of English is for learners to develop a confident and competent independence in their use of language for communication and in their enjoyment of language in its various written and spoken forms. The development of English skills, and its study as a subject, is such an important and essential element to learning, that this is considered in further detail in Chapter 10 as the chief illustrative example of how four-dimensional principles work at a subject level.

Developing rigour, confidence, ambition: mathematics

Mathematics is like a window on the world, revealing a vast and elegant abstract substructure which underpins its entirety. Also deeply practical, maths is integral to all scientific, engineering, medical and economic endeavours.

Learning maths develops and exemplifies the importance of rigour like no other subject, as every part of mathematical understanding holds together, reliant on its links and connections within the whole. Rigour is an essential element in ensuring depth in learning, and maths shows how getting it right really matters, because what I learn today I will rely on as I build tomorrow. The overarching aims of maths teaching need to be to provide a secure and rigorous foundation of knowledge and understanding, an ability to reason logically and the capability of applying all this to solve problems. Just as English skills are foundational to learning across the curriculum, so too maths skills are essential in many other subjects, particularly the sciences.

Putting down strong roots of learning is the essential starting point for rigour in maths. The earliest years require the laying of utterly reliable foundations of knowledge, such as an accurate grasp and recall of number facts, for example, as well as understanding the foundational concepts underlying this knowledge, including notions of symbol, shape, measure and pattern.

Most schools use bricks, counters or other practical equipment to begin with in maths, which enable children to build up a feel for an essentially abstract subject. The use of the abacus, for example in China, for developing numerical work, demonstrates the power of starting with the concrete to develop the abstract. Extensive practice with the abacus when young facilitates the internalisation of a reliable computational aid. For anyone who has watched ten-year-old Chinese maths champions compute multi-digit multiplication and division sums in their heads faster than numbers can be keyed into a calculator, the efficacy of the method is beyond doubt.

While many methods of teaching move directly from the concrete to the abstract, some effectively include an intermediate level of diagram to help bridge this gap securely. The important thing is ensuring that understanding is secure, and that visualisation can take place, there being no merit in moving through these stages unless the child is evidently ready to do so securely. Practical maths, which helps to root maths in reality, continues to have a place as more advanced concepts are introduced, with children out of doors measuring the height of a tree by applying their understanding of trigonometry, or grappling with measures of capacity at the classroom sink.

Some argue against the need to learn facts in maths, suggesting that they can easily be looked up when needed or technology used to calculate as necessary:

how many of us use long multiplication in everyday life, is the question rhetorically asked, the implication being that its teaching is redundant. Secure foundational knowledge remains essential irrespective of new technologies which may indeed assist those engaged in mathematical endeavour at a more advanced level. Maths is a complex construct: trying to build understanding without strong and secure foundations is likely to create inherent instability.

This is not to say that curricula never adapt. The generation before me was still using slide rules to calculate, and I remember being taught to use books of logarithms for complex calculations, long since relegated to the annals of history. These were tools, not concepts, however, which have been replaced. Of course calculators have their place, as did slide rules and log books once upon a time; but these handy tools cannot and must not replace conceptual understanding, best acquired through thorough and carefully chosen exercises, 'intelligent practice',[12] which provides hands-on familiarity with how numbers work, and how patterns evolve, in turn enabling mathematical instincts and flair to develop.

Equally maths can, and should, generate a unique confidence, a key element of the character trait of positivity. Confidence is grown by maths because it is a subject in which perfection is attainable – perhaps the only subject in which an answer to even a complex question can be completely and flawlessly correct. We know that success breeds confidence, so ensuring the achievement of successful outcomes in maths must be a matter of priority in order that pupils can carry on positively with their learning. The emphasis on all pupils being able to master maths must be welcomed, and seen through in practice. Fostering confident enjoyment also leads to a genuine fascination with the subject for its own sake.

Sometimes worry is expressed about lots of ticks in a maths book indicating that the work is too easy. Actually, a chief goal of maths is to get it right: in the long run if our budding mathematicians are going to be engineers, doctors or accountants we want them to get it right every time. Practice has its place in maths as long as children are practising what they have understood in order that they develop a memory for it. The old adage has it that practice makes perfect; more likely that practice makes permanent. While practising the wrong method is disastrous, practising getting something right is invaluable. Rigorous and appropriate practice, which cements understanding at every stage and as each new topic is introduced, enables secure learning and builds with the future in mind. It also means that the essential application of mathematical knowledge to problem-solving can take place using reliable and trustworthy tools.

Because of the inherently black-and-white, right-or-wrong, quality of maths, the experience of success is particularly important in order to boost confidence; working at the right level for this to be achieved is critical. I recall early on in my teaching career meeting children whose confidence in maths was so low, that even if they were asked to choose any number between one and ten, they would hesitate for fear of getting the answer wrong: lack of confidence can completely impede progress. Paradoxically, it is this tireless characteristic of maths to 'be wrong' that is both so important for the development of good learning habits and understanding rigour, and yet can make it so daunting for some young learners. As a result, children need to be taught how to get their maths right: doing so gives them confidence. The course of study, and lessons within it, must be carefully designed to meet the learning needs of each child so as to allow pupils to perform successfully with assurance to the best of their respective abilities, the experience of success once again breeding the confidence on which it builds.

Practice can establish something firmly in the memory, be it recall of multiplication tables or the method of factorising an algebraic expression, and practice questions need to be easy enough for them to be right pretty well every time (plenty of ticks here). The application of facts and techniques in order to solve problems, however, is a different matter. Problem-solving is an essential part of maths in all its topics, and indicative of the presence of, and ability to apply, real understanding. Application questions need to be sufficiently challenging to be just about within reach at full stretch: less challenge is too easy, more is demoralising. The teacher needs to exercise expert judgement for this to be pitched just right.

Maths is a logical construct which becomes increasingly abstract and complex as it advances, an obvious example of a 'spiral curriculum' where each new element of learning in a topic depends and builds on what has gone before. Ambition is thus cultivated because the construct which is maths is endlessly intricate, increasingly sophisticated and always beyond our full grasp. Within each topic or level of learning, there is always more to be explored, harder problems to solve or more complex challenges to be tackled.

For some learners, maths provides a wonderful opportunity to take initiative and think for themselves, moving forwards rapidly and confidently. Some pupils have a natural flair for the subject which is to be capitalised upon, encouraged and celebrated. And although it is perhaps the only subject which can result in a score of 100 per cent, there is always further to go, more that can be done and new and more challenging concepts to be explored which grow incrementally more abstract, complex and demanding.

For those pupils with an instinctively mathematical turn of mind, maths provides unique opportunities for intellectual stretch. Maths must be taught in a way which encourages pupils who naturally excel to stretch really high, tackle intellectually demanding concepts and problems and push themselves on as far and as fast as possible. There is no room for boredom for such pupils in maths as there is always further that they can be taken, and no end of entertaining puzzles to solve and intriguing challenges to grapple with. Such pupils do not necessarily need an accelerated curriculum which rushes ahead, never providing real stretch, however, but rather, more demanding problems, challenges and investigations – of which there are always plenty – should be set in each topic, at each level, encouraging pupils to think for themselves, determine their own solutions to challenges and even formulate their own problems or design their own investigations.

Mathematical investigations, such as determining the number of hops frogs take to leap across a lily pond, given stringent rules of engagement, and discovering the underlying mathematical formulae, will be incorporated as one of a variety of approaches used to cement knowledge, ensure understanding and develop engagement. Finding patterns, formulating mathematical explanations, presenting findings and communicating understanding are all important skills learnt through investigation.

Fostering an independent love of learning and an appreciation of any subject for its own sake is a hugely important driver within teaching. Maths lessons taught in this way create a sense of appreciation and awe at the beauty of maths in all sorts of ways, such as by studying Fibonacci numbers,[13] for example. The simplicity of logic is appreciated watching algebra unfolding. The creative power of reason becomes apparent as pupils move from manipulating simple positive integers towards an understanding of irrational and imaginary numbers and seeing the new possibilities that they create. The power of maths to forge graphical representations, generate statistics or formulate a probability, and its powerful role in the life of the citizen by so doing, are appreciated.

Typically, maths is the subject in which the greatest spread of ability is noted in schools; all children must be taught in such a way as to enable maximum success, as strong mathematical proficiency is imperative for all pupils as they move through their education and beyond. Just as being well educated means being good at reading, so also to be well educated is to have experienced success and acquired a sense of achievement which leads to a long-term confidence and competence in maths. Not everyone finds maths easy, but a good education should serve to ensure sound mathematical competence that lasts a lifetime and can be applied as needed, whether in the world of work or simply to the everyday economics that we all need to live with.

Developing curiosity, investigation, reasoning: science

Like maths, science shines a light on the patterns and structures underlying the world in which we live, readily accessed through practical exploration, investigation and experiment. Science fosters children's natural curiosity about their surroundings and encourages investigation and the disciplined logic of reasoning.

Curiosity is a chief element in developing strong roots of learning and fostering depth of engagement. With science playing a key role in this, it should be taught in such a way as to provoke fascination and foster enjoyment.

Science is apprehended through sensory experience – observing, measuring, and testing – and as such is most effectively accessed via a practical route. Being all about the real world in which each of us lives, experience should be first hand as much as possible. Children typically love practical elements to learning and science provides the perfect opportunity for this, whether by being out and about exploring school grounds, or investigating the inside of an apple. Within science, children will need to be taught about the scientific method, how science itself grows through investigation, observation, testing and reasoning. As these skills are learnt about, and practised, so they develop.

Practical science of course sits within a wider body of essential knowledge and skills. This means that while pupils grow in their understanding of how to plan for and carry out their own practical investigations, and apply reasoned logic when analysing their findings, this has to be within the context of developing understanding of received scientific theories and models. Here again, we see the part that science plays in forging depth of engagement through collaboration. We build on the learning of others. Our understanding always sits in a bigger context of established concepts and principles. Our reasoning grows from that of others, and we need to apply ourselves with diligence to understand it fully.

Creativity and communication skills are no less fostered in science than elsewhere across the curriculum. Devising how to make a model to show seed dispersal or the structure of a cell, or devising an experiment to measure a rate of change, require imagination, ingenuity and attention to detail in order to be done well. Learning the protocols of experimental write-up, and devising the best way to present experimental results, necessitate and foster clear and effective communication. The scientific method has a unique place in children's learning, and a unique contribution to make.

Science needs to cover topics within the separate, traditional areas of biology, chemistry and physics. Once these are taught separately, which usually occurs in the early secondary years, pupils' knowledge and understanding is likely to deepen. As a result, the more thorough and rigorous their learning will be, and the more capable they will be of making essential connections within and between these traditional disciplines.

Like maths, science promotes rigour through an inevitably spiral curriculum. One of the great skills of the science teacher is to be able to simplify a scientific concept in an age-appropriate way, without any distortion of the truth: teaching younger children science is thus in many ways more scientifically demanding than teaching older children. There is no excuse for teaching something in such a way that it has to be unlearnt later. 'Everything should be as simple as it is, but not simpler', said Einstein. A scientific principle, concept or idea should be taught in such a way as to lay a firm and reliable foundation on which the next layer of detail and complexity can be laid – putting down deep and secure roots of learning.

The application of scientific discovery and understanding has transformed modern life. Children need to grow up knowing not only about the world in which they live, but also how knowledge of that world and understanding of its processes can lead to technological advance and widespread development. They need to understand the scientific basis for medicine, architecture, engineering, technology and computing, and the implications of science for the individual and community. If they are to be well educated, they need to realise what constitutes the scientific process, grasp the concept of scientific theories and models and ideas of sample size and significance and understand the nature of scientific progress: the body of scientific knowledge is not only growing, but changing, continually being challenged and refined.

Science should capture a sense of wonder at the complexities and intricacies of the natural world and marvel at the grand sweep of the cosmos and its vast universal laws. Science should be enjoyable, fun, interesting and engaging, but given its study of the wonder-filled world in which we live, it should also be awe-inspiring and breath-taking. As such, science is very much part of the pupil's spiritual development.

Developing understanding, perspective, empathy: humanities, including history, geography and religious studies

The humanities subjects help to develop both an understanding of the world and a sense of perspective. They encourage empathy with others and allow children to grasp the significance of place, time and faith to the local and global community.

In doing so all the humanities subjects contribute to the cultivation of knowledge, understanding and appreciation of the rich and diverse world in which we live, and help to foster some of the skills necessary for studying it. In humanities, pupils learn about their own place in the world and how this relates to peoples of other times, places and faiths. The character trait of respect for others is fostered as pupils discover differences and similarities, understand how peoples connect with each other and their environment, and appreciate the significance of local, national and global factors in such interactions.

Historical study, of course, stretches back into the past, encompassing chronology, consequence and change, as well as helping pupils to understand the significant role that individuals and communities can play in shaping events. Together such knowledge and understanding contribute to the ability to make sense of complex and dynamic change in individuals, within communities and across the globe. Both key events from the past, which provide an essential frame of reference, and more gradual changes in ways of living, have their place in historical study, the latter perhaps accessed through exploring local archives or grandparents' photographs.

Geography puts our place in the world into perspective, as members of the local community as well as of the global. In part, this is achieved through understanding our connection to the physical land on which we live. The world's many and diverse physical features, landforms and environmental factors all find their place in the study of geography, alongside consideration of sustainability and ecological awareness. These latter areas sit at a neat intersection between physical and human geography, providing insight into the lives and environments of the peoples of the world, their communities and ways of life.

Religious studies enables pupils to develop awareness, knowledge and understanding of the influence that religion has on a personal, national and global scale. In also providing the opportunity to explore and reflect on the ideas that a religious response might give to the questions of life, it plays an inevitable part in developing spiritual understanding.

To understand the world in which we live, its cultural and social development, its history and its current issues, pupils need background knowledge and appreciation of the major world faiths – including Christianity, Islam, Hinduism, Buddhism, Sikhism and Judaism. In addition, it is equally important that pupils gradually acquire a similarly rigorous and honest appraisal of other world-views, including atheism, humanism, materialism and secularism, and an appreciation of the contribution they have all made to both development and conflict. Pupils need to understand that ideas are potent, religions are not all the same and moral codes vary; they need to understand points of difference as well as shared values if they are to make sense of the world in which we live. They should be encouraged to discuss these differences in a respectful spirit, tolerant of those whose views differ from their own.

History, geography and religious studies must be valued as academic disciplines in their own right, not least to ensure that the factual knowledge necessary to understanding our own place in space and time is rigorously communicated and securely absorbed. Children need to have a grasp of the sequence of major historical events affecting their country, for example, or have some factual knowledge of countries neighbouring their own, or have some sense of the scale of the world's population, if they are to be able to make sense of, and form judgements about, the world in which they live.

Pupils also need to be encouraged to make links between and within the humanities disciplines, however: it is not difficult to see, for example, how a study of the geography of India is not only enhanced, but is rendered more rigorous, by an understanding of the history of the country and the religious beliefs of those who live there. Perhaps uniquely in the humanities, through the primary and early secondary years, pupils need a grasp of both the big picture and the small print; they need to know about the great sweep of global history, but also about how one act of courage or carelessly spoken word can determine the course of events, for better or worse.

With such a wealth of information to delve into, being selective is a necessity, and it stands to reason that the selection will differ depending on context. Principles need to be applied as to how content should be prioritised. Here a balance needs to be struck in developing knowledge, experience and under-standing of a pupil's own context (historical, geographical and religious) and the broader sweep of worldwide studies. No one can know everything about their place in the world but having a secure understanding of one's own local identity within a global context provides a ready point of reference from which to explore similarities and differences with others. True across all the humanities subjects, religious studies provides a good example in this respect. The religion which has been most widely held and had the greatest influence on a school's community should command the greatest depth of study, and others should follow.

Over the past two thousand years, Christianity has influenced life in England more than any other religion, philosophy, or world-view. It has led to the formation of the legal system, the nature of the monarchy and the expansion of education; numerous charitable causes owe their existence to Christian reformers and visionaries, as does the National Health Service; the great ceremonies of state are Christian in form and content; wars, battles and crusades of one sort and another have been waged in its name, and the Christian faith has been relied on, publicly and privately, in times of conflict, anguish and trouble. As Eric Pickles, Secretary of State for Communities and Local Government said in 2012:

> Christianity in all its forms has shaped the heritage, morality and public life of Britain . . . Religion is the foundation of the modern British nation: the Reformation is entwined with British political liberty and freedoms, the King James Bible is embedded in our language and literature, and the popular celebrations of the Royal Wedding and Diamond Jubilee placed the Church side by side with our constitutional monarchy.[14]

For children to understand England, Great Britain or the United Kingdom, or the history, literature, art and architecture of Europe, they need to understand Christianity.

Some communities, however, including some within England, may be more deeply and directly influenced by another faith: in such a case, this may provide a ready starting point for their study. We all need to have an understanding of our own place in the world to use as a point of reference if we are to try and understand that of others. Civic responsibility, however, must always be upheld, and understanding and respect for those among whom we live always be engendered.

In the humanities, benefit is gained from first-hand experience wherever possible, as pupils pursue an evidence-based approach to help them appreciate similarities and differences, evaluate change and progress, and understand the beliefs and values of the peoples of the world, thus promoting the unity of human-kind and respecting the uniqueness of cultures.

Developing communication, connection, respect: modern and classical languages

Languages are about communication with others through the spoken and written word, connection with others across time and space, and respect – recognising what we share in common with other people while learning to value the differences. The first aim of teaching other languages must be to encourage a love of languages, both modern and ancient, and a competency in their exercise.

In many ways the earlier children start to learn another language, the easier they find it – and certainly the less self-conscious they find themselves. If my own experience as a pupil is anything to go by, starting a first foreign language concurrently with the move to secondary school, and the potential insecurity and uncertainty that brings with it, can be disadvantageous to some children in the development of linguistic confidence and competence.

The more natural children see the speaking of other languages to be, the better; opportunities to capitalise on those children who have a language in addition to English are considerable in this respect, and should not be overlooked. Statistics from the National Association for Language Development in the Curriculum (NALDIC)[15] indicate that there are more than one million children between the ages of five and 18 in UK schools who speak in excess of 360 languages between them, alongside English. The 2013 figures published by the Department for Education[16] show that the first language is known or believed to be other than English for one in six primary school pupils, and in some London boroughs over three-quarters of all pupils are either bilingual or have English as an additional language.

While there has been admirable focus on diminishing the attainment gap between such pupils and their English only-speaking peers, the ability to speak another language, in itself, should be seen as a considerable advantage for the child and the country in which they live, something to be cherished and fostered. Believing children to be uniquely gifted extends to the range and variety of languages that they speak. The development of reading and writing skills in languages spoken other than English is often the next step needed in these children's development of their first or additional language. Schools can be imaginative in their creation of opportunities to develop and celebrate linguistic skills. For example, at designated times, children can produce written homework in a language of their choice and this work can be celebrated in display. Parental involvement or that of local community groups or university specialists may be invaluable in supporting such work.

Valuing additional languages spoken at home may encourage pupils to pursue language study beyond the years in which it is compulsory, as may the early introduction of modern languages into the school curriculum. When and which modern languages are taught varies. I learnt French from the age of eleven, but where I now teach all children learn Spanish from the age of four. They then add French from the age of eleven, the latter building successfully on the former which is considered to be easier to pick up with its phonetic spelling and simpler grammatical constructions; it is also spoken by considerably more people, worldwide. In many English schools, French, being the language of our nearest neighbours, is still the first learnt language, with German also a popular choice as the most widely spoken language in Europe. Although these three then are the main modern foreign languages studied at GCSE, happily, there is also opportunity for this qualification in many other languages from Bengali and Urdu to Modern Hebrew and Polish. Mandarin, Russian and Arabic are also popular choices, particularly for older pupils.

When it comes to classical languages, having suffered considerably following the demise of academically selective grammar schools and the introduction of the National Curriculum in which Latin did not feature, recent years have seen a steady rise in the number of schools teaching Latin. The total figure now stands at around 1,000, according to the University of Cambridge Schools Classics Project,[17] itself established in 1966 to try and stem the decline of Latin teaching already underway. In recent years the number of state schools teaching Latin has overtaken the number of independent schools doing so. Anecdotal evidence suggests that some parents' rule of thumb is to judge the quality of a school's academic provision by the presence on the timetable of either Latin or Mandarin, both being seen as demanding and rigorous academic disciplines.

The academic discipline of modern (European) languages is underpinned by the study of classical languages and, despite my own less-than-successful school Latin career, I have seen that when taught well Latin serves to sharpen powers of logic and discrimination and increase all-round linguistic competence. An erstwhile colleague of mine used to recount how an hour of Latin would mark the start of every day for him at school. Mine now introduces Latin from the age of nine, and incorporates into its study elements of classical civilisation. Knowledge of ancient civilisations gives depth and perspective to the discussion of contemporary issues, and assists in our understanding of who we are as a people. Some study of the classics, whether or not that includes a substantial language element, is beneficial in a rigorous ambitious education aspiring to excellence.

The teaching of languages provides further opportunities to foster confidence and enjoyment, both in their practical use and in appreciation of the underlying structures. Learning other languages raises awareness of grammar and idiom, and develops analytical and problem-solving skills, enhancing academic achievement as a result. Translating necessitates paying attention to detail and fostering rigour.

The possibility of residential trips abroad takes learning beyond the classroom and offers exciting opportunities for first-hand experience and adventure. Pen-friendships with overseas schools or conference calling making use of IT lay down foundations of communication and pave the way for lifelong connection and empathy.

Developing logic, creativity, problem-solving: computing

For the current generation of children, information technology (IT) is as natural a part of the world as are books and bicycles – arguably more so. Born into a digital world, from the earliest moments of play children now engage with digital toys, graduating rapidly to all manner of mobile and wired digital devices. For these pupils, IT is neither special nor novel; it is simply an integral part of any world they have ever known. IT is also likely to be a highly significant element of the world they will enter as adults, so that not only will good IT skills and understanding be important for employment, but for playing any part as a fully integrated and responsible citizen. Further, however, the current generation of children will rapidly become the architects of future technological advance.

Computing magically combines logic and creativity in problem-solving, while also enabling competence and confidence in the use of developing technologies. Computing has the two-fold aim of helping pupils to understand how computers work, and ensuring that they are equipped with the strong computer skills needed in almost every discipline, and certainly in everyday life beyond the classroom.

The first of these two components, known as computer science (or computing science) aims to develop problem-solving and logical thinking skills. Computer science offers a unique opportunity to stimulate creativity, curiosity and interest as an academic discipline in its own right. A major component of this is programming, in which pupils have to organise their thoughts in a formal, unambiguous and structured way; in computer science, pupils have to think about their thinking – and it is utterly dependent on rigour.

Learning the basics of computer science can start in the earliest years of school, and it is remarkable how sophisticated pupils' ability can be in this subject area by the time they enter their teens. Once children know what the building blocks are for programming and understand the structures which they form, they can acquire the skills necessary to become architects of novel applications themselves. Hence, for example, knowledge of control sequences and the Python programming language gives the opportunity for pupils to create their own nascent versions of artificial intelligence; an understanding of binary, hardware and logic gates can lead to the creation of computers themselves. It is thus also intrinsically creative, and combines elements of linguistic skill as well as the application of logic. Interestingly despite its highly rigorous approach, it can be very popular even with pupils who find other academic disciplines more challenging. As such, it is a most useful contributor to academic breadth.

While a chief goal in computing is for pupils to become 'creators not consumers', the second element might best be described as digital literacy. This has the aim of imparting the skills needed to survive and flourish in the 'Information Age'. Pupils need to receive a foundation in the operation of the most widely used software packages and computing devices in order that they can use these tools effectively. They need to be taught the operational fundamentals of computers and programs, which can be transferred to future developments in technology. They need to know how best to use digital devices, software and the Internet, understanding their power, strengths and limitations so that they can be used responsibly, safely, creatively, effectively and efficiently. Unease over a possible link between excessive use of IT (particularly social media) and mental health concerns reinforces the goal of this teaching to ensure that children grow up to be masters rather than servants of IT: pathological dependency is to be actively avoided. Nevertheless, strong IT skills need to be honed which are transferable and applicable across the curriculum, enhancing opportunities for accessing widely divergent banks of information as well as for the presentation and communication of ideas.

Developing design, modelling, evaluation: engineering

In a report published in 2016, the Institution of Mechanical Engineers, supported by the Royal Academy of Engineering, called for children to be taught about engineering and the manufactured world from primary age upwards.[18] I include a section on engineering as although it is not a commonly taught school subject, it has a very great deal to commend it as such. Combining the intellectual, creative, practical and social elements of learning, the engineering process enables pupils to apply their scientific, mathematical, computing and design knowledge – and skills – to solve a variety of problems. In engineering, children are typically encouraged to find and develop their own areas of strength while working in collaborative teams. It thus very neatly fits into the four-dimensional model of learning with its emphasis on the individual as a uniquely contributing member of the learning community.

Engineering also stimulates strong roots of learning, fostering curiosity, creativity, initiative and rigour, while valuing and promoting a cross-curricular, outward-looking, problem-solving approach. The subject lends itself ideally to supporting strong values of responsibility, recognising that good engineering solutions are those of benefit to the community – both local and global – and the environment.

Engineering is an unusual subject in sitting at the crossroads between other subjects. It is a creative subject but rests firmly on the academic foundations of science and maths; it is a problem-solving subject with a strong design and artistic element; it is a practical subject but requires excellent communica-tion and presentation skills, both written and spoken; it relies on a sound understanding of humanitarian and sustainability considerations, and the needs and aspirations of communities. Typically, pupils enjoy working together on real projects and coming up with their own potential solutions to genuine problems.

Engineering equips pupils with experience of using academic knowledge to be creative, and testing their solutions against strict criteria, through tackling projects from the problem and design stage through modelling and modification to implementation and evaluation, applying knowledge, understanding and skills gained in other subject areas.

By including the subject of engineering here, it also provides the opportunity to consider for a moment how a new subject area might be included in the curriculum. This is particularly pertinent given the freedom now enjoyed by all schools to determine at least part of their curriculum, and the concurrent calls from various concerned parties that their area of interest be included. It may be helpful briefly to consider the process involved in the introduction of engineering into our curriculum.

First, since a number of children were already attending an over-subscribed and highly successful after-school engineering club, it was felt that it would be valuable to explore the possibility of extending this opportunity further to create provision for all. Specialists from local universities and businesses were consulted over a two-year period, and advice taken from the professional bodies.

Consideration was given as to whether and how engineering would meet four-dimensional criteria if introduced. High-quality and ambitious projects could ensure heights of excellence, and the subject undoubtedly added academic breadth to the curriculum. The teamwork element and application of maths and science would be likely to foster depth of engagement and have lasting impact. A detailed proposal put to governors was unanimously agreed. Specialist science teachers in school were already enthusiastic, and representatives from the professional bodies were consulted as a draft syllabus was devised and a specialist lead teacher recruited.

Such initiatives cannot be undertaken lightly, but curricular innovation is essential if provision is to be as good as possible to keep pace with a changing world. All our seven- to thirteen-year-olds enjoy an hour of engineering per week.

SUMMARY BOX 8.1: The components of a broad academic curriculum

A broad academic curriculum:
English + maths + sciences + humanities + languages + technologies

---

Is it all simply academic?

Across the academic subjects we can see a wealth of facets that develop the mind in many ways and which resonate variously with different learners: communication, expression, creativity, discovery, rigour, confidence, ambition, logic, reasoning, investigation, empathy, perspective, connecting, problem-solving, research and design, to name but some. The development of the mind through the study of academic subjects is likely to be the major part of any school curriculum, not least because of the vast sum of human knowledge and understanding that succeeding generations have passed down, and that children need to know when and how to access.

Academic study develops mental faculties, although as we have seen, also of course contributes to the development of the spirit and character as well. Similarly, all areas of school life contribute to academic development whether directly or not. Learning to play a musical instrument, interpreting a character on stage and playing a tactical cricket match all require application of mental agility and intellectual rigour. But primarily, they serve a broader purpose, and provide a wider, richer context in which the academic sits. Real breadth, and the development of the whole person – body, spirit and character, as well as mind – requires serious attention to be paid to the arts, sports and pastoral areas. It is therefore to these that we now turn.

Notes

1   www.legislation.gov.uk/ukpga/1988/40/contents, accessed 28 July 2017.
2   www.publications.parliament.uk/pa/cm200809/cmselect/cmchilsch/344/344i.pdf, accessed 28 July 2017.
3   www.education.gov.uk/consultations/downloadableDocs/040713%20NC%20in%20 England%20consultation%20-%20govt%20response%20FINAL.pdf, accessed 28 July 2017.
4   www.gov.uk/government/publications/national-curriculum-in-england-framework-for-key-stages-1-to-4/the-national-curriculum-in-england-framework-for-key-stages-1-to-4, accessed 28 July 2017.
5   The Royal Society for the Encouragement of Arts, Manufactures and Commerce.
6   www.thersa.org/action-and-research/rsa-projects/creative-learning-and-development-folder/opening-minds/, accessed 28 July 2017.
7   www.civitas.org.uk/archive/press/PRcurriculum.html, accessed 28 July 2017.
8   www.educationengland.org.uk/documents/pdfs/2009-IRPC-final-report.pdf, accessed 28 July 2017.
9   www.readyunlimited.com/wp-content/uploads/2015/09/An-Introduction-to-the-Cambridge-Primary-Review.pdf, accessed 28 July 2017.
10 The 2014 version of the National Curriculum replaces the word 'adult' with 'later', the only change in its aims.
11 www.tes.com/news/school-news/breaking-news/sugata-mitra-schools-should-scrap-3rs, accessed 28 July 2017.
12 See, for example, www.ncetm.org.uk/public/files/19990433/Developing_mastery_in_mathematics_october_2014.pdf, accessed 28 July 2017.
13 The Fibonacci sequence is the numbers 0, 1, 1, 2, 3, 5 etc., where each successive number is made by adding the two previous numbers together. The sequence has many interesting properties and occurs widely in elements of the natural world as well as being used in computer programming.
14 www.telegraph.co.uk/news/religion/9538561/A-Christian-ethos-strengthens-our-nation.html, accessed 28 July 2017.
15 https://naldic.org.uk/the-eal-learner/research-and-statistics/#eal-learners-in-schools accessed, 28 July 2017.
16 www.gov.uk/government/statistics/schools-pupils-and-their-characteristics-january-2013, accessed 28 July 2017.
17 www.nuffieldfoundation.org/cambridge-school-classics-project-1966, accessed 28 July 2017.
18 www.imeche.org/docs/default-source/1-oscar/reports-policy-statements-and-documents/big-ideas-the-future-of-engineering-in-schoolsaa34ac8d54216d0c8310ff0100d05193.pdf?sfvrsn=0, accessed 28 July 2017.

9

The four-dimensional curriculum

Breadth of attainment in the wider sphere

Having considered breadth across the academic subjects, the broader learning context must also be considered. A four-dimensional curriculum serves to develop the whole person, soul and body as well as mind, and does this through a rich curriculum beyond the academic.

Education in ancient Athens and twentieth-century France

I was fortunate enough to study Education for the second part of my degree, and the most memorable and fascinating parts for me were the lectures and study to do with comparative education. Were we to visit any French classroom at this moment, intoned the lecturer, not only would every nine-year-old in the country be drawing a picture of a cat, they would all be drawing the same cat, its same tail curling to the left of its same body. Then again, had we lived in fifth-century (BC) Athens, been of the right class and gender, the *trivium* would have been our educational diet (grammar, rhetoric and logic) followed by the *quadrivium* (arithmetic, geometry, music and astronomy), all washed down with a healthy helping of physical education, which itself played an important part in the mental and moral development of the highly prized 'rounded' citizen. On the other hand, had I chanced to live in another century, been born into a certain type of family and had a good enough governess, I might have acquired all sorts of skills in botanical drawing, embroidery and dancing: it was evidently not to be.

The academic may sit at the heart of the curriculum, but generations have recognised that to be well educated goes beyond purely developing the mind and sees to the development of the artistic and cultural elements of our beings, our physical strength and agility, and our moral sensitivity and responsiveness.

This continues to be reflected in the National Curriculum's call for Spiritual, Moral and Cultural development, recently re-emphasised as SMSC education (the extra element being social) together with the physical. There is little doubt in the rhetoric that calls for these, but less certainty, I think, as to what they mean in practice in the curriculum. In addition, since they are rarely used as a measure of educational success, they may apparently, or actually, be regarded as being of significantly less importance than the academic components of the curriculum.

However, they also all feature in the four-dimensional curriculum, which identifies directly their purpose and delivery. Having considered the academic side of the curriculum, consideration is now given to other areas of the four-dimensional curriculum, starting with the performance and creative arts: art, music and drama and the role that they can play in development of the spirit. Second the role of sport will be discussed, and third those elements of the curriculum which contribute directly towards the development of character and social and moral awareness. All contribute to roundedness and breadth within the curriculum.

Developing the spirit: the importance of the arts

Without doubt, within the academic subject areas of the curriculum there is diversity and breadth. Logic, curiosity, creativity and empathy are all variously cultivated within the academic subject areas, and much else besides. The arts subjects, however, add another whole dimension to learning, which perhaps might best be described as the cultivation of the spirit – including, but not limited to, spiritual, cultural and moral areas of development.

Creativity is a deep part of our being as humans. The arts help develop creative disciplines both of the mind and heart but they also sooth, encourage and help develop the spirit through the creative process of making and sharing, enabling us to reach out beyond ourselves, beyond what we can perceive directly through our physical senses, to a knowing that is felt in our heart and in our soul, to what the soul of the eye sees.

Creative identity, and the artistic process of making, have a very special place in the holistic development of every child, every human, and in the development of their character. Part of life's meaning is to see; being creative also helps us to relate, to see humanity with purpose and direction. Being creative helps a child to exalt the ordinary and give creative value and worth to the world around them.

Developing imagination, realisation, seeing: art

The nurture and enriching of artistic ability is a most wonderful responsibility and opportunity within a good education. Exploring elements of fine art, such as drawing, painting, collage and sculpture, helps ignite creative gifts and fan them into flame. Art helps to develop and articulate the imagination, since at some level a work of art is always an expression of a concept or a representation of something in the world around us or some other imagined world. Art enables us to look at things (both ideas and objects) in a new light, and to see deeper into the world around us. If we believe all humans to be by nature creative, then the fostering of creative ability is an essential part of developing our identity and being more truly human.

Art is also a discipline, and it helps to foster spatial awareness, perception of colour, tone and composition, and skills in drawing, painting, printing and sculpting. These traditional artistic disciplines may be partnered by a new range of opportunities provided through creative technologies. Depending on what is available these might include, for example, the application of photography, computer-aided design, laser cutters and 3-D printers, all of which can be used to create, enhance and enrich new forms of art from stop-frame animations to multi-media design. These combination``s help to open wider creative horizons and pathways for the pupil.

In addition to developing their own artistic skills through art lessons and the practical process of making, pupils also learn a discerning art appreciation through the creativity of others – makers of art, craft and design. Such study helps pupils to discover the value and diversity of art work in the contemporary world, as well as through art history. Pupils develop an appreciation of the influence that many artists and art movements have had on the world around us and understand how art continues to influence and shape our culture, as well as reflect it. The study of art encourages powers of appreciation, opens insights into cultural heritage and identity and develops the aesthetic in both analysis and description, helping the pupil develop a wider range of personal creative empathy.

Visits to galleries and museums, where children's eyes are opened to new worlds of artistic expression, are invaluable. Speaking of one of its paintings chosen for the youngest of children to explore, The National Gallery describes *River Landscape with Horseman and Peasants*, painted in about 1660 by Albert Cuyp, as one of the greatest seventeenth-century Dutch landscapes. 'It is the largest surviving landscape by Cuyp, and arguably the most beautiful. The entire scene is bathed in gentle sunlight, harmonising the natural, animal and human elements. Children can enjoy discovering cows, sheep, ducks, horses and a hiding dog'. The session promises exploration of various themes including places, objects, living things and contrasts.[1] Art fosters appreciation of the aesthetic, and of beauty.

It is also true that artistic imagination, creativity and ability are also of great practical value in their application to design. The recent trend towards recognising the importance of cross-curricular STEAM (science, technology, engineering, art and maths) projects, as opposed to merely STEM (without the art) projects, highlights the important part that art can also play as part of wider educational endeavour.

The arts give expression to something deep within all of us. While art and design are of practical value, they also enable us to explore and express truths about the world in which we live beyond a purely functional and prosaic description. The human spirit is inherently creative and imaginative and needs to be fed.

Throughout all of art history, from the earliest cave paintings via Byzantine mosaics and African tribal masks to American colonial art and abstract expressionism, people have felt a desire and need to express themselves, to openly share their ideas and the things they hold dear through word-free visual representation. As John Berger observed, 'Seeing comes before words. The child looks and recognises before he can speak. All creation is the art of seeing. What matters are the needs that art answers'.[2]

Developing listening, composing, performing: music

Music is at once joyous and reflective, allowing for the expression of deep feeling and rich emotion whether through listening, composing or performing. Perhaps because it is the most abstract of the arts, music reminds us of another world beyond the purely physical. We are moved to tears by a plaintive violin; our spirits are raised by Dave Brubeck's foot-tapping *Unsquare Dance*; we find release and relaxation in our favourite pieces, be they by Beethoven or Clean Bandit.

Music also allows us to express ourselves. As Mendelssohn famously wrote of his *Songs without Words*:

> People often complain that music is too ambiguous; that what they should think when they hear is so unclear, whereas everyone understands words. With me it is exactly the reverse, and not only with regard to an entire speech, but also with individual words. These too seem to me so ambiguous, so vague, so easily misunderstood in comparison to genuine music, which fills the soul with a thousand things better than words . . . Only the song can say the same things, can arouse the same feelings in one person as another, a feeling which is not expressed, however, by the same words.[3]

For Mendelssohn, at least, music represents a richer, higher form of language than words, one which 'fills the soul'.

Music, of course, has its academic elements and is richly linked to mathematics and physics, reflecting the pattern and order of the world in which we live, but it is so much more than this as well. Music is woven into the fabric of the world, and so is the birthright of every human soul. All children need to be given the opportunity to sing and make music, to listen to and appreciate music. Sensitivity is needed to accommodate any children with hearing impairment but all need to know, experience and access as far as possible their rich musical heritage; this should not be the preserve of the luckily advantaged, because musical heritage is a bequest to the entirety of the next generation, not just to a privileged few.

All children should enjoy a broad music education that promotes a lifelong love of music. They should be introduced to a wide variety of music which they experience through listening, appraising, performing and composing. From the youngest age, the emphasis should be on enjoyment and appreciation while increasingly covering a wide variety of topics, including the basics of musical notation, singing, composition, improvisation and performing as well as studying some Western music history, World Music and contemporary music.

Ideally, every child in school should experience the joy of singing in a choir, and where it is possible individual tuition should be available on orchestral instruments as well as piano, singing, guitar and drum kit; for those who take individual music lessons, opportunity should be provided to play in and perform with one or more ensembles, depending on what opportunities can be made available.

Highly talented musicians need to be given opportunities to perform on a wider stage and should be encouraged to participate in regional and national events. Ideally, music and drama should work closely together in effecting and celebrating the performing arts. Working together musically develops team spirit and underlines the value of community: musically, the whole is always greater than the sum of the parts.

And musical productions can bring great joy to those who perform in them. Back to our children's primary school, and despite its limited resources and (relatively) time-poor school day, during the years our children were there, the one dependable 'extra' that was eagerly awaited each year was the school musical. Somehow, despite the obvious obstacles of a nineteenth-century school hall, which doubled up as the dining room and had only a limited platform as a stage, they managed to arrange for vast numbers of children to take part with inordinate enthusiasm and remarkable panache in musical plays from *Annie* to *Honk*. Wonderful costumes emerged from the hands of skilled parents, and wonderful performances were coaxed out of nervous children by enthusiastic and dedicated staff. Music and drama go hand in hand, bringing joy to the hearts of all those who participate, and smiles to the faces of parents watching, guaranteeing that for all of them 'the sun'll come out tomorrow – bet your bottom dollar there'll be sun . . .'.

Developing improvising, expressing, presenting: drama

Whether working on original or scripted pieces, drama promotes confidence and camaraderie through improvising words and actions, expressing individuality and presenting both solo and group performances. The aim of drama is surely to provide enjoyable and creative opportunities for all pupils to develop confidence in self-expression. Their learning in this subject is an active experience which is physically, emotionally and intellectually rewarding. Games, exercises, improvisation and scripts can all be used effectively to enable the development of creativity, imaginative thinking, speaking and listening and interpersonal skills. Humour and empathy, communication and cooperation are key elements, as are gaining an understanding of theatre and presentation skills.

Confidence is developed through performance, and as described with primary school musicals, performance also brings a great sense of camaraderie, satisfaction and pleasure for those taking part. High-quality productions, from early years Nativity plays through to staging of Shakespeare, or even learning to run an entire production company, enable pupils to learn what the essential ingredients are for the achievement of excellence: hard work, attention to detail, imagination, creativity and teamwork, to name just some.

Such opportunities may variously be open to all, or on occasion provide special opportunities for those with a particular dramatic flair. Dramatic talent, like any other, needs to be identified, valued and fostered; this can only happen if opportunity is given to all. Particularly able pupils should be encouraged to pursue opportunities in local and national theatre, or be encouraged to take part in local festivals. Some pupils may benefit from individual solo or shared speech and drama lessons, which can provide an excellent means of capitalising on a child's gift in one case, or in another, help to develop greater confidence and skill in public speaking and presentation.

Plays, of course, are just that: an opportunity to play. Drama enables exploration of actions and their consequences, the intended or unexpected results of words and gestures, in the safe context of the stage. As such it has a rich moral seam running through it, allowing children to understand the violent force of love in *Romeo and Juliet* or the power of suggestion in *An Inspector Calls*.

And just as with the other arts, drama also enables pupils to access and appreciate their heritage, to enjoy watching and studying plays as well as staging them. Pupils need to be taught how to watch a play intentionally, and they should learn to have a sense of respect and awe for those who can turn the lifeless, black-and-white, two-dimensional words on the page of a play script into a colourful pageant playing out before our eyes that can trick us into utter absorption in another, entirely make-believe, world.

Physical development: the role of sport

The difference between a school that takes sport seriously and one that does not is disproportionately marked. Sport does not confine itself politely to the hours allocated on the timetable, but spills over into pre-season and after-school training sessions, fixtures, tournaments, meetings, competitions and even, for the lucky ones, tours. Visually, in a school that takes sport seriously, it dominates the landscape, since sport takes up so much more physical space than any other teaching; sports facilities on-site are immediately visible to visitors; and always welcoming spectators, sport brings parents into schools like nothing else, ensuring that no other teaching has the same profile.

This phenomenon is further enhanced by pupils' instinctive enthusiasm for sport, in all its many facets. From a gymnastics display to a tug-of-war, from a football friendly to a rowing regatta, sport is loved by participating pupils. How many of our collective early memories are comprised of the traditional sports-day races: three-legged, egg-and-spoon or sack?

Of course, a number of sporting activities include an element of the arts. It is a moot point where, in the progression from drama to mime to dance to gymnastics to trampolining, the transition occurs between the two broad areas. But for sure, both the arts and the sports contribute to the four-dimensional curriculum.

What is it that sport has to offer to the curriculum that we expect a good education to provide?

Developing fitness, agility, coordination: physical education (PE)

The body in which we run around, controlled somehow by mind and spirit, is self-evidently intrinsic to who we are. A holistic education cares for development of the body as well as the mind and spirit.

PE effectively educates the body, training in suppleness, fitness, coordination and agility. It also educates the mind to think about how best to look after the body, gaining some understanding as to how it works, and knowledge as to how to eat healthily and keep physically fit. It teaches children why such fitness matters and how best to maintain it.

If the aim of PE is to develop excellent levels of physical fitness and coordination, the emphasis needs to be on the fullest possible participation and enjoyment, and as a result include as great a variety of activity as possible. Within this we should expect to find swimming (not least for reasons of safety), and might also expect to see some elements of traditional sports such as gymnastics and athletics. Clearly what is on offer must depend on the range and extent of facilities and expertise, but in some schools PE also extends to include experience of activities such as dance, basketball or badminton.

Special provision must obviously be made for those who can participate in sport to only a limited extent, whether temporarily or permanently. While some limited physical activity, such as swimming, may prove possible, this will not always be the case, and here as elsewhere every child must be treated as an individual, particular sensitivity being shown to the most physically disadvantaged. Opportunities may present themselves for more physically able children to help others and a caring attitude in this respect is always to be encouraged.

The main aim is to nurture ability in every pupil and to encourage each to achieve his or her potential as often and fully as possible. Pupils may take part in competitions at school, locally or even nationally, depending on the resources available. PE clearly plays an important part in a rounded education, providing opportunities for the pursuit of excellence and encouraging breadth of attainment as a result.

Developing teamwork, fairness, competition: Games

It may initially seem a false distinction to make, but many schools distinguish 'Games' on the timetable from 'PE', the primary aim of the former being to provide opportunities for pupils to take part in and develop a love of competitive team sport. Thus while PE primarily develops the body, Games develops character. Games teaches children the benefit of teamwork, the importance of fairness and a healthy appreciation of competition, qualities that are also invaluable in other areas of life.

Competitive sport is not universally admired by schools, and some seek what they perceive to be a less confrontational approach to physical education (more akin to PE alone). Nevertheless it remains a significant feature in many schools and those who advocate it regard the social, cultural and character-building elements of it as being of enormous value.

Through competitive sport, fair play and sportsman-like behaviour are promoted, central to the cultivation of integrity and respect. Working hard towards success, driven with a desire to do as well as possible, encourages distinction in performance. Cultivating the right mental approach to competitive sport means that children see first-hand the importance of getting the basics right every time (a hall-mark of rigour), and of focusing on positive thinking. Developing cooperation, essential for success as a team, children learn how to channel their energy towards a common goal. Fostering initiative and service, participation in team sport also encourages pupils to value dependability, commitment and loyalty, while also learning to train hard, think tactically and give of their all. It is therefore not hard to see the value of competitive sport in the development of character.

A games department that is a strong advocate of competitive sport, and is working at the highest level, will try to find fixtures against other schools for as many children as possible. While some children may reach national standards – and certainly should be given the opportunity to do so if they are performing at this level – the aim should be to have as many children as possible participating in matches at the level appropriate to their skill development. Of course one of the benefits of competition is learning the lifelong lesson that there are winners and losers, and experiencing what it feels like to be on either side of that divide. Rudyard Kipling's apt words, written on the wall of the players' entrance to Centre Court at the All England Lawn Tennis and Croquet Club where the Wimbledon tennis championships are held: 'If you can meet with Triumph and Disaster/and treat those two impostors just the same', remind us that neither failure nor triumph is all that it seems, and certainly neither should define us. Perseverance is learnt through disappointment, compassion through success.

Schools which take sport very seriously for their girls and boys may expect to field teams in netball, hockey, tennis, cricket, rugby and soccer – even from the age of seven or eight in some cases – and some schools may even put out a rowing eight. Learning the rules of such sports through participation provides pupils with undeniable cultural capital. Competitive sport, however, can be far more modest – a rounders team can still represent an enormous and highly significant opportunity for children to feel the thrill of selection, participation and contribution. Coping well with the joy of winning and the disappointment of losing, responding appropriately to the honour of being chosen as captain or despondency at de-selection, at any level of play, builds character and resilience.

A school that values breadth of attainment and variety of achievement will want to include sport. For many children it gives them an opportunity to excel and gain a sense of success: for some it will be their chief means of doing so.

Pastoral elements of the curriculum

Pastoral elements of the curriculum variously include: tutor times, which may incorporate personal, social, health and economic education (PSHE) and citizenship; school assemblies; and lessons dedicated to promoting social, moral, spiritual and cultural (SMCS) development. In addition, all English schools are required actively to promote what are described as fundamental British values.

Every part of school life needs to send the same messages in these respects: we aim to promote spiritual, moral, social and cultural development and help to prepare all pupils for the opportunities, responsibilities and experiences of life; we need to help pupils to be resilient rather than brittle in dealing with change. However, although every subject contributes to the holistic development of the pupil, the pastoral elements of the curriculum pay special attention to the development of character and an overall sense of well-being. Thus while many of these elements of development and learning are inherent throughout the curriculum, time will also be specifically dedicated to them, to some extent.

Pastoral elements of the curriculum need to be designed and planned carefully to enable pupils ultimately to become happy, well-adjusted, modern teenagers (and in due course, adults), friends and family members in today's demanding society. It is also true that a child who is happy will be a better learner, more willing to participate actively in his or her learning and to keep trying, thus ensuring greater experience of success and consequent happiness – another virtuous circle in learning.

Developing support, behaviour, well-being: Tutor times and PSHE

Tutor times (or form times), when the specific children in the care of their pastoral tutor meet together, enable supportive relationships to form between tutor and tutees, and within the group. Tutors (or form teachers) can keep an eye on pupils' effort and progress, behaviour and happiness. In addition, the tutor group as a whole, or individuals within it, may take part in specific acts of service to the community, whether through 'buddying' younger children, for example, or helping to look after the school site. A tutor programme might specifically include PSHE as part of its provision.

Particular emphasis might be placed on developing any of the character traits described in the four-dimensional model, developing pupils' abilities to tackle the challenges of life and learning. PSHE programmes can encourage children to understand their own feelings and behaviours, and those of others. Developing emotional literacy helps them take more responsibility for their own behaviour and choices, and to understand and value kindness, sympathy and compassion.

Developing respect for the opinions of others, and making decisions on what they believe to be right, including how to live safe, responsible, considerate and healthy lives (including online), can be built into such lessons, as well as being promoted across the entire curriculum. In such ways children can be encouraged not just to talk about problems, but to solve them confidently by making informed choices face to face with people or through healthy, safe, social networks. With a focus on health and well-being, age-appropriate Sex and Relationship Education (SRE) is often taught within a PSHE programme, perhaps collaboratively with science.

Separate or integrated lessons may focus on elements of citizenship, enabling pupils to understand the structures, history and values of the society in which they find themselves living.

Developing spiritual, moral, social and cultural development: assemblies

Recent years have seen an explicit requirement for English state schools to foster the spiritual, moral, social and cultural aspects of education. While the government states that 'All National Curriculum subjects provide opportunities to promote pupils' spiritual, moral, social and cultural development', it continues by stating that 'Explicit opportunities to promote pupils' development in these areas are provided in religious education and the non-statutory framework for personal, social and health education (PSHE) and citizenship. A significant contribution is also made by school ethos, effective relationships throughout the school, collective worship, and other curriculum activities'.[4]

This reference to collective worship refers to the requirements first instigated by the 1944 Education Act that all state schools should hold a compulsory daily act of worship. Regularly and variously challenged by secularists[5] and pragmatists,[6] the law nevertheless currently remains in place. Whether a daily (or indeed any) act of worship is regarded as being a realistic or desirable part of school life, in schools where they do occur, at the very least they encourage pupils to look beyond the immediate, to transcend the mundane and for a few moments of each day reflect that the world may not revolve around me as an individual, or even us as a community. The four-dimensional model endorses these benefits as enabling pupils to recognise the spiritual element of life as a whole, and to recognise themselves to be spiritual and moral, as well as physical, intellectual and social, beings.

In a school with a Christian foundation, through assemblies or services celebrating the Christian festivals, pupils are encouraged to celebrate the gifts of creation, life and love; they appreciate the need and provision of forgiveness, reconciliation and grace; they will be helped to foster a sense of hope, meaning and purpose. Assemblies (as opposed to services) may tend to focus more on personal development and community life, encouraging pupils to develop a growing sense of appreciation, responsibility and respect for themselves, each other and the wider world. Assemblies may reflect on those character traits which the school seeks to promote such as respect, positivity, service and compassion; success across a variety of endeavours may be marked and celebrated.

It is not just in assemblies and services that such values are cultivated and celebrated. The four-dimensional lesson, in whatever subject, should foster a sense of appreciation – an enhanced aesthetic, spiritual or moral awareness, a sense of wonder or awe.

The foundational values at the heart of the four-dimensional model assume a moral framework or world-view. As a result, pupils will be taught that we live in a moral world and that we each have the responsibility to discern right and wrong. Moral issues affecting the school and the wider world will be regularly addressed in pastoral time but in other parts of the curriculum as well: many, if not all, lessons explore moral and ethical issues across the range of subjects, from fair play in Games to fair trade in maths. Whether explicitly faith-based, morals come to us through traditions with long-established histories and experience from which we can learn and grow. Moral teaching should give life, hope and grace.

When integrity of character is fostered, pupils are expected and encouraged to act in a way which demonstrates self-respect and respect for others. Whether in lessons or assemblies, they are encouraged to develop the ability to reason logically, to understand cause and effect in the moral as well as physical world, and to offer considered, reasoned views. Pupils learn how the rule of law supports a moral code, protecting what is good and acting to halt or prevent that which is wrong.

Within the four-dimensional framework, pupils are encouraged to see themselves as members of a community which flourishes through understanding and appreciation of diverse viewpoints, and fostering a spirit of service and collaboration. All pupils need to be given the opportunity to participate in community events, older children supporting younger ones in reading, joint fundraising activities or community social action. Integration with the local community is to be encouraged whenever possible, from supplying art work for local building site hoardings to participating in projects with other schools.

Through English and modern languages lessons, the performing and creative arts, and humanities subjects, pupils have access to, and learn to appreciate, the achievements of the Western cultural tradition, but also those of other cultures.

Through history and the other humanities subjects, pupils learn about the various factors contributing to the local, national and global environment in which they find themselves growing up.

Pupils may variously be given opportunities to celebrate and enjoy elements of traditional British culture – such as the aforementioned Pancake Day – and other cultures, such as the Chinese New Year, both of which might typically be marked in assembly, feature in a lesson or be reflected in a lunch menu.

British values

With the introduction of the 'Prevent' strategy in 2011, all schools in England are required to actively promote and embed the fundamental British values of democracy, the rule of law, individual liberty and mutual respect and tolerance of those with different faiths and beliefs.[7] While some caution may be felt if it appears that political concerns are being addressed through schools, these four values (also held beyond Britain itself, of course) should be in line with the values and practices of any school, and can be welcomed as such.

Democratic values, lawfulness, respect and liberty should be expected to run through the school like water in a river, and should be caught as well as taught. Believing every member of the community to be of equal and inestimable worth, democracy is promoted in the life of a school that adopts the four-dimensional model, or that reflects its principles. The origins of British parliamentary democracy are taught through history, and pupils may learn about the current political process through visits to the school by Members of Parliament, or visits to the Houses of Parliament. Pupils should be encouraged to engage in discussion of matters of concern to the whole school community, and where possible pupils should take part in surveys or consultation on matters which affect the whole school. Members of the school community may have a voice through electing members of a school council, or representatives with responsibility for eco matters or such like.

Acknowledging all members of the school community to be mutually dependent, needing supportive cooperation to live and work successfully, the rule of law should also be promoted through teaching and practice. Teaching will promote our national laws which ensure that all people living in Great Britain can enjoy their life in a safe and organised manner, while enjoying the freedom and liberty fundamental to British life. Simple, basic rules governing the behaviour of all members of the school community allow a school to run safely and successfully, while recognising and encouraging the expression of individuality within this framework.

While specific lessons may actively promote understanding of the rule of law, the practices of a school – from following instructions in a maths test to following an agreed order of priority going into lunch – endorse the rule of law in practice. Consistency of these principles, interpreted compassionately and sensitively, is foundational to supporting the varied needs within the community.

Individual liberty is also regarded as a fundamental British value and, if we believe that every pupil is uniquely gifted, with a distinctive and personal profile of strengths and creativities to be valued and fostered, this too will be promoted. Endorsing the character traits of integrity and respect ensures that pupils are taught the importance of taking responsibility for their own actions, standing up for what they believe to be right and not being subject to coercion. Pupils must be encouraged to think through and express their own opinions sensitively and to be respectful of those of others.

Wherever possible, across the curriculum, pupils should be encouraged to make personal, creative and individual responses and to appreciate the responses of others. Creativity, individuality and diversity are to be celebrated, and a wide range of opportunities for children to express their own personality should be offered.

If every member of the school community is believed to be equally inherently precious, but also mutually dependent, respect and tolerance will be promoted. The respect due to all fellow human beings will be taught and referenced in lessons, assemblies and tutor times; the curriculum will promote understanding and appreciation of a variety of cultures within and beyond those represented by the school community. Whatever religious or non-religious ethos a school may nourish, due respect should be given to those of other faiths and beliefs.

Finally, belief in our mutual dependency and responsibility means that charitable work should focus attention on variety of need within the local, national and global communities, and encourage support of the less advantaged whoever or wherever they may be. Sometimes pupils may be fortunate enough to travel within or beyond the UK, gaining a broader perspective and appreciation, and it is becoming ever easier to form direct links with other specific schools at home and abroad through the internet and application of mobile technology.

SUMMARY BOX 9.1: The components of a broad wider curriculum

A broad wider curriculum:
the arts + sports + pastoral elements

The practicalities of implementing breadth

Self-evidently, the time that children spend at school is limited. In England, at the time of writing, state schools have to be open for 190 days each year, but the hours they operate are unspecified. Figures from the Organisation for Economic Co-operation and Development (OECD), published in 2014, indicate that on average primary school children in England are in receipt of '861 hours of compulsory instruction time per year'.[8] Despite the considerably longer holidays, the longer working day of an independent school may result in the total number of hours of tuition being closer to 1,000.[9] Whichever the sector and whatever the context, however, it is clear that time is limited and priorities have to be set carefully as to how that time is divided up.

Within the four-dimensional model of education, there are four broad areas of the curriculum. These all support the holistic development of the child in various ways, but equally each will have a predominant facet which it supports. The first, the academic, chiefly supports development of the mind or intellect. Second, the arts chiefly support development of spirit through culture and aesthetics. Third, sports support physical development, and fourth, the pastoral curriculum areas particularly support development of the heart (character or moral development).

We may instinctively feel that the fourth of these is intrinsically the most important, and indeed the model indicates that the cultivation of character traits, individually and within the community, is central. The National Curriculum lists moral development of pupil and society first in its list. Pastoral time in all its various facets, which most obviously promotes this, must not only be allocated, but protected. There also needs to be a recognition that every single part of the school day and every facet of school life contributes to the cultivation of character and to care for the individual within the community.

In terms of practical timetabling, the lion's share of time in the week will always be given to the mental development of children. Strong academic provision, in support of good mental development, must be a priority, not least since academic qualifications remain the key to future opportunities for young people. At the most foundational level, pupils need to be able to read and to write, to be mathematically competent and to be computer literate. These are essential both for wider study, and to enable participation in, and contribution to, life in the modern world. The further development of the mind through wider and deeper academic study enables greater knowledge and understanding to be built up. This in turn enables greater opportunities to participate in, and contribute to, life and society, and greater choice as to how that might occur. There is a vast accumulation of such knowledge and understanding to be passed on to each new generation, and that takes time; it also requires expertise which schools are in a position to provide. For all these reasons, the academic must be a priority in terms of allocated time.

Despite the assertion of providing a rounded education, schools governed by the National Curriculum are assessed in narrow terms. If a school is going to be judged by its scores in reading, writing and maths, securing the best standards here will inevitably be a chief focus. The introduction of the literacy hour in 1998 and the introduction of the national numeracy strategy in 1999 with its daily maths lesson served to place the emphasis firmly on these areas of learning, and given the structure of the school day for some schools, by the time they have had a morning assembly, and an hour or so each of English and maths, the morning is over. Afternoons provide time for other subjects, which may be timetabled either on a carousel or together by way of cross–curricular projects.

A state primary school's teaching day may run approximately along the following lines:[10]

- 9.00–9.30 registration and assembly
- 9.30–10.30 lesson 1
- 10.45–12.00 lesson 2
- 13.15–15.15 lessons 3 and 4.

In this scenario, maths and English (and associated activities such as reading), together with assemblies, take up the entirety of the morning lesson time, leaving the afternoon hours available for the teaching of other subjects (Table 9.1).

It was certainly the case that in our children's (high-performing) primary school, great emphasis was laid on the pupils' English and maths, to very good effect. They were very well taught and their knowledge, understanding and skills in these subjects were typically very good. It is probably true, however, that other subjects largely played second fiddle: all the bases were covered, but not necessarily in a great deal of depth, and not with any particularly special emphasis.

In other schools (such as specialist academies) there may be a more detailed hierarchy in terms of allocated time, and consequent opportunities for some, even several, other areas of strength to be recognised and developed. Operated by the City of London Educational Trust, a proposed primary academy in London will offer a 'specific focus on mathematical ability and financial literacy'[11] for example, while at Dixon's Music Primary, 'Every week, each pupil receives instrumental,

TABLE 9.1 Subject allocation in a school with a twenty-four-hour teaching week

SUBJECT ALLOCATIONS BY YEAR IN HOURS PER WEEK IN A STATE JUNIOR SCHOOL

SUBJECT	YEAR			
	3	4	5	6
English (includes reading and spelling)	6¼	6¼	6¼	6¼
Maths (includes tables and mental arithmetic)	5	5	5	5
Other subjects (includes Arts, Crafts, Computers, History, Science, Gymnastics etc.)	10	10	10	10
Pastoral (includes registration time and assemblies)	2½	2½	2½	2½
TOTAL	23¾	23¾	23¾	23¾

vocal and ensemble tuition in a mixture of small and large group tuition which is delivered by specialist music teachers'.[12]

If the best possible provision is to be made to cater both for the whole child and the wide range of individual gifting within the community, the greater the breadth of opportunity and the more ambitious the expectations within those opportunities, the better. Although time resources are very limited in some schools due to the structure of their working week, time reserved and protected for specific academic subjects beyond maths and English is highly valuable. We have already noted how each of the other academic subject areas (sciences, humanities, languages and technologies) makes a unique contribution to pupils' development. A fixed timetable (albeit flexible enough to being set aside for enriching learning opportunities) protects against the temptation to focus learning time narrowly on maths and English in the run-up to exams or assessment.

In addition to the academic, time allocated to the arts (both visual and performing) and for sport (both physical education and competitive team sport) is also highly valuable, and should also be dedicated and protected as such. Teachers will be conscious when they teach that had the children in their classes been born into a different age or tradition, instead of sitting stoically emblazered behind a desk, they would variously be running round barefoot, climbing trees or learning a trade by observation and participation. That is not the world in which our children live, but trying to bear in mind that some children's instinctive strengths and interests may more naturally lie in their physical or artistic activity than the academic helps us to ensure that we make good provision for them to develop their unique gifting, not to the exclusion of secure academic performance, but alongside it.

The spiritual, moral, aesthetic, cultural, mental and physical elements of education do not map readily onto specific subjects. Moral lessons may be learnt through assembly, but they may equally be learnt through reading a novel or captaining a sports team. Cultural lessons may be learnt in a music lesson, but may equally be learnt in a tutor time or geography lesson. Just as children are indivisible, holistic beings, so too the curriculum – and even more so the teaching – needs to have a holistic coherence even if it is broken down into timetabled subject-specific sessions for pragmatic purposes. And of course the same values and principles need to run through every part of the curriculum, like that lettering through the seaside stick of rock.

The prep school where I currently work has thirty timetabled hours a week to allocate, the school day looking as follows:

- 08.25–10.25 two one-hour lessons followed by a break
- 10.45–12.45 two one-hour lessons followed by lunch
- 13.40–15.40 two one-hour lessons followed by optional after-school activities.

Time is allocated very specifically across all the year groups (see Table 9.2), with every hour being timetabled for even the Year 3 children. This not only

TABLE 9.2 Subject allocation in a school with a thirty-hour teaching week (at the start of the school year, Year 3 children are aged seven and Year 8s are twelve)

SUBJECT ALLOCATIONS BY YEAR IN HOURS PER WEEK IN AN INDEPENDENT PREP (JUNIOR) SCHOOL

SUBJECT	YEAR					
	3	4	5	6	7	8
English (includes 30 min library time in all years)	6½*	6½*	5	4	4	4
Maths	5	5	4	4	4	4
Sciences (includes physics, chemistry and biology topics)	2	3	3	3	3	3
Humanities (includes history, geography and RS)	3	2	3	3	3	3
Languages (Spanish in all Years, Latin from Year 5 and French from Year 7)	2	2	3	3	4	4
Computing (includes digital literacy and computer science)	1	1	1	1	1	1
Engineering	1	1	1	1	1	1
Art	1	1	1	1	1	1
Music	1	1	1	1	1	1
Drama	1	1	1	1	1	1
PE	1	1	1	1	1	1
Games	2	2	3	4	4	4
Pastoral (includes assemblies, tutor periods and PSHCE)	3½	3½	3	3	2	2
TOTAL	30	30	30	30	30	30

* includes 60 min reading

ensures that a balance is protected within learning, but on a practical level enables maximum use to be made of specialist facilities for art, computing or sport. The allocation of time to subjects prioritises the academic but allows for generous provision for physical education, the arts and pastoral time.

This table clearly shows the opportunities to broaden the curriculum which a longer school day provides. The younger years still have at least an hour each of English and maths each day, following a primary school pattern but, in addition, are able to enjoy plenty of the wider academic subjects (with specific dedicated time), the arts and sports, as well as having dedicated pastoral time. As the children become older the amount of English, maths and pastoral time reduces, while languages and sports increase. A broad, balanced and rich curriculum is achieved, which is age–appropriate and provides for both continuity and development.

Subject areas are not exhaustive and however long the school day may be, the process of curriculum design is, of necessity, selective. Nevertheless, however expansive or limited the standard curriculum offered may be, every school can enrich its curriculum through occasional or regular off-timetabled days, after-school clubs or extension activities, which provide wonderful opportunities otherwise very difficult to fit in.

Beyond the timetable: enrichment, extension, activities and awards

The curriculum only takes children so far, however broad, balanced and extensive it may be: there is much beyond it. Off-timetable, enrichment days held once or twice a term enable all sorts of opportunities which otherwise would simply not occur. Use can be made of in-house, parental or local expertise. Teachers can share specific interests, areas they studied while students or hobbies about which they have become particularly knowledgeable. If a school is unable to offer a subject on a regular basis, it can offer it on an enrichment day. We have found this to be extremely successful, and have managed to have days on languages not otherwise studied, such as Japanese, sciences not otherwise studied, such as astronomy, and other subjects which draw on various disciplines, such as architecture.

Enrichment days enable the timetable to be collapsed so that time can be given to extended research or large-scale studies. These may be the best days for outings to museums or trips to galleries, for study of natural formations in the landscape or historic houses, for dressing up as Greeks or spending the day as Victorians. On some days, visits to farms or factories enable children to understand the origins of their food or manufactured goods, while on others they can have access to extraordinary elements of their heritage, whether it be the crown jewels or Hadrian's Wall.

Another benefit of enrichment days is the opportunities that they provide for cross-curricular work. Having argued the value of subject allocations on the timetable, I would nevertheless strongly argue the necessity of children being able to make connections within and between subject areas. Tracking the journey of a cocoa bean from its humble tree-origins to its ultimate corner-shop destination can draw on and develop knowledge of geography, science and mathematics and require the application of information-mining and communication skills. A day spent looking into the writing of Jorge Luis Borges can consider both the art of story-telling and the skill of translation; it can use both Spanish and English text; it can result in creative writing or dramatic interpretation. A study of the number seven can consider the origins of the names of the days of the week, the symbolism of seven in literature and some challenges concerning prime numbers in maths. Cross-curricular work mitigates the effects of a polka-dot curriculum which fosters entirely separate pockets of knowledge making no connections between them.

Typically, such *enrichment* opportunities are open to all the children in a year group, and help to support the principle of breadth for all. Similar off-timetable opportunities, however, may sometimes be provided for just some children, those who would especially benefit from a maths master class, writing poetry with a native speaker of their first language or attending an orchestral day at another school. While all children need access to rich and challenging learning opportunities, such *extension* activities can be a key way of ensuring that pupils' individual gifts are valued and provided for. They are therefore an important component in the pursuit of excellence for all and for attainment in various different disciplines and arts. Here too is where selective sport fits into provision: if a child has a gift in playing a team sport, there is nothing wrong – and indeed much that is right – with them being given the opportunity to exercise it, provided that commensurate opportunities are provided for others to identify and develop to the full their talents. A 'pyramid of opportunity' (Figure 9.1) enables all pupils to have full access to some level of activity, but ensures that further, increasingly challenging opportunities are accessible for the decreasing number with exceptional talent in a given area.

Off-timetable activities may include after-school or lunchtime clubs, some of which may be open to all and others of which may be by invitation. Sometimes a club caters for those children who are yet to identify a particular talent or special interest within any regular school subject, so that photography, app-design or chess provides an opportunity for a talent to emerge and be fanned into flame.

Many national and international schemes are available for schools to participate in which enable extra-curricular activity to be organised in a structured goal-orientated manner, providing great incentives to young people. Participation in the Duke of Edinburgh Award Scheme, for example, enables pupils to develop outdoor skills, individual talents, community service and physical skills,[13] while the Arts Award[14] provides opportunities for young people to develop creativity and leadership skills and link with creative arts professionals. Similarly, the CREST Awards[15] give young people opportunities to explore real-world science, technology, engineering and maths projects. Such awards are all valuable

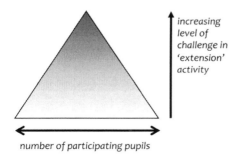

FIGURE 9.1 A schematic representation of the 'pyramid of opportunity'

not only in encouraging young people to take part in such activities, but to do so in a structured way which enables them to reach high and go far.

A good education finds every way to encourage breadth of attainment, recognising that we are all different, all have something to contribute and there is great joy to be found in the discovery and exercise of whatever that might be. In a community with a shared, positive outlook and wide opportunities, there should be much to celebrate.

Inevitably, the extent to which this is actualised is dependent on the quality of the constituent elements. The primacy of pastoral time, of maths and English, the essential contribution of the other academic subjects, the arts and sport, and the wonderful contribution that can be made beyond the standard curriculum, may be agreed, but within these elements how can high quality be ensured? It is necessary to drill down into the detail of how a subject is taught.

Notes

1 www.nationalgallery.org.uk/learning/teachers-and-schools/sessions-for-eyfs, accessed 28 July 2017.

2 *Ways of seeing*, by John Berger (pub. Penguin, 1972).

3 From a letter to Marc-Andre Souchay, Berlin, 15 October 1842.

4 http://webarchive.nationalarchives.gov.uk/20130123124929/http://www.education.gov. uk/schools/teachingandlearning/curriculum/a00199700/spiritual-and-moral, accessed 28 July 2017.

5 See for example, The National Secularist Society: www.secularism.org.uk/collective-worship.html, accessed 28 July 2017.

6 See for example, the 2015 publication from the Westminster Faith Debates: http://faith debates.org.uk/wp-content/uploads/2015/06/A-New-Settlement-for-Religion-and-Belief-in-schools.pdf, accessed 28 July 2017.

7 www.gov.uk/government/uploads/system/uploads/attachment_data/file/97976/prevent-strategy-review.pdf, accessed 28 July 2017.

8 *Education at a Glance* 2014 – © OECD 2014.

9 At our school, pupils have a 30-hour learning week (including assemblies and pastoral time) for 33 weeks, and up to 10 additional hours a week of after-school activities.

10 Information based on http://projectbritain.com/schday/Start.html, accessed 28 July 2017.

11 www.cityoflondon.gov.uk/services/education-learning/schools/Pages/City-of-London-Primary-Academy-Islington.aspx, accessed 28 July 2017.

12 www.dixonsmp.com/, accessed 28 July 2017.

13 www.dofe.org/what-is-dofe, accessed 28 July 2017.

14 www.artsaward.org.uk/site/?id=1346, accessed 28 July 2017.

15 www.britishscienceassociation.org/crest-awards, accessed 28 July 2017.

10

The four-dimensional subject

Achieving heights of excellence

The way in which each subject is approached is fundamental to achieving excellence. Pursuing the practical detail of teaching, the four-dimensional model has implications for individual subjects or areas of study. Subject expertise is a complex mix of knowledge, understanding, skill and appreciation, usually mediated via knowledge-based topics or units of work. How these are chosen and the ways in which they are taught are key factors in the pursuit of excellence and consequent development of expertise. The evidence of learning is seen in the resulting output. As these processes are considered below, examples are drawn from across the subjects, with the most detailed being from English. This is due to its uniquely foundational nature and distinctive flexibility with regard to content.

The virtues of being a not-so-natural scientist

I was something of an all-rounder academically at school – a jack-of-all-trades and certainly master of none. My O-level grades, as they were then,[1] had been fairly uniform across the subjects, and when it came to my A-level choices I felt that I wanted to retain a good spread across the disciplines, or so I said. Actually, the simpler truth was that I wanted to do what I enjoyed, and what I enjoyed was history, maths and English. That was what I said to school. Not so, I was told: you must study either Arts or Sciences, and – they added for good measure – as you are a girl you should do Science, because by the time you graduate there will be lots of jobs for female scientists. As a piece of careers advice it was probably rather limited, but it was well meant, and maths, physics and chemistry it was, to be followed by a degree in Natural Sciences. It turned out that I was not a very natural scientist, but I found my niche in the study of history and philosophy of science, a subject which I found utterly fascinating and which returned me somewhat to my love of history, while managing to combine elements of the maths and English (well, plenty of reading and writing anyway) that I also enjoyed.

Although my first teaching job picked up on the science degree I had, I quickly moved into teaching maths. I loved the puzzle of having to work out how to explain something in the best possible way so that it was simplified but not distorted, how to lay rigorous and stable foundations on which to build, how to engender confidence in those who were less certain and yet cater for the brightest mathematicians who were fast and instinctive. I loved the fact that when teaching maths everyone trooped in at the beginning of the lesson not being able to solve simultaneous equations, recognise conic sections, prove a theorem or whatever, and – provided I had done my job well – they all trooped out after an hour being able to do so. It was a great feeling.

On my return to teaching, it was in the English classroom that I found myself, and before long I was teaching the top set of the top year, preparing them for the quirky, one-of-a-kind scholarship exams that the big independent senior schools still love to set: these must surely be the last preserve in school education of examinations without syllabi, of open-ended challenges which require in equal measure eclectic knowledge, mature-beyond-years insight and that most indefinable of all qualities, flair. The English papers, taken by pupils of just twelve or thirteen years of age, last an hour or more, and generally consist of one text to read (unseen, from any century and by any author) and one question to answer (which could be absolutely anything) on it. The one question for me was: how should I teach it?

Here I returned to my scientific roots, got hold of every single scholarship exam paper from any school I could find and put them in chronological order by text extract and decided that was how I was going to teach. The texts and the fiendish questions on them provided the nautical navigation chart as my class and I embarked upon a voyage of discovery across the historical sea of literature.

For sure it was an unusual approach to apply a somewhat scientific (that is, a methodical, systematic) approach to the teaching of English literature to twelve-year-olds, but it certainly provided academic challenge and engendered high-quality output. In addition, by the end of the course they knew that Chaucer came before Shakespeare, that *Jane Eyre* was a book but Jane Austen was an author, and that it was Oscar Wilde who wrote *The Ballad of Reading Gaol* whereas it was Jeffrey Archer who wrote *A Prison Diary*. Not only could they successfully sit the exam, but to some extent or other they had begun to get to grips with their literary heritage. This was neither easy, nor easy to do well, but both ambition and quality had been ensured, the two opposite sides of the excellence coin.

A four-dimensional curriculum, with its academic heart, and essential endorsement of the arts, sports and personal development, particularly helps to ensure the educational principle of breadth being secured. As explored, each subject uniquely contributes to this. The way in which a specific subject or topic is tackled within the four-dimensional model enables a consideration of how, in

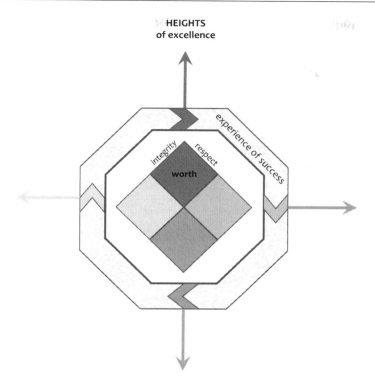

FIGURE 10.1 The principle of height and its elements

particular, the educational principle of height (with its dual components of ambition and quality) can be realised in practice (Figure 10.1).

Subject expertise

Planning the teaching of any subject with the aspiration of excellence requires a clear vision of the goal for each stage – what we might think of as the level of expertise being sought. Formulating such a vision entails knowing the subject well, appreciating its constituent elements, analysing and selecting from them and identifying the necessary progression and continuity required for success.

'Education is foundationally devoted to knowledge, its acquisition and transfer', says professor of philosophy, Dallas Willard. Knowledge has a factual component, but is more than information. According to Willard, 'For ancient philosophers knowledge was essential to the ability to navigate the world, to live and thrive in it, since the possessor of knowledge was empowered to accurately engage the world and its conundrums as they actually are in reality'.[2] Such a definition may be closer to what we might call wisdom, in that it suggests ability to respond to and use knowledge well, in addition to simply having acquired knowledge.

FIGURE 10.2 The four elements of learning within subject expertise

Four elements of learning

To reflect this rich sense of learning, and tease out its elements, it is useful to consider expertise in a subject as a rich and intertwined mix of what we might call knowledge, understanding, skills and appreciation (Figure 10.2).

To become proficient in a subject, at any level, entails grasping a unique blend of these four elements. Expertise will obviously be demonstrable in different ways in each subject. In competitive sport, expertise will be demonstrated through knowing the rules, understanding tactics, exhibiting technical skills, appreciating the importance of team work and so on – all evidenced when playing in a match. By contrast, in Latin, expertise will be evident in knowledge of vocabulary, for example, understanding grammatical rules, skilful translating and appreciation of accuracy.

Knowledge

Used in this sense, as part of the whole, 'knowledge' may be regarded as the capacity to represent things as they are. It is based on a mix of thought and experience, and includes, but is not limited to, facts and information.

Of the four elements, a specific emphasis on knowledge has been reflected in government statements on education in the UK in recent years. 'At the heart of our reforms has been a determination to place knowledge back at the core of what pupils learn in school', stated Education Secretary Nicky Morgan in 2015; she continued, 'For too long our education system prized the development of skills above core knowledge'.[3] Dr E.D. Hirch of the University of Virginia, founder of Core Knowledge, has been influential in promoting a highly specific, knowledge-rich curriculum internationally. 'We will achieve a just and prosperous society', he says, 'only when our schools ensure that everyone commands enough shared knowledge to communicate effectively with everyone else'.[4]

This emphasis on knowledge has led to a revival of the education essentialism debate – the place and nature of core knowledge in the curriculum. Views vary (and change) as to how much knowledge should be included in the core curriculum (often presented, as indicated above, as being opposed to time spent learning skills), and exactly what that knowledge should be. In some subjects, including maths and science, the nature of the knowledge deemed to be at the core, will often be that which is foundational – that is, the knowledge which is required in order that the next logical stage of understanding can be built securely.

The importance of in-depth core knowledge is also sometimes contrasted with a broad, wide-ranging, and implicitly shallow, curriculum. While some schools explicitly advocate 'depth before breadth' in the curriculum,[5] Hirsch has described breadth versus depth as a 'premature polarity', stating that 'we should teach a diversity of subjects that will lead to broad general knowledge, and we should also teach in some depth a moderate number of specific examples'.[6]

History provides a useful example here, since by its extensive nature it has to be taught selectively. However, giving children a long-term overview of history is hugely valuable in developing breadth of understanding. When they study one period in more rigorous detail, encouraging depth, they can do so intelligently against a coherent backdrop context.

Understanding

The word 'understanding' indicates ability to perceive meaning and significance from facts and information, to interpret and infer. Its etymology suggests standing under or – more accurately – surrounded by, which helps to grasp the fuller sense of being able to see through 360 degrees, to pull ideas together from a variety of sources, the resultant whole making greater sense than the sum of the parts.

In my O-level music exam, I had to write an essay on the use of the orchestra in Brahms' Variations on the St Anthony Chorale. The only thing that I can now remember was that I had memorised twenty facts about his use of the orchestra, which I wrote down, a fine example of factual knowledge at the time (although all twenty facts are now entirely forgotten). I hope very much, however, that I found some way to make sense of these pieces of information as a whole and that I had understood something of Brahms' purpose, process or his overarching goal as he wrote, and why indeed his use of the orchestra in that piece was especially significant. The twenty pieces of knowledge needed to be knit together into some kind of coherent narrative for understanding to be demonstrated, something I suspect was not achieved in my case.

What this demonstrates is that the elements of learning cannot be taken in isolation from each other. Knowledge is essential, but so is the understanding which gives it shape and context. Furthermore, it requires subject skill to find out the knowledge, build it into understanding and communicate effectively.

Skill

As the example above demonstrates, the ability to do something, such as write an essay on a piece of music, is not isolated from, nor independent of, either knowledge or understanding. The essay required my twenty pieces of knowledge, understanding as to how they fitted together and skill to communicate this in a compelling and interesting essay. Knowledge and skill are not to be perceived as being oppositional, but rather need to be developed in tandem, each reliant on the other to develop effectively. It is not possible to think of any skill in complete isolation from content, although it is true that many skills can be applied in more than one context. Just as breadth and depth are not contrary learning ideals but complementary principles, the same is true of knowledge and skills.

Across the subjects, skills range from the very academic (such as the ability to structure a music essay, dependent on pieces of accurate factual knowledge and a good understanding of how they connect and impact each other) to the highly practical (such as the ability to discern the sound of a trumpet when listening to an orchestra, dependent on knowing the names and qualities of brass instruments and having some understanding of different timbres).

Skills are often described as transferable. In practice, some skills are more transferable than others – accuracy skills such as spelling and handwriting, for example, are highly transferable across written subjects. Being able to measure accurately, first learnt in maths, will be very useful in science and engineering. Performance skills learnt in drama may be transferred to public speaking when making a science presentation. Other skills are transferable in rather more limited contexts, such as discerning the sound of the trumpet as described above, transferable to a variety of musical contexts but less applicable beyond that.

It also has to be remembered that every context is subtly different, so even highly transferable skills need to be applied with discernment: the structure of an essay on a historical episode will depend on the events under discussion and the writer's understanding of them; it may be very different from the structure needed for an essay on another period of history, and even more different from the structure of an essay exploring the plot in a work of fiction.

Transferable skills are important, but so of course is transferable knowledge. The ability of pupils to apply knowledge, and indeed understanding, gained in another context is also a highly valuable educational ability, and as we have noted already, one which enhances learning across the disciplines; it is also a skill in its own right.

Appreciation

The final element in the mix is 'appreciation'. This concerns the development of attitudes, values and respect and has much connection with the development of individual and community character traits, and Willard's 'ability to navigate the world, to live and thrive in it'.

Appreciation is also inextricably linked to the other three elements. Appreciation can extend from recognising the elegance of a universal mathematical formula (requiring knowledge), to respecting the courage of a historical figure (reflecting understanding) or valuing the importance of proofreading (entailing skill). It is not difficult to see how the poignancy and power of a poem may be appreciated through learning it off by heart for recital, a task that involves knowledge of the words, understanding of their meaning, and skill in recitation: the four elements are closely intertwined.

Equally importantly, a subject may be a key contributor in developing pupil attitudes and character traits, from compassion which grows through a study in history or geography, to perseverance which grows through an ambitious approach to learning.

SUMMARY BOX 10.1: The components of subject expertise

Subject expertise: a unique blend of
knowledge + understanding + skills + appreciation

In terms of ensuring the development of knowledge, understanding, skills and appreciation across a subject, and hence the development of expertise, choices have to be made as to what will be studied.

The four-dimensional model reminds us that excellence is a potent combination of ambition and quality. Ambition is ensured at subject level through the way in which topics are chosen for study, and what is included within them.

Ambitious choice of topics

Ambition is one side of the excellence coin, and for a subject to be taught and learnt in an excellent way, subject content needs to be selected with ambition in mind. In practice, most subjects are divided up into topics (or units of work). The choice of topics, the order in which they are studied, and the length of time spent on them, serve to achieve the development of subject expertise.

Topics are most frequently defined by their knowledge component, which directly leads to the development of understanding, and through which skills are rehearsed and appreciation fostered. To achieve excellence, topics must be carefully chosen, taking various factors into account.

Logical and sequential order

In some subjects the order of topics is critical because one builds on the next. Within maths, for example, understanding of number, measure and shape has to be the starting point, because other topics build on them, and it is self-evident that whole numbers need to be understood ahead of fractions or decimals. In due time, simple statistics, followed by ideas such as ratio and proportion, will be added to the mix, and eventually algebra, trigonometry and calculus: the order cannot be reversed.

In Latin, the past tenses will be taught after the present tense, incorporating knowledge already gained. In other subjects, the order of topics may be chosen because the understanding developed at one stage can be built on later: children may investigate primary and secondary colours in art before an exploration of line, tone and texture, for example. Skill levels will also build up systematically through what is taught, from simple push passing in hockey to practising passing under pressure, for example.

Maths follows a spiral curriculum, as do similar subjects, in which broad areas of study, such as number and measure, or within them, specific topics such as fractions and decimals, are repeatedly returned to, each time revising the learning of the previous visit and adding to it in depth and sophistication. There is probably an element of this in every subject. Map work will feature every year in geography at some point, each time building on previous learning as more complexity and detail are included. Spelling may be taught 'spirally' every week, and poetry will be included on a regular basis within an English curriculum, as well as play scripts and prose.

The principle of excellence means that these topics, and the material included within them, will be chosen so as to build most convincingly and ambitiously on what pupils already know. The aim is for children to reach as high as they can in their learning by building successfully on what has already been learnt, and in turn laying excellent foundations for the next layer to come.

Cross-curricular links and collaboration

Great benefit can be had from making cross-curricular links, and when the order of topics is less critical this may be a factor. An introduction to African drumming in music might be included in a term during which children study African art, or the geography of Africa.

Cross-curricular collaboration across a range of subjects may enable bigger projects to take place. Pooling time from art, music and drama may enable a musical theatre production to be staged, which also features children's art work in scenery, props or costume. A study of robotics in computing could link with an engineering problem to be solved, while Greek theatre might be explored in drama to link in with a study of Ancient Greece in history.

The skills learnt through one topic in English, such as writing a newspaper report, may be taught at a particular time in the year so that they can be used in a humanities topic later that term. Careful planning across and between departments can enrich children's learning, avoid duplication of material and hence ensure greater heights of excellence.

Balance and variety

With breadth a central feature of four-dimensional education, where there is room for further choice, balance will be a factor. Within the sciences there will be a balance each year between topics in biology, chemistry and physics. Similarly a range of history, geography and religious studies topics will be covered in the humanities. Within any one of these subjects, there will be variety when possible – from weather systems and ecosystems to plate tectonics and tourism, there is so much to be chosen from that there should never be an unnecessarily narrow focus or any tedious repetition.

In English, literature will be chosen for varied study which makes accessible our children's heritage, from across centuries and continents, fiction and non-fiction, including speeches, biography, travel writing, poetry and plays. Detective fiction with its idealised solutions, dystopian novels which depict the world as we would prefer it not to be, and science-fiction which create an as-yet unrealised world, all have their place.

Topics may be chosen on the grounds that they provide opportunities to develop subject-specific understanding and skills. Historical contextualising may be facilitated through a chronological approach in history, starting with pre-history and early civilisations, while an understanding of continuity may be fostered through the immediacy of investigating recent local and family history, so both may be included at different times.

Such principles ensure heights of excellence without building a distorted or lop-sided edifice of learning.

Use of textbooks and published schemes of work

A pre-written course of study or textbook can be a very helpful means of navigating the development of subject knowledge, through pre-selected and ordered topics, and provision of well-edited teaching resources. However, it always has to be assumed that our pupils may be capable of more than we or others might expect; ambitious choices should bear this in mind. We should ask ourselves whether our children could be working from a pre-published spelling list, mental maths book or languages text intended for older pupils, as almost always the answer for at least some pupils will be that they can, at least in part.

Whether or not such schemes or textbooks are used, however, home-grown or individually sourced supplementary material is likely to be needed both for richer variety and to meet the specific needs and interests of individual learners and so take them higher in their learning.

Topics can of course become more or less fashionable. When I started teaching maths, sets, matrices and number bases were all included in the syllabus. Dropped some years ago, the latter of these has made a comeback in computing lessons, children now having to be able to work in binary and hex again. Enrichment days or similar may provide valuable opportunities for the inclusion of material currently off the mainstream syllabus, but which nevertheless promotes excellence. Formal proofs in geometry (my favourite part of maths at school), for example, are currently out of general circulation, yet teaching children the formal method for proving that there are 180 degrees in a triangle encourages rigour and an appreciation of the significance of going back to first principles.

Knowing a subject and knowing about a subject

One question sometimes pondered is the extent to which pupils are learning 'to know about' or 'to be'. Are they learning *about* history, for example, or are they learning how *to be* historians? A similar question can be asked of geography, or science teaching.

Perhaps two factors can be borne in mind. First, all children live in a real world which is historical, geographical and scientific in character. Having knowledge and understanding of that world helps all of us to live more effectively in it. Second, although not all children will go on to become professional historians, geographers or scientists, understanding the nature of these disciplines enables a greater appreciation of the questions they address and the type of answers they can provide.

This suggests that including both approaches is beneficial in the pursuit of excellence.

Personalised choices

Content choices can sometimes be made in response to particular opportunities, interests or challenges. The Olympic Games provide such an opportunity every four years, but some teachers, like myself, will be lucky enough to have rarer events to inspire their students. I recall the excitement generated around the appearance of Halley's Comet, regular as clockwork, just three years into my teaching career: it will next be seen in 2062, a long time to wait.

Choices as to what is included in a subject can sometimes be made on an individual basis. The four-dimensional model values the uniqueness of the individual child, and recognising this, decisions as to what is recommended for personal reading, for example, will inevitably depend on the individual children. I might recommend that one of my Year 8s reads Dodie Smith's *I Capture the Castle*, but that another reads Stevenson's *Strange Case of Dr Jekyll and Mr Hyde*. The provision of a personalised reading list can be a turning point for even the most reluctant of readers, ambitious for the individual through making sensitive and accessible suggestions.

Across all academic subjects, children need to be able to access information from written texts in order to learn. Finding information from text is easier for children who have background knowledge in the subject about which they are reading: the child with an underlying interest, whether in football or animals, finds it easier to retrieve information from a text on that subject than the child who does not have this interest.[7] This means that the more children know, the more they can read; of course the more they can read, the more they will know. In other words, reading feeds on itself and the more it is fostered, the more it will flourish. One implication of this is that those who read less at home need to be supported with reading more in school, but teachers can also support their pupils by knowing them well enough to capitalise on their interests and respond to their situations.

The principle of excellence within the four-dimensional model implies ambitious choices of input. However, the model also recognises that such choices will inevitably be different in different contexts and for different individuals.

SUMMARY BOX 10.2: The components contributing to ambitious choice of topics

Ambitious topics:
logical and sequential order + cross-curricular links
+ balance and variety + published and unpublished work
+ knowledge of and about a subject + personalised choices

Ambitious approach to topics

For each topic, once chosen, clarity is needed as to what the aims are in terms of knowledge and understanding to be acquired, and skills and appreciation to be developed. These aims will determine how much time is spent on a topic: not everything requires half a term's worth of lessons. In addition, there needs to be a clear sense of the approach taken to meet these goals, since the way in which they are tackled also contributes to excellence.

Setting and meeting aims

Having established the unit of work to be studied, aims must be set to ensure maximum knowledge and understanding, and the best possible development of skills and appreciation. Suppose, for example, that *The Hound of the Baskervilles* is the ambitious text chosen for a unit of work with eleven-year-olds. Aims will be many, but might include: knowledge of classic detective fiction; under-standing layers of meaning; being able to write a short essay; and appreciating how an author can impact the reader.

At the end of Chapter 6, children will read Dr Watson's sinister description of the late evening scene viewed from his window: 'Beyond, two copses of trees moaned and swung in a rising wind. A half moon broke through the rifts of racing clouds. In its cold light I saw beyond the trees a broken fringe of rocks, and the long, low curve of the melancholy moor'. Understanding layers of meaning necessitates being able to read between the lines, call on ideas and information located across different parts of a text, recognise allusion by drawing on latent knowledge, and pull all this together to make deductions – rather like Sherlock Holmes himself. The essay might include demonstrating understanding of the power and effect of simile and metaphor, irony and caricature, understatement and hyperbole. Through interpretation, extrapolation or analysis, children will learn to perceive what is implicit rather than explicit, and realise how carefully the author has crafted his tale to impact his reader. These are ambitious aims which build on and develop knowledge, understanding, skill and appreciation.

TABLE 10.1 Stages in the development of aims within reading

AGE IN YEARS	AIMS	
	READING	WRITTEN RESPONSES
7	Read accurately Understand simple texts Express views about events and ideas	Write full-sentence answers to questions on text
	Read accurately and fluently Use strategies to understand meaning Understand main points Express preferences	Write full-sentence answers to questions on text
	Read increasingly expressively Understand events and characters Understand ideas Use inference and deduction	Various lengths of written responses including full-sentence answers
	Understand fiction and non-fiction Locate and use information Identify ideas and themes	Various lengths of written responses including short paragraphs
	Identify layers of meaning Comment on significance and effect Make personal responses to texts Develop ability to summarise	Various lengths of responses, including short essays
13	Make personal and critical responses to poems, plays and novels showing awareness of themes, structure and language, selecting, comparing and synthesising information	Various lengths of written responses; inclusion of embedded quotations

This is a cumulative process which takes place over many years, so opportunities to respond to such literature need to be appropriate to the age and stage of the learners. *Sherlock Holmes* in Year 7 will be just one step in that process. Table 10.1 shows the progression in aims for reading and written responses that might be expected to develop, between the ages of seven and thirteen.

Encouraging personal response

Ambitious input in terms of topics and aims will not achieve excellence without personal engagement from the learners.

> A word is dead
> When it is said,
> Some say.
> I say it just
> Begins to live
> That day.[8]

Emily Dickinson's words challenge us to consider the importance of personal response from the listener or reader, in order for 'dead' words to come alive. To learn *well* is to dig deeper, to respond intelligently – both intellectually and emotionally – and as a result to grow in maturity. Personal response must also therefore be engendered, through the way in which a topic – and whole subject – is approached.

Across the curriculum, teachers must open their pupils' eyes to the wonder of their subject, to the magic of music, the elegance of maths, the grandeur of science, the power of drama, and the drama of sport, to elicit a personal response. In English classes, teachers foster a realisation that language is an extraordinarily potent tool: words have power. Through language, nebulous dreams, thoughts and ideas can begin to take recognisable, identifiable and repeatable shape and form. And through the gift of language, they can make the journey from the mind of one to the mind of another.

Words can describe in glorious graphic detail the world that is, the world that is not, the world that could be or even the world that could not be. Language creates whole new worlds peopled with characters who variously make merry, make mistakes or make mayhem; characters who do good, who do harm, who do nothing; characters who live, who love, who die.

And while a million such words are spoken and lost every day, a million more may be written and kept. Through this process a great reef of imagination, wisdom and wit accumulates organically, growing gradually into our literary heritage. This literary heritage is a virtual library, containing tomes of poetry, prose and play scripts, works of beauty and profundity with the power to make us weep, laugh and ponder.

Our literary heritage is a gift bequeathed to us by our ancestors, sufficiently cherished by them to be handed on, by and large intact and within reach. The task of each generation in this respect is to follow suit, if we are not to let our descendants, or indeed our ancestors, down. This provides a ready illustration of the role of the teacher whatever the subject.

As we strive towards heights of excellence, the purpose of teaching is to bring together two distinct entities – the learner and the object of learning – and introduce the one to the other, in such a way as to maximise engagement, benefit and enjoyment. In this case the two entities in question are the writings of previous (and contemporary) generations, and one or more members of this new generation. For such an introduction to be effective, young people need to be brought to the literature and the literature needs to be brought to them. The teacher acts as a mediator, carefully choosing texts that stimulate the imagination, feed the intellect and wherever possible bring joy to learning.

This principle can be explained with an analogy. If my friend wants to get to know Scotland, I can describe to her in great and glorious detail my many holidays there. Alternatively, I can take her to Scotland and show her round what I think are some of the most iconic and breath-taking locations. One way she knows about Scotland; the other way she experiences and starts to know Scotland for herself. As teachers, our task is that our pupils should *know* their subjects rather than simply *know about* them. We facilitate an introduction which encourages personal response by enthusing, expressing our own fascination and ensuring suitable challenge. It is partly this sharing of genuine personal enthusiasm which contributes to what is often described as inspirational teaching.

Ambitious material should have been introduced to children that is just about within their reach at full stretch. Once the introduction is facilitated, pupils then need to be given room to respond personally. Intellectual response requires taking some initiative in (and responsibility for) their learning, stepping up to the challenge because they have been enthused to do so. This needs just the right amount of intellectual challenge – too easy and no initiative is required, too hard and initiative cannot close the gap.

Developing good character

'Fairy tales do not tell children the dragons exist', said G.K. Chesterton. 'Children already know that dragons exist. Fairy tales tell children the dragons can be killed'.[9] Every part of our teaching influences the holistic development of the child, and the way in which topics are approached influences attitudes and character. This is true in all subjects. In history we teach about the abolition of slavery; in maths we teach about taxation; in sport we teach about winning and losing; in engineering we teach about sustainability – attitudes are formed.

The approach to teaching a topic needs to engage and stretch, but it also needs to develop a sense of responsibility, respect and integrity. Year 8, reading Steinbeck's *The Pearl*, grapple with ideas of ambition, materialism, racism and corruption. As they question, debate and reason together, referencing fictional episodes to support their assertions, critical thinking and the ability to make ethical judgements are developed.

Reading Coleridge's *The Rime of the Ancient Mariner* helps children see that great and small actions act like chemical reagents in the laboratory of literature, and result in profound consequences and soaring emotions; these are experienced vicariously, safely from a distance, but nonetheless vividly. As a result, reading also fosters empathy, and by extension, respect. Fleur Adcock's *Immigrant*, Denise Levertov's *Settling* or Seamus Heaney's *Digging* enable pupils to think about heritage, rootedness and alienation, and develop empathy for those on the move in life. Henry King's *Sic Vita* or Robert Frost's *Out, Out–* provide the opportunity to reflect on the preciousness and fragility of life itself.

These examples taken from literary choices make the point clearly, but the way in which every topic is approached, from learning about deforestation in geography to learning about the sections of an orchestra in music, in the four-dimensional subject, can be taught in such a way as to encourage the development of character, central to the model.

SUMMARY BOX 10.3: The components of an ambitious approach to topics

Ambitious approaches:
setting and meeting aims + encouraging
personal response + developing character

The broad sweep of development occurs over a long time-scale. Ambitious choice of topics, carefully delivered to ensure maximum personal response and benefit, leads to a gradual growth in expertise. Having looked at how a topic can be taught through an ambitious approach, it is now possible to consider how expertise develops. Considering reading as the chief example, we can see the important stages in this process.

Growth in expertise

We learn to read so that we can read to learn. But reading is also part of the whole ongoing education which continually acts as a gateway to broader intellectual, emotional and ethical maturity, as across all the subjects, children learn to understand themselves, their neighbours and their world more fully. Reading is central to the whole learning enterprise.

Reading acts in the same way as the root system of a tree, providing firm anchoring and provision for healthy educational growth, or as the foundations of a house, enabling the structure of learning to stand. Good reading enables strong learning across the curriculum, and builds reliable foundations for future learning. The earlier children master reading, and progress through stages of increasingly challenging content, the better it therefore is for their development as learners in every respect.

While school usually provides the starting point for a child to learn to read, the value of the home–school partnership in developing and honing the ability to read must be mentioned. Parents can provide far greater opportunity for one-to-one support in helping their children to read than can possibly be made available in a school (although any such gaps at home will need to be filled as far as is practical at school). Parents may be surprised at the recommendation that they continue to read with their children for some time after they seem to have mastered the art. But this is necessary because reading is far more than knowledge of how to decode words into sounds, and reading together triggers conversation which promotes greater understanding of what is being read. Of course, the sharing of books into the teenage years can also be hugely enjoyable and is always to be encouraged. I remember how pleased I felt when one pupil asked to take home after each lesson the novel being read in class, as his father was keen to read it each evening, and another mentioned that she had just bought a copy of the same book for her mother's birthday.

Learning to read is not equally easy for all children, however; an unnatural process, reading is to speaking as performing a gymnastics routine is to walking. While speaking is acquired naturally through listening, without having to be taught, reading is always a result of having been specifically educated. Teachers may sometimes determine that additional help or specific intervention is required to assist in the process of learning to read, and many diagnostic tools are now available to schools to help ascertain whether this is the case.

With whatever support and intervention is required, the first step towards the ultimate goal of independence and sophistication is accuracy. Parents instinctively repeat a word that their child is learning to say, correcting and reinforcing a right understanding, thus building up not only an accurate, but a confident, use of the word. As adults, we know that we have to have heard (or read) a new word being used accurately in context before we can confidently reuse it ourselves in speech (or writing).

As a general rule, when citing a piece of knowledge, drawing on some understanding gained or deploying a skill, confidence without accuracy is misplaced, a recipe for disaster; but accuracy alone without confidence can unnecessarily limit further development and opportunity. Both must therefore be actively and carefully fostered. Once accuracy and confidence are established, then fluency (regular, reliable use) can follow.

In reading, once fluency is established, the next goal is enthusiasm. Every child should be encouraged to have a book 'on the go'. Reward schemes to support this may be helpful, encouraging pupils to read widely as they move up through the school, along with providing lists of recommended books, peer book reviews and schemes to encourage children to try new genres. English teachers may start every lesson with five minutes' quiet reading, or time may be set aside regularly for them to read aloud to their classes. The school may organise an 'extreme reading' competition whereby pupils submit photographs of themselves reading during the holidays in unlikely or exotic locations. Evenings about reading may be held for parents to attend. There are many ways to promote reading: the critical thing is for it to be promoted one way or another, so that reading takes root.

Such enthusiasm is to be promoted in the development of expertise across all subjects, from art to computing to swimming. As teachers, we need to recognise that as enthusiasm develops, so does depth of engagement, and we should do all we can to foster it.

As children grasp the power and impact of language, and enthusiasm builds, reading expressively is perhaps the start of recognising literature as an art form in which language can be crafted for maximum impact. This is the moment when the learner clearly starts to engage personally with their learning as a unique individual. Exactly the same pattern is evident in the development of writing: once accuracy and confidence are established, fluency and enthusiasm follow; expressiveness can then give voice to personality. This sense of ownership and the expression of individual flair can be seen across other subjects too, from drawing in art to stylish scoring in soccer. Enthusiasm for any activity supports the hours needed to establish individual excellence both in terms of ambitious goals and high-quality, expressive output.

With choices growing through individual expression, children start to appreciate quality: the 'best' words are those which maximise impact, and communicate as effectively and clearly as possible. To make such judgements develops the critical faculty, fostering independence in making good choices, and results in sophistication.

The progression and accumulation of expertise in listening, speaking, reading and writing in English is indicated in Table 10.2. Each follows the same pattern

TABLE 10.2 Development of areas of expertise in English, showing a pattern common across all subjects

AGE IN YEARS	LISTENING AND SPEAKING	READING	WRITING
5 ↓ 13	accuracy confidence fluency enthusiasm expression appreciation independence sophistication	accuracy confidence fluency enthusiasm expression appreciation independence sophistication	accuracy confidence fluency enthusiasm expression appreciation independence sophistication

of development, but at any given time they will have reached differing levels of maturity. Self-evidently, knowledge, understanding, skills and appreciation gained in one area of expertise impact all the others, true to a differing extent across all subjects.

Development of an area of expertise within any subject follows a similar pattern. The goal of becoming increasingly accurate, confident, fluent, enthusiastic, expressive, appreciative, independent and sophisticated applies to playing the flute, problem-solving in maths or serving in tennis. The commonality is in purposefully paced and staged progression through to maximum independence and sophistication in each area.

In such a way subject expertise develops, feeding on ambitious content and enabling high-quality output as an end result. For alongside excellence being achieved through topics being chosen and delivered with ambition in mind, and expertise being developed through the growth of knowledge, understanding, skill and appreciation, there is a final contributor to excellence: quality of output.

Excellence through high-quality output

In all subjects, high-quality learning is evidenced by high-quality outcomes which provide a chance to gauge and celebrate progress. This might be a beautifully sculptured piece of art, an exquisitely performed trampolining routine, a meticulously mapped piece of geography fieldwork or the honing of authentic accent in a Spanish class. It might be a board game showing understanding of historical events, a poster showing the results of a science experiment or a computer programme in which characters jump from one level to the next. Within maths, high-quality output is demonstrated by the application of high-level knowledge through sophisticated reasoning to solve the most challenging of problems or explore the most demanding of investigations. Making use of rigorous and imaginative resources, such as those provided by Cambridge's NRICH Project,[10] enables excellence, as defined in this way, to be achievable and demonstrable at every age and stage of children's mathematical development.

In many cases, in the academic subjects, the final outcome will be in the written form, and this is certainly often true in English. Exploring the components of writing provides an example of the multifaceted nature of excellent output. Expertise in writing is characterised by ambitious output executed to the highest of developmentally appropriate standards. It will exhibit clarity and economy of expression and independent, sophisticated style. Once again the two-fold character of excellence is in evidence: ambition and quality.

Widely applicable across a range of subjects, five elements of excellent written output will be considered in turn: precision, content, organisation, style and accuracy.

Precision: meeting task requirements

The first and most obvious element of output is that it has to meet any specific requirements given, and the best output will meet those requirements precisely in order to fulfil the purpose of the task. Suppose that the task is to compare and contrast two pieces of writing on London, one a section of prose by Dickens and the other a sonnet by Wordsworth. The essay needs to reference both texts, explaining and describing what they have in common, how they are different and the impact this has on the reader.

Meeting the precise requirements of the task, however obvious that may seem, is the first element of a good outcome by which learning is evidenced. Whether it is writing up an experiment, maths investigation or piece of geography field-work, if the task is not clearly understood, clarification needs to be sought because without understanding the task and all its requirements, it cannot be done well.

Content: including high-quality ideas

The second element of excellent outcome is the quality of ideas thought about and included. The quality of ideas of course also needs to be judged on the basis of the task set. In a piece of creative writing, high-quality ideas will make the piece engaging for the reader. Experiences gained are key contributors to such ideas, combined with creativity and imagination. Very young children often enjoy writing their news accounts of the family weekend, but as children progress and mature, high-quality writing is increasingly borne of their literary experience. In reading great books, children meet a whole variety of experiences, settings, characters and events far beyond their own personal experiences. This can lift pupils' own creative writing to an entirely new level, from the heart-rending diary of a chimney sweep after reading Blake's *Songs of Innocence and Experience*, to witty character studies based on Wilde's *The Importance of Being Earnest*. Reading good literature feeds the imagination and fosters a creative ability to use language with clarity, precision and impact. Writing widely is important as well as reading widely: character studies, journal entries, diary extracts, descriptions of settings (real or imagined), dialogues between characters, interviews with protagonists, fact files, parody and imitative writing all have their place in encouraging children to produce imaginative and creative output freely, with ambition and drive.

Across the other subjects quality of ideas is equally important. Whether comparing different faiths in religious studies, completing a log-book entry in engineering or composing a letter to a Spanish pen-friend, the inclusion of high-quality thinking is essential to excellence.

Structure: organising material

However precisely a question has been addressed, and however brilliant the quality of ideas, the material included has to be purposefully ordered for good

TABLE 10.3 Progression in the development of structure in writing

AGE IN YEARS	STRUCTURE EVIDENT IN WRITING
7 ↓ 13	Some structure included, e.g. beginning, middle and end Written in paragraphs Starting to develop structure within and between paragraphs Well-structured, developed paragraphs which flow from one to the next Essays include introduction and conclusion; some sophistication such as flashbacks in narratives Structure effectively adapted for variety of purpose; carefully controlled pace

communication of ideas to take place. Structure controls pace and aids the flow of ideas, through links within and between paragraphs or sections of text. Organisation of material into a purposeful structure across the whole piece is a high-level skill, especially if combined with large elements of free choice and personal creativity in writing.

The way in which children are taught and expected to structure their writing must therefore progress as they mature, so that they eventually reach a sophisticated level of structure which is purposeful, controlled and adapted for the specific purpose of the piece. Table 10.3 shows the structure of writing that we might expect to see develop in extended writing in English.

Style: expressing ideas effectively

A fourth important contributing factor to high-quality writing is style. This certainly starts to become of greater artistic interest as children are encouraged to progress in their choice of words, shape of sentences and variety of diction. Do their word choices communicate atmosphere and emotion; are imagery, allusion and vocabulary chosen to paint the most vivid picture? The humble newspaper report provides a useful example: very young children can be taught to write a newspaper report about an event, imagined or real; as they mature they may move from reporting key facts under a headline, to including interviews with witnesses, or providing speculation as to what might happen next; with greater age and maturity still, they may be challenged to write a satirical newspaper article which comments on a serious point through the use of irony, caricature, hyperbole and humour.

Equally important is gaining sufficient maturity and judgement as to be able to match the appropriate style of writing to its content and intended purpose: it is self-evident that science experiments, historical accounts and fantasy stories require different styles of writing to be effective pieces of communication. Writing is a transferable skill, but like all such skills, it needs to be transferred judiciously and thoughtfully, demonstrating knowledge and understanding in doing so. In addition, language in both written and spoken forms gradually evolves: the split infinitive is no longer the horror it once was, and young writers need to learn to be sensitive to the living nature of language: literally, apparently, may be now be used for emphasis, and does not necessarily *literally* mean 'literally'.[11]

Accuracy: freedom from technical errors

The final element of high-quality output is accuracy. Although in the digital age it might be argued that the ability to write is now redundant, in practice this is not yet the case, and nor is it clear that it ever will be. Writing remains the simplest visual form of verbal communication in many contexts, requiring, as it does, nothing other than pencil and paper. It is also relatively secure, economic and fast. Although many adult occupations currently require typing skills rather than handwritten communication, for most children the handwritten form remains highly accessible and effective as a first introduction to learning the rules of writing and therefore the essential starting point in written communication. Typing follows as and when it is a help or a necessity. Well beyond the confines of the literacy lesson or English classroom, across the academic subjects, writing is a large component of output, and its quality matters. The ability to put pencil to paper and communicate effectively in doing so remains essential.

There are four elements to accurate written work: handwriting, spelling, punctuation and grammar. Like all areas of expertise, handwriting is acquired in a progressive manner, although of course the rate of development varies. Table 10.4 shows the progression in the development of handwriting which most children follow.

This table references children writing with fountain pens from some point around the age of 8. Personal experience suggests that teaching children to write with a fountain pen improves the quality of their written work in almost all cases. Mastery of a fountain pen helps to ensure a neater and more consistent script because the pen has to be held at a specific angle. The nature of the pen requires

TABLE 10.4 Progression in the development of handwriting skills

AGE IN YEARS	DEVELOPMENT OF HANDWRITING SKILLS
7	Form letters clearly and neatly, write words evenly with letters joined
↓	Write with a joined even script using fountain pen
	Have fluent, even, upright joined writing
	Write neatly with increasing speed
13	Have stylish handwriting at speed

skill and attention for its use and results in a more controlled style. A few children, particularly those who are left-handed, may get on better with some other form of pen, but since we introduced the use of blue-inked fountain pens in exercise books across all subjects, the quality of presentation of children's work has improved enormously.

The acquisition of a joined, fluent script which is clear to read, and achieved with an increasing sense of effortlessness, is a considerable aid to spelling. To write a word accurately is, of course, to spell it correctly. For this to become an automatic part of muscle memory is a great aid. Most people do not need to think how to spell their name: they spell it automatically, and this is the goal for the writing of all common words.

As is frequently noted, some children find this element of their learning more demanding than others, and for a few it presents a really serious challenge. Much can be done to support children in their learning of spelling, and indeed all children need to be taught to spell, not least, as the rules (and exceptions) of English spelling are complex.

In some cases, if handwriting or learning of spelling are proving to be a significant barrier rather than an aid to learning, a learning support department may conclude that the use of a laptop for writing or even voice-activated software may be recommended. A school needs to have clear policies in place for such eventualities (bearing in mind that typing, like handwriting, needs be taught) so that every child is supported in the best possible way in their learning.

For most children, progression in spelling through the pre-examination years follows an orderly pathway which ensures maximum but secure progress, seeking to establish both ambition and aiding high-quality expression. Children move through the stages at different rates, but Table 10.5 indicates the general pattern of learning to spell. Younger years may learn with the help of weekly spelling lessons, homework and tests, with this reducing as the children get older, according to need. As well as a progression in the pattern of teaching, there is also progression in the pattern of marking of spelling errors in extended writing. The goal is consistent accuracy and a continuing expansion of vocabulary. With additional emphasis being laid on both spelling and grammar currently in the UK, many new resources are available to support teachers in teaching spelling. The use of standardised spelling tests may be used to help determine whether more specific and advanced help is needed.

Such skills are useful only insofar as they are employed in children's writing. Children's writing style needs to mature, and their vocabulary grow, as their word-level work develops. Pupils needs to be taught progressively and gradually to include more powerful verbs for impact, adverbial phrases for detail, expanded use of imagery and the inclusion of idiom, metaphor or caricature for effect, as all the while their vocabulary expands. The inclusion of precise, ambitious vocabulary is always to be applauded, as are attempts at spelling such words correctly. Accuracy must be fostered by teachers so that confident, fluent use can follow.

TABLE 10.5 Progression in the teaching and marking of spelling

AGE IN YEARS	SPELLING SKILLS BEING TAUGHT	ACTIVITIES	MARKING: the following should be corrected if spelled incorrectly; children should follow up errors, as indicated by the teacher
7	Regular words using patterns; apply spelling rules such as adding suffixes; learn high-frequency irregular words	Weekly spelling lesson, homework and test	Common words; simple phonetic words; short regular words; the most common high-frequency irregular words
	Learn further high-frequency irregular words; continued application of spelling rules	Weekly spelling lesson, homework and test	Common and short regular words; high-frequency irregular words; words which follow taught rules
	Further application of rules and conventions; use of root words; -ible/-able endings, ent/ant endings; common homophones	Weekly spelling lesson, homework and test	Common words, short regular words, high frequency irregular words; words which follow patterns
	Attempting unusual spellings using known rules; learning exceptions to spelling rules; dictionary work	Weekly spelling lesson and fortnightly class test	All of the above and specific technical vocabulary; others at teacher's discretion
	Emphasis on expansion of vocabulary; thesaurus	Weekly spelling lesson if needed and tests half-termly (or as needed)	All spelling errors (or teacher discretion)
13	Writing should display consistently accurate spelling; a continuation of vocabulary expansion	Spelling as needed, and test termly (or as needed)	All spelling errors (or teacher discretion)

Punctuation and grammar are largely concerned with organising ideas into coherent sentences which make the clearest sense. Typically, informal speech does not follow the rules of written punctuation; that is, even the most articulate of speakers tends to employ a variety of sentence fragments, word strings and whole sentences when speaking in order to communicate effectively. Formal writing is very different, following strict protocols and rules. Punctuation is essential for clear, unambiguous written communication, which unlike the spoken form has to make do without intonation; like the other accuracy skills, punctuation needs to be taught in order that technically accurate, high-quality written work can be produced.

As far as possible, children should be taught to get their work right from the outset; that is, as soon as they start school, whenever they write their name, they use a capital letter, as they do as soon as they start being expected to write a date or a title. Learning to write in correctly punctuated sentences is harder, especially since such writing does not replicate speech. This skill therefore needs to be taught systematically and progressively, as do rules for the use of more complex punctuation such as commas, apostrophes and colons.

Every school needs to establish what is being taught when, in order for such a systematic coordinated approach to be adopted, and with the increasing emphasis in English schools on grammar and punctuation much material is available commercially to assist in this. Table 10.6 shows how punctuation and style might be expected to progress.

With the increasing emphasis being placed on accuracy skills generally, the formal teaching of grammar is also enjoying something of a resurgence in English schools, having missed out at least two generations in many schools.

The thinking behind teaching grammar is that 'explicit knowledge of grammar . . . gives us more conscious control and choice in our language'.[12] Knowing what a modal verb is (such as *must*, *should*, *might*), for example, encourages children to think about its use in their speech, and they will therefore employ it more readily in their writing, thus 'aiming for a smooth transition to sophisticated writing'.[13]

Grammar involves teaching children a technical understanding of how the English language works. For the national tests in England at age eleven, children need to have grasped the meaning of technical grammatical terms including those for parts of speech, types of clauses and categories of sentences. The rationale is that having such understanding will enhance children's ability to write with precision, accuracy and sophistication, all features of high-quality written output.

The component elements of high-quality output

An English task may be to write a fifty-word mini-saga or a five-chapter novella, a poetic original or a humorous parody. In every case, as well as fulfilling these task requirements, for excellence to be achieved the ideas included have

TABLE 10.6 Progression in punctuation goals and elements of style

AGE IN YEARS	PUNCTUATION GOALS AND ELEMENTS OF STYLE
7	Write in clear sentences using capitals, full stops and question marks correctly Join sentences with and/but/because Use commas in a list Use the apostrophe for contraction
	Start and join sentences in varied ways, correctly punctuated Use various conjunctions in compound sentences Start on punctuation of speech: new line for speakers; use speech marks Use the apostrophe for possession
	Use simple, compound and complex sentences with conjunctions Add phrases to enhance meaning Punctuate speech fully Use exclamation mark
	All basic punctuation fully secure Manipulate sentence structures for effect Include subordinate clauses and use commas as grammatical markers
	Use complex sentences securely; use semi-colon and colon appropriately Use sophisticated techniques (e.g. varied use of person and tense) Have secure use of complex sentences Use semi-colon and colon confidently
	Use rhetorical or poetic style Make secure use of embedded quotes Adopt different types of diction for effect
	Writing should have a good, balanced flowing style with the following characteristics: – purpose: content well suited to the task – variety: varied sentence length and shape, e.g. inclusion of direct and indirect speech, verb before subject and so on – style: use of strong verbs and nouns, avoiding unnecessary adverbs and adjectives – clarity: tautology and repetition avoided – structure: ideas well organised and effective paragraphing – precision: vagueness avoided and ideas expressed precisely
13	Writing should be clear and precise and demonstrate consistent accuracy of grammar, punctuation and spelling

to be engaging, the expression stylish, the pace and structure manipulated for maximum effect, and the whole piece written flawlessly.

Only if all five of these elements are in place is excellence achieved: that stellar alignment of high ambition and flawless standard. This is what it means to achieve excellence: to reach up as high as possible, to produce an ambitious, engaging, entertaining, original, surprising piece of writing while also ensuring that technical quality is maintained. Such excellence is achieved through setting ambitious goals, reached by purposeful, progressive input.

The same is true across any academic discipline: in maths the question must be answered using relevant concepts and knowledge, and the more complex it becomes, the greater the importance of style, or elegance, and the structure of the mathematical argument; accuracy is always essential. In writing up a science experiment, a humanities essay or a description in French, the same elements matter: that the question be answered precisely, drawing on appropriate ideas and material, in a style appropriate to the subject, in an organised and orderly manner, as accurately as possible.

SUMMARY BOX 10.4: The components of excellent output

Excellent output:
precision + content + style + structure + accuracy

Doing all this achieves heights of excellence: a well-written essay, with the above characteristics, comparing and contrasting two seventeenth-century poems, demonstrates ambitious output of the highest quality; and it is achievable by a twelve-year-old. It is possible only with adequate breadth of input: the literary material will be chosen with a view to extending understanding and appreciation. The manner and means of learning require, but also help to develop, deep roots of intellectual engagement – in this case grasping the analytical techniques needed for appreciating literature to the full. A lifelong ability to work with language and develop its use is born: the knowledge, understanding, skills and appreciation gained are all transferable and widely applicable. In other words, all four educational principles of the four-dimensional model are ensured through treating a subject in this way.

Across the subjects, excellence is demonstrated through high-quality, ambitious output, whether in the form of an essay, a football match or painting. The output is achieved through the medium of highly ambitious topics and approaches to them which develop knowledge, understanding skills and appreciation. The component elements of subject excellence are shown below (Figure 10. 3).

FIGURE 10.3 The components of subject excellence

Treating a subject in this way results in the four practical outcomes we expect to see from a good education: experience of success, variety of achievement, good habits of study and a love of learning. How all this is achieved in the practicalities of an actual lesson is where we look next.

Notes

1 O-levels, 16+ subject-based qualifications, were introduced to the UK in 1951 and replaced by GCSEs in 1988.

2 *The Divine Conspiracy Continued*, chapter 9: Knowledge and Education (pub. Williams Collins books).

3 www.gov.uk/government/speeches/nicky-morgan-why-knowledge-matters, accessed 28 July 2017.

4 www.coreknowledge.org/ed-hirsch-jr, accessed 28 July 2017.

5 See, for example, www.goresbrookschool.org.uk/About-Goresbrook-School/Curriculum and http://arkbentworth.org/curriculum-aims, accessed 28 July 2017.

6 *Breadth versus Depth: A premature polarity*, From *Common Knowledge*, Volume 14, Number 4, 2001, E.D. Hirsch, Jr: www.coreknowledge.org/mimik/mimik_uploads/documents/22/BreadthVSDepth.pdf, accessed 28 July 2017.

7 This topic is covered at some length in *Seven Myths about Education*, Daisy Christodoulou (pub. Routledge, 2013), in which the importance of latent knowledge in the understanding of text is described.

8 *The Complete Poems of Emily Dickinson*, published Boston: Little, Brown, 1924.

9 *Tremendous Trifles* (1909), XVII: 'The Red Angel', paraphrased.

10 https://nrich.maths.org/, accessed 28 July 2017.

11 A change in use recognised by the OED in its 2011 edition.

12 www.gov.uk/government/uploads/system/uploads/attachment_data/file/335190/English_Appendix_2_-_Vocabulary_grammar_and_punctuation.pdf, accessed 28 July 2017.

13 *Ibid.*

11

The four-dimensional lesson

Encouraging depth of engagement

Heights of excellence are sought at the level of subject planning – through identifying subject expertise to be developed, providing challenge through ambitious content and through ensuring output of the highest quality. These ideals, usually planned behind the scenes, become a reality in classroom lessons where the four-dimensional model has applications on a daily basis. All four principles are in evidence at this micro level, but it is particularly in lessons that depth of engagement is fostered.

Medieval art and the Dead Sea honey pot

One of the most memorable lessons I have ever witnessed was when I took a group of ten-year-olds to our local museum of fine art. The curator led the children through an exploration of medieval religious art. They sat spellbound at her feet round an early sixteenth-century painting of the Annunciation attributed to Bernart van Orley. Part way through the lesson she explained the symbolism of the lily in medieval art. Apart from that I do not recall her telling the children anything, and yet they came away having learnt an enormous amount: they were full of knowledge about medieval religious art, had gained an understanding of how and what it communicated, had developed their ability to look at works of art and interpret a painter's meaning, and gained an appreciation of the skill involved in producing such wonderful works and why it is that they are so highly treasured today. How was this depth of engagement achieved? The answer lies in the fact that the entire session consisted of asking the right questions, skilfully encouraging the children to look, to think for themselves, to work things out and to grapple, grasp and conclude. It was a master class in teaching as well as in the history of art, and it was utterly compelling.

A finely formulated vision, perfectly communicated across a school, a well-structured timetable to implement a broad and balanced curriculum, and excellent subject plans that promote progression of expertise, ambitious content and sophisticated output, are not enough to ensure a good education. Even adding in pristine facilities, sports fields manicured within an inch of their lives and all school policies perfectly in place, is still insufficient. Education is delivered in bite-sized chunks of lessons – perhaps ten thousand or so for every child in the school years currently under discussion. Without good lessons, we do not have a good education.

It is in the daily reality of classroom lessons that education takes place, lesson by lesson, week on week, year after year. Those adults who work most closely with children in the provision and delivery of these lessons on a daily basis have the opportunity to make an enormously positive difference in the lives of those in their care. This is why a school's single most valuable resource is its teachers.

One of the great privileges of working in school leadership is the opportunity to appoint new members of teaching staff. It is particularly enjoyable observing interview lessons, especially if the interviewees have the freedom to give a lesson on a topic that really interests them personally. As a result, I have discovered the joys of a new T.S. Eliot poem, have learnt fascinating facts about problems surrounding the honey-pot tourism site which is the Dead Sea, and learnt about new technical aspects of hockey which will stand me in good stead should I ever find myself back on the pitch.

What was it about the best of these that made them really good? Using the four-dimensional model, it is possible to ascertain that a good lesson is first one which ensures that heights of excellence, facilitated through good subject planning, are delivered effectively. Second, a good lesson supports breadth, as part of the wider picture of learning across the curriculum, as well as within the subject itself and the particular topic under consideration.

Third, a good lesson aids the construction of deep roots of learning (Figure 11.1) that enable depth of engagement. These build on previous learning and provide a reliable platform for future growth. A good lesson both incorporates interaction and fosters initiative, as pupils serve each other in their learning. Good habits of study are formed on a lesson-by-lesson basis.

Fourth, a good lesson encourages long-term learning, in the immediate future and stretching ahead to days and years to come. Practical outcomes are that in a four-dimensional lesson, a pupil experiences success, achievement is evident and varied, good habits of study are fostered and a love of learning is encouraged.

These aspirational principles and expected outcomes will be fleshed out and facilitated through the setting of clear goals for learning and the implementation of robust and purposeful pedagogy.

Goals for progress in learning

There has been a useful re-focus recently on the importance of pupils making progress in their learning in every lesson. In a paper published by The Sutton Trust, researchers emphatically state: 'Great teaching is defined as that which leads

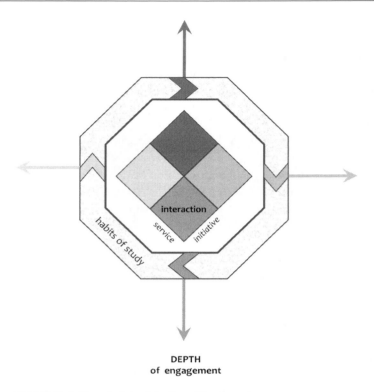

FIGURE 11.1 The principle of depth and its elements

to improved student progress'.[1] This may not be easy to demonstrate (and is certainly not always easy to measure) just as in the course of a day it is not easy to demonstrate a physical increase in height, but pupil progress nevertheless rightly remains both a legitimate and essential goal of teaching, and by extension, every lesson.

Reflecting the educational principles of the four-dimensional model, progress should be expected in the four distinct elements of learning already identified (knowledge, understanding, skill and appreciation), although the balance between them will vary from lesson to lesson.

Through a consideration of the four elements in turn, it is also possible to see that each is particularly closely linked with one of the four dimensions of learning (Figure 11.2).

Heights of excellence and progress in knowledge

Being absolutely central to the educational endeavour, when planning or reflecting on a lesson the first thing to be considered is the progress made in development of pupil knowledge. It may variously be gained via experiment,

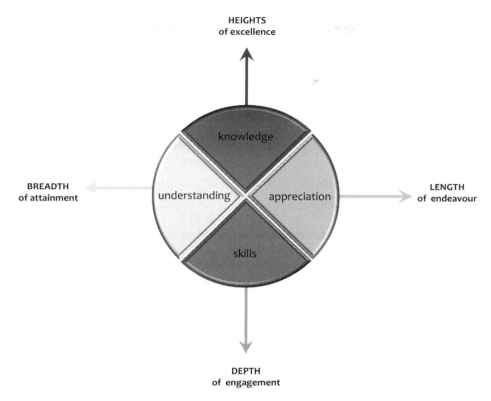

FIGURE 11.2 The relationship between the four elements of learning and the four educational principles

observation, demonstration, from books or the Internet, through discussion (which may include the contribution of individual children's own personal knowledge) or directly from the teacher. Just as was the case in our museum trip, sometimes the role of the teacher is to ask such pertinent questions as to enable the children to discover answers for themselves. This requires great subject understanding on the part of the teacher, and also great skill in knowing the questions to ask and the direction in which the answers need to move in order for the children to learn.

By whatever means it is imparted, at the end of a lesson, it is legitimate – and important – to ask this question: what do the children know now that they did not know before? Or what additional detail do they know now that they did not know prior to this lesson, or how has their knowledge become richer, fuller, more precise or more greatly consolidated? Knowledge is key to learning, essential for progress and foundational for responsible action.

Excellence entails both ambition and quality. Without progress in knowledge, neither aspect of excellence can be achieved.

Breadth of attainment and progress in understanding

While acquisition of knowledge is essential, the second and distinct area in which lessons should facilitate progress is that of understanding. This involves being able to use knowledge to explain a process or sequence of events or connection between different ideas. It is also essential to promote this, teaching pupils to piece knowledge together as part of a logical or coherent whole.

For understanding to be promoted, pupils should know how to use knowledge to think critically and imaginatively about issues and subjects encountered. At the end of a lesson, the teacher should be able to consider what process or idea the pupils can explain that they could not have explained (or have explained as fully) before the lesson, or how they can think about a subject more richly than before. Pupils should be able to make connections between ideas, and within and across subject areas, if their understanding has grown.

As with knowledge to be gained, the processes and explanations which need to be understood in a lesson or scheme of work must be determined by the teacher, and are typically those which themselves form together into a greater and stronger edifice of learning. In this way, progress in understanding contributes to the principle of breadth, enabling a growing network of ideas to be linked, developed and matured.

Depth of engagement and progress in skill

Progress in both knowledge and understanding is essential in a good lesson, but is not sufficient. The third area in which children should progress in a lesson is that of skill, the ability to do something which they could not previously do, or could not do as well.

As noted already, some skills are highly transferable, and others less so, but at the end of a lesson, irrespective of how transferable any skills learnt may be, a teacher should be confident that pupils have progressed in their ability to do something, to apply their knowledge and understanding in some way. They may have developed a more rigorous way of working, their curiosity and research skills, the ability to work collaboratively or honed an element of their creative ability.

They are now able to do something that they could not do before at all, or can do something with a greater degree of skill, competence or confidence. As pupils' skills develop, so their engagement in their learning deepens and develops, and good habits of study become secure.

Length of endeavour and progress in appreciation

The fourth question to be asked at the end of a lesson is: what do my pupils newly, additionally or increasingly appreciate, value or respect? A history lesson may help a child to appreciate the complexities of cause and effect, or the law of unintended consequences. A science lesson may help a class to appreciate the wonder of the universe, marvel at the knowledge of ancient astronomers or grasp the elegance of a scientific law. A games lesson may help a pupil to appreciate the importance of fairness and playing by the rules, or the finesse of a well-placed drop-shot. A drama lesson may help a group to appreciate the power of gesture and the impact of facial expression.

Being closely aligned with the development of character, such attitudes may include, but are evidently not confined to, those within the moral sphere. All these lessons above may help in appreciating the value of perseverance, compassion, positivity or individual distinction. As we saw earlier, the values that run through a school fill its every part including every lesson, and so at any time pupils may be learning to appreciate more fully the importance of personal integrity and mutual respect, the place of initiative or how an attitude of service plays out in practice.

Progress made in appreciation develops the character of the learner as attitudes take shape that will contribute to a lifetime of learning.

In practice progress should be made in each of these four areas in each lesson, although the balance between them will vary considerably between lessons and between subjects. It is useful however to cross-check in the teaching of more practical subjects, such as art, that knowledge and understanding are progressing, and in the more academic subjects, such as languages, that skills are being developed. Developing attitudes, such as appreciating what really matters in different contexts, may be among the most useful, yet hardest to define, areas of progress. Table 11.1 gives some examples from various curriculum areas to show how these four spheres of progress can work out in practice.

SUMMARY BOX 11.1: The components of progress in a four-dimensional lesson

Heights of excellence and progress in **knowledge**
+ breadth of attainment and progress in **understanding**
+ depth of engagement and progress in **skill**
+ length of endeavour and progress in **appreciation**

Teaching for learning

Progress by pupils in the above four areas – knowledge, understanding, skill and appreciation – can helpfully be described as good learning. Such learning only occurs, however, through the provision of good teaching. There are five specific characteristics that can be identified as contributory factors to lessons in order that good teaching, and by extension, good learning and progress, all occur within

TABLE 11.1 Examples in the four areas of progress for different subjects

SUBJECT: LESSON	LESSON AIMS IN AREAS OF PROGRESS			
	KNOWLEDGE PUPILS WILL KNOW . . .	UNDERSTANDING PUPILS CAN EXPLAIN . . .	SKILLS PUPILS WILL BE ABLE TO . . .	APPRECIATION PUPILS WILL VALUE/ RECOGNISE . . .
English: writing poetry	about placement of key words at the end of lines	how a poem makes sense; grasp further differences between prose and poetry	create a poem using given vocabulary	playing with words and creating a work of beauty; appreciate each other's writing
Maths: area of a triangle	the area of a triangle is given by the formula: $A = \frac{1}{2} \times base \times height$	what is meant by the 'base' of a triangle, its (perpendicular) height and why area is given by multiplying them together and halving the answer	apply formulae to calculate the areas of various triangles and solve associated problems	the use of a formula; grasp the significance and beauty of a universal rule
Science: flame tests	which elements burn with which colours	why flames are different colours	carry out experiment safely, developing practical lab skills	practical lab work; appreciate and enjoy the beauty of the colours in the flames
Drama: use of gesture in Mime	the meaning of 'gesture' – and give examples	why gesture is so important on stage	use gesture effectively in performance	the power of non-verbal communication
Games: developing the overhead serve in tennis	more fully about the follow-through part of the serve	why follow-through makes a difference to the quality of the serve	include follow-through in their own serves	a good serve when they see one; recognise the part played in that by the follow-through

the four-dimensional approach. These five are: engagement, challenge, rigour, support and purpose.

Engagement through captivating, pacy, interesting lessons

Children need to be engaged in their learning in order to learn. That is to say, they need to be connected with the lesson, participating in it and concentrating on it in order to benefit to the full and make maximum progress. In fact, it is in each individual lesson that the third educational principle, depth of engagement, is developed on an hourly basis.

There are a number of ways in which engagement can be achieved. I recall the crippling fear which motivated me in some lessons at school, the anxious desire to please my teacher in others. Neither of these is ideal, for different, but obvious, reasons. The best way, of course, is for there to be genuine engagement with the subject matter itself; this does not happen by accident.

For a lesson to be engaging, it needs to capture children's attention and imagination in the best possible way at the outset. Like setting sail on any venture in life, starting off in the right direction gives the greatest chance of ending up in the right place, and the start of a lesson needs to be particularly captivating. There are many ways in which this can be achieved, but chief among the ingredients are the enthusiasm of the teacher for the material to be taught, and for the process of engaging the children with it. As we saw with the teaching of literature, the teacher's role is akin to introducing two friends to each other who have not met before – here, the subject matter and the children being taught. The importance of knowing pupils well in order to choose the best approach and material has already been noted. The teacher's engagement with the two, and interest and passion for each, are most important, more significant than methodology or particular teaching technique. The teacher must communicate enjoyment of the subject, fascination with it, enthusiasm for it, if those attitudes are to be acquired by the children.

A good lesson requires challenge for all pupils at some point, which is why cultivating interest and enthusiasm at the start is so important before the going gets tough. A second element to ensure retaining engagement is that of pace. The pacing of a lesson must be carefully controlled by the teacher so as neither to leave those behind who are finding the material more challenging, nor to let those who are stronger stagnate and become impatient, or worse, bored. A good lesson should be pacy – that is, feel as though it is moving quickly so as to retain interest and momentum, while not leaving anyone stranded.

It is the job of the teacher to make the lesson interesting. Some topics may be of great personal interest to the teacher. Enthusiasm can shine through in a lesson and really make it sing, and where choices can be made without compromising consistency, it can be helpful for teachers to be given the freedom to include content about which they are really passionate or in which they have expertise. Truly inspirational teachers are those who inspire a love of their subject

– and a broader love of learning – in their pupils. Teacher enthusiasm and ambition rub off and pupils become equally enthusiastic and ambitious. In this way curiosity in the subject is fostered and encouraged, an essential component ensuring depth of engagement and cultivating good habits of study.

Even when the topic being taught is one of particular personal interest to the teacher (and most teachers have such topics), communicating this enthusiasm still requires energy and commitment. How much more are these required when the topic is of less inherent interest to the teacher (or indeed the class). For topics with less intrinsic appeal, the teacher has to make additional effort, and exercise even greater imagination in how to present the material to be covered. Humour – even nonsense – can often help out those topics which might be drier; English grammar lessons on subordinate clauses can involve children completing sentences: '. . . because the dog ate my homework'.

There is no reason for a lesson not to be fun. Enjoying a lesson does not distract from learning in it, but loss of engagement certainly does. This is not to say that lessons are characterised by flippancy, or that learning can take place without hard work; but it is to say that disengagement with the subject matter is to be avoided at all costs.

Challenge through ambitious, intellectual, demanding lessons

The second essential element in a good lesson is appropriate challenge. This has already been touched on in the consideration of what constitutes excellence, where it was argued that excellence is about a potent combination of ambition and quality: standing on tiptoe, reaching out at full stretch and eventually grabbing hold and securely grasping.

The first element of challenge is ambition. The challenging lesson has the right amount of stretch in it for the children in the class. The teacher is to have ambitious, but attainable, goals in sight. In the art lesson this may be to move to work in a more difficult medium or with greater realism; in swimming it may be to beat a personal best or move on to butterfly stroke; in maths it may be to solve more testing problems or understand more complex proofs. Good lessons aspire to excellence, and when this is achieved are characterised by ambition and a commitment to quality.

One successful approach in the pursuit of ambition is the cultivation of 'top-down excellence'. Rather than teaching 'to the middle' and differentiating with the provision of extension material for more able children and support material for less able pupils (an approach which had become an orthodoxy in recent decades), this approach sets the goals at the highest point for all pupils and then provides scaffolds and support to enable access for all. The challenge is presented first, with steps to meet it available as required, rather than expecting children to work through the steps, regardless of whether or not they need to, and get on to the challenge only 'if they have time'. This of course also avoids pre-judging at the outset which children can reach, and will therefore be offered, the toughest gaol. Such methods have gained wide support through the work of Bob Cox,[2] whose prize-winning books *Opening Doors to Quality Writing* provide innovative approaches to exploring quality texts as stimuli for children's writing. Planning is pitched from the top; expectations are high for all; opportunities are available for all.

Ambition also takes the form of greater intellectual complexity. Recent growth of philosophy in schools, such as through P4C,[3] offers pupils the chance to grapple with and debate complex questions or flummoxing dilemmas: What is art? Does it matter whether a language becomes extinct? Has technology made the world a better place?

Fostering intellectual ambition might entail strengthening critical thinking skills by working through 'de Bono's hats',[4] a technique to enable consideration of process, facts, creativity, benefits, cautions and feelings in any problematic or complex context. The utilisation of Bloom's taxonomy to encourage higher cognitive thinking, pupils moving 'upwards' from a base of knowledge and understanding through application and analysis to synthesis and evaluation, has been widely encouraged, and many teachers find its approach to encouraging pupils to think for themselves most helpful.[5] There are many such models on offer: Thinking Schools[6] list nineteen in their 'thinking toolbox', which includes 'habits of mind', 'ignorance logging', 'clustering' and 'the thinking sandwich', to name just some. Teachers also of course foster intellectual ambition through their own instinctive individual, idiosyncratic approaches, which makes the journey through the school day so much more varied and interesting for the pupil.

Intellectual challenge is not easy, one model of learning indicating the necessity and value of moving from initial clarity through 'the pit' of confusion in order to reach a higher level of understanding.[7] Such models support the 'growth mindset' work of Dr Carol Dweck, which identifies that 'in a growth mindset, people believe that their most basic abilities can be developed through dedication and hard work – brains and talent are just the starting point. This view creates a love of learning and a resilience that is essential for great accomplishment'.[8] The growth mindset emphasises the importance of deter-mined perseverance to accomplish ambitious individual goals along the learning journey.

It is also important that lessons provide opportunities for pupils to take responsibility for their learning. Opportunities need to be provided for them to take initiative in the way that they learn and in how they tackle challenges. Carefully crafted open-ended tasks, which can be responded to in different ways, encourage intellectual initiative, an important character trait within the model and essential for a later flourishing life. One task I have sometimes set my class is to devise any way of summarising the first six chapters of a particular book: they have created models and children's picture books, made memory boxes and story boards, written newspaper reports and diary entries. Sometimes pupils will set their own challenges or devise questions for others to answer. Sometimes a teacher will wait for a pupil to ask a question, and sometimes may even suggest they work out how to answer it for themselves.

Lessons need to be challenging for pupils, but pitching work at the right level of difficulty so that pupils feel the struggle will be worth it is a skill and an art. Challenge is allied to interest, as well as difficulty. The importance of generating interest has already been considered under the heading of engagement. Interest is not just cultivated through work being fun, helpful as this may be, but also – in the right context – through work being hard. These two are not contradictory: there is pleasure to be had in something difficult being achieved, as any regular cryptic cross-worder will attest.

Challenge is achieved through ambition, and is characterised by difficulty, complexity and high levels of demanding interest. In such ways, the challenging lesson stimulates the mind. It takes pupils to places they have not been before intellectually, and it encourages them to grapple and to struggle. Carefully and professionally handled, the challenging lesson develops in individuals a determined perseverance which brings a pupil through to a place of greater depth of engagement as well as further knowledge, understanding and clarity of thought. With mutual respect within the learning community, and a compassionate spirit, learning can safely take place through mistakes and error as well as success: a positive attitude rather than perfection is the prerequisite for individual distinction in the challenging lesson. It is in such ways that good habits of study are formed.

Rigour through accurate, thorough, academic lessons

Rigour was defined and described in Chapter 5 as a key component of depth of engagement. At the heart of every good lesson lies rigour; it is to be found in each and every maths, science or English lesson, as well as in the arts and sports, on a daily basis, as the roots of learning are being put down. The onus is on the teacher to ensure that through good roots being formed, the best possible habits of study are nurtured and the best foundation is laid for future learning.

If an individual lesson is rigorous, it is accurate: teacher subject knowledge needs to be sound and secure. Questions posed by children to the teachers need to be answered accurately; words need to be spelt correctly; ideas need to be explained precisely. It follows too that children are encouraged to work in the same way: answering questions precisely and accurately, whether verbally or in writing.

In a rigorous lesson, children are only taught what is right: it may sound obvious, but they are not given misinformation. It is not always easy to explain something complex in a simple yet technically correct way, but this has to be part of the skill of the teacher, and is essential if secure roots of learning are to be put down. We do not want children relearning later because they have been mistaught and misled now in a bungled attempt to simplify a concept.

In addition, rigour implies thoroughness. If additional knowledge needs to be given in order that the explanation is complete, then that should occur.

The research published by the Sutton Trust, already referenced, identified that a teacher's pedagogical content knowledge has the strongest impact on student outcomes; this includes knowledge of the subject itself as well as knowledge of the ways in which students will access and think about the ideas and material. The second factor to have a strong impact in pupil progress is the quality of instruction. This includes effective questioning, use of assessment, scaffolding and other elements already noted here, such as careful pacing of learning.[9]

By providing thorough teaching of this nature, the teacher ensures that thorough learning is taking place. Can pupils work through examples correctly? Can they explain the idea back to the class in their own words? Can they construct their own problems (and solutions) to demonstrate sound understanding of the concept?

The rigorous lesson never shies away from being academic, of using technical terminology, of sharing the more profound insights the teacher has into the topic at hand. In this respect, the arts subjects and sports lessons are just as rigorous, of course, as academic subjects. In a school in which all areas of attainment are valued, no one area has a monopoly on rigour: highly qualified and enthusiastic games teachers may be among the most precise in their explanations of techniques needed for improved performance, and musicians famously exploit a complex, technical, largely Italian vocabulary of their own, to support precision.

Support through kindly, disciplined, positive lessons

The fourth characteristic of a good lesson is that it is supportive. That is, the children are, and feel, fully supported in their learning. The teacher is there to help the children to learn – and in so doing, develop good strong habits of study – and needs to create an atmosphere in the classroom which is most conducive to this happening. This means engendering and enabling a classroom environment which is both happy and studious. Children need to be happy in order to be able to learn most effectively, but they are also happiest in school when they feel they are learning and achieving: each attribute supports the other. In the happy and studious classroom, in which pupils feel supported, they are confident to take the risk of being fully engaged in challenging work. The 'support challenge matrix',[10] often cited as a leadership tool, identifies that achieving a good balance between providing support and offering challenge is both liberating and empowering. Such an atmosphere can be sensed immediately on walking into a classroom.

There are four major things that children need to do to learn: listen carefully, follow instructions closely, work as hard as they can and think for themselves. They need to know that if they do these four things, they can expect to make very good progress in all areas of their learning: the onus is on them. The teacher's supporting contribution lies in clear communication and instruction, promotion of hard work within the group and facilitating personal initiative of each pupil.

The atmosphere created needs to support children in being confident to ask for help if they need it. My job as a teacher is to instruct and explain: if there is something that pupils have not understood, they should be confident to let me know so that I can offer support by explaining the point differently or in more detail. Such additional explanation should always be offered in a kindly and respectful manner.

It has already been noted that an education based on the foundational value of every pupil (and teacher) being inherently precious expects and encourages mutual respect. In the ideal lesson, everyone is working together towards the same goal: four-fold progress for each pupil. Such progress is most likely to be made when children sense the respect of their teachers and peers, such respect breeding confidence in the learner. In a classroom this is evident in the way that teachers and pupils speak to each other. Relationships should be kindly and positive, with the teacher setting the tone through polite and respectful, but also warm and friendly, communication with the class. Of course, taking the opportunity to share a joke, or show some humanity, can help relationships to flourish, any tension to be relaxed and work to prosper.

A supportive learning environment is positive, and a positive classroom environment is one which predominantly focuses on what is being done well. In one of the first conversations I recall having with a parent early on in my teaching career, a mother told me that her son responded better to praise than to criticism. I was mortified, taking the rebuke as intended, but it is a lesson I have not forgotten. In fact, I have yet to come across anyone who responds better to criticism than to praise. Apart from anything else, knowing what we have done well is often more instructive and useful than knowing what we have done badly unless, at the same time, explanation is offered in how to improve.

This is why, when giving feedback either to children in their books or to parents in reports, strengths in a child's learning need to be identified, and then the next steps that they need to take to progress need to be explained. For this sort of feedback to be fully supportive it also needs to be precise, specifying exactly what was done well and articulating the detail of what needs to improve. Here too, the tone should be kindly, as it should be in verbal classroom communication.

A supportive lesson is also a disciplined lesson – the classroom will be neither happy nor studious if it is not. The teacher needs to accept responsibility for the learning environment of the classroom, and be fully confident of it. A disciplined working environment enables all children to feel secure and to know that they can get on with their work unhindered.

If every pupil develops integrity, they will work hard, reliably and honestly; their value as a person warrants nothing less. As already noted, however, each of us, including every individual child in a school, is still a work in progress, not the finished article. This means that in practice, children do not work with integrity or the self-discipline it demands all the time – indeed, some will struggle to do so any of the time. In this case the teacher must take responsibility for the classroom atmosphere, and assert discipline on it. I am always nervous when I hear teachers being advocated to 'control' their classes, although I understand the intention, because it does not seem to me that any of us has the right to control another human being – and doing so has led to some disastrous and tragic consequences. Our language as well as our practice needs to be cautious in this respect, but equally we must ensure that until such time as self-discipline is fully developed in all pupils, the teacher makes up for the shortfall. Good discipline is never self-serving, there for its own sake. Rather, the ultimate goal of any such classroom discipline is to make itself redundant because every member of the class has developed self-discipline – born of a sense of worth and personal integrity, the foremost character trait identified in the model.

In the first instance, good classroom discipline is ensured by the teacher communicating clear expectations, in a firm, kindly and respectful manner, at the outset of the lesson. This communicates that certain identified boundaries are in place and are fully secure. Just as a lesson needs to start off by being engaging, so a lesson needs to start off by being disciplined. For this reason, classes may line up outside their lessons in silence, stand behind their chairs when they enter, sit when invited to do so, and raise their hands to answer a question. Such boundaries, when firmly in place, enable children to feel secure, confident and supported. Children do not like anarchy, they do not like insecurity and they do not like to feel that the boundaries shift – just one reason why they may test them to see what happens.

A supportive lesson is a disciplined lesson, but such discipline requires patience, strength of character, resilience and energy on the part of the teacher. Disciplined lessons may look effortless, because everyone works hard, addresses each other politely, gets on happily and achieves success, but in fact they are always the result of conscious effort.

It must be acknowledged that the challenges to achieve good levels of discipline will be considerably greater in some schools than in others, however. While it is the responsibility of every teacher to maintain the learning environment in the classroom, discipline is always a school-wide concern which requires consistency within and between classrooms. If a pupil is intent for whatever reason on disrupting learning, teachers affected must be fully and demonstrably supported by the school's senior leaders. Parents can make an enormously positive difference by being supportive of a school's disciplinary policy, and working with the school to overcome children's behavioural problems, but where sadly necessary, protection must always be provided against abusive or aggressive pupils or parents.

In practice, even in a school of well-motivated and largely compliant children, no lesson is disciplined without the teacher imposing their standards and boundaries clearly, firmly and positively on the class. Within such boundaries there is freedom, space and flexibility for individualism and creativity to flourish.

Teachers can reinforce with positivity in a number of ways: telling children what to do ('work quietly please') rather than reinforcing what not to do ('you're talking again') is just one of many practical ways in which good classroom behaviour is supported. The modelling of good behaviour – from arriving at a lesson on time, to speaking clearly but quietly, and to treating every pupil as being of equal worth – should go without saying.

It was allegedly Elbert Hubbard who said 'You can lead a boy to college but you cannot make him think', and anyone with an interest in education knows that with the very best will in the world (and the very best lessons), a teacher cannot do the work of learning for the child.

What we can do as teachers is to make our expectations as clear and manageable as possible, and to support pupils in reaching for those goals.

An emphasis needs to be placed on the contribution that children make to their own learning, on the grounds that if they take maximum control of the input, the outcome is the best possible. It can be very helpful to have some means of letting pupils know how their effort is regarded, or how well their habits of learning are developing. This may be provided through a score, grade or qualitative comment, at regular intervals. Depending on the age of the pupils, specific guidance along the lines shown in Table 11.2 may need to be provided to describe clearly those habits of study which need to be developed.

If we feel that a pupil's effort is not as good as it could or should be, we can be explicit in identifying one or more specific learning habits on which to work. Setting the challenge to a pupil of being the first to arrive at his maths lesson every time may be just the sort of precise guidance needed for helping turn effort round. Providing a daily report sheet with specified personal targets, to be signed by each teacher through the day, may provide the reminder needed to form good habits.

Whether it is good behaviour or good work that a pupil may find a struggle, or both, an education characterised by integrity and respect, honours and supports

TABLE 11.2 Habits of study to be encouraged

HABITS OF STUDY

Excellent effort means developing good habits of study, including . . .

    Punctuality – arriving on time and ready to learn
    Readiness – fully prepared and equipped
    Careful listening to teacher and others
    Full concentration in class
    Participation and answering questions
    Collaborating with others
    Following instructions and starting promptly
    Working carefully and attending to detail
    Displaying creativity and curiosity
    Thinking independently and taking initiative
    Reflection on learning and responding to feedback

personal initiative and determined perseverance in a spirit of compassion. In valuing the unique identity of the individual, there will be neither favouritism towards those who find school easier nor a giving up on those for whom it is a challenge. Rather, every child is tenaciously supported, encouraged and equipped to work hard towards individual distinction in whatever area that may be.

Purpose through organised, intentional, resourced lessons

The fifth and final characteristic of the good lesson which promotes learning in all four areas is that it is purposeful – that is, it is carefully and thoughtfully planned.

A good lesson is well organised in terms of choice of activities, the length of time spent on them and the pacing through the lesson. In the spirit of breadth, there should be variety of approach across a lesson, and even within types of task. In discussion and questioning, a teacher may ask for 'hands-up', or may go round the room asking each pupil in turn, or may select alphabetically, or randomly. When reading a novel with a class, it need not be read in the same way in every lesson or even during the course of one lesson: at times the teacher may read to the class, while they listen or take notes; at others they may read aloud individually a page each, or a paragraph each, perhaps a sentence each, round the room from punctuation to punctuation mark, or as a play script in which one narrates and others take the part of characters. The same is true in every subject: variety and creativity of approach must be modelled by the teacher.

A well-planned lesson also has balance between task types: written, verbal, practical; working alone, working in pairs, working in groups; working in silence or discussing as a class; working indoors, working outside; practical and theoretical; supported work or assessment. Collaboration and creativity are fostered through careful provision of such opportunities in lessons, where pooling of ideas and approaches is encouraged as much as individual expression, and open-ended tasks complement closed tasks. Some topics may lend themselves to a longer, project-based approach and others to a number of short time-frame tasks within a lesson; some may involve working with considerable constraint and others with great freedom of expression and opportunity. I might ask a class to write a fifty-word mini-saga or a page in the form of a *lipogram* (an entire text written without using a specific letter, such as 'e', for example); alternatively, I might ask them to write the opening of a novel or produce a creative response to a poem in a format of their choice. Such variety contributes to depth of engagement and hence the formation of strong habits of study. In playing to the different strengths of individuals, such diversity of approach also facilities breadth of attainment and helps to ensure variety of achievement.

Sitting behind the choices a teacher makes in planning is intentionality. These choices are made with specific ends in mind: the elements of four-fold progress. Teachers must be creative in coming up with their own ideas to ensure such progress, which in the best and most collegiate of schools are freely shared among colleagues to enriching effect. I may teach the same topics year on year, but there will be ways of improving how I teach, to include new resources or references to items currently in the news or international consciousness. Learning is alive, never arid or fossilised, but dynamic, responsive and purposeful, principles firmly embedded but practice continually morphing for each new generation and situation.

Finally, the good lesson is carefully, safely and thoroughly resourced. Everything needed is trialled and prepared in advance, with practical equipment set out and home-made resources printed and stapled into booklets. Any resources not from published textbooks or other reputable edited sources, especially those downloaded, need to be very carefully checked for accuracy and suitability, as well as copyright. The quality of resources must reflect the aspiration to excellence just as every other part of the lesson should.

Etched onto the window of our engineering workshop are the words, 'Measure twice; cut once'. This is apt for the planning of lessons too: teachers have one chance to teach each lesson, and the quality of the lesson will be a reflection of the quality and care of our planning: we need to think twice and teach once. And in our choice of teaching materials and methods, we need to be willing to sacrifice the good if it is the enemy of the best. This requires not only the provision of effective departmental plans considered in Chapter 10, but also the individual responsibility of each teacher to work out how those plans will be implemented on a lesson-by-lesson basis to the best possible effect.

SUMMARY BOX 11.2: The components of a four-dimensional lesson

engagement through being captivating, pacy, interesting
+ **challenge** through being ambitious, intellectual, demanding
+ **rigour** through being accurate, thorough, academic
+ **support** through being kindly, disciplined, positive
+ **purpose** through being organised, intentional, resourced

---

The benefit of collegiality: learning from each other

Schools are communities in which every member should be acknowledged to be continually learning. This of course includes the teaching body. For some matters, such as safeguarding, or health-related concerns, training from outside professionals is essential. In many other areas, being able to listen to those with specific expertise in an area of child development or subject knowledge can be enormously useful and may often be inspirational. Schools need to plan their staff training, professional development and opportunities for attending meetings and conferences carefully with this in mind. Personal research projects, based on both reflective practice and wide-ranging reading of professional journals, can also bring huge benefit to individual teachers and their classes as well as informing whole-school development plans.

Perhaps it is because teachers spend more of their time working in isolation (from their peers) than in many other professions, that when they get together there is a tendency to talk about teaching: by and large we enjoy learning from each other. So while we can all learn from those working outside our own context, I still never fail to learn from observing and discussing the work of my fellow practitioners in a collegial atmosphere.

Lesson observations

The primary goal of such collegial activity is to ensure that a school is providing the best learning opportunities for all pupils, in order to maximise pupil progress. This is therefore both an essential activity and a shared responsibility. Observing each other's lessons enables teachers together to safeguard and pursue the highest of standards, especially as the ideas behind the lessons are shared and observations fed back to each other as colleagues. Such peer observations also help to ensure that every child is getting a fair deal – that provision is tailored to need as closely as possible, but is as equitable as is manageable. Observing lessons, and being observed teaching, also help to ensure that standards are kept high as we learn from and implement the best of each other's ideas.

Such observations might be used to focus on a particular element of learning, such as developing understanding of a concept or the acquisition of a particular skill. They can also be used for focusing on a particular element of teaching, whether introducing an app or the use of question-and-answer. Again, observations can also be used to focus on a whole-school development target such as use of classrooms as teaching spaces, or improving the participation of all children, or developing listening skills.

The progress that we would expect to see in knowledge, understanding, skills and appreciation has been outlined above, together with the elements of teaching that might be expected to be evident in a good lesson. These are high standards to aspire to and it should always be remembered that to observe another teacher is a privilege, an opportunity for both practitioners to learn and develop as professionals.

Assessing output

It is not just through the observation of lessons that pupil progress can be monitored and ideas shared, of course, but also through close consideration of output. Once again, this tends to be most useful when all teachers are involved in the process, whether looking through exercise books informally at lunchtime, the spontaneous sharing of a breakthrough piece of work a pupil has produced, or the more formal moderation of assessments and exam papers.

Pupil exercise books are a shop-window of their learning: although they do not tell the whole story, they do tell part of it (very visibly), and as such are a useful tool in reflecting on practice. Looking through pupils' books gives teachers the chance to reflect not only on their pupils' work but on their own. My pupils' output challenges me to ask whether I am expecting excellence. Have I set ambitious tasks, and do my pupils know what is required to do them well? As well as sufficient explanation, pupils also need to be given sufficient time to do the task to a high standard, so that it is not rushed or incomplete, but fully finished and polished. Is this what a colleague would see looking at my classes' books?

Just as the lesson needs to start in a disciplined and engaging way, so written work needs to set off in the right direction. It matters that the date and title are spelt correctly, and are correctly capitalised, even in young children's written work, so that good habits form. Such points need to be routinely corrected if they are not in evidence. If I am aiming for rigour, I should also habitually correct spelling and punctuation errors, making professional judgements based on age, ability and learning needs of individual pupils.

Written work provides evidence as to whether clarity is being endorsed: at the most basic level, letters must be formed carefully, spaces left between words, and digits written one per square in maths books, for example. Good presentation should be promoted, with sharp pencils and the use of rulers in evidence. Teachers' written comments must be easy to read if they are to be of any use, and marking must not compromise the integrity of the pupils' effort to present well.

The most effective praise from teachers in books is precise, identifying specific areas of strength in a piece of work. Similarly, the most useful marking includes explicit and clear next steps ('Include more detail in explanations', 'Show every step in your working' or 'Use the most precise vocabulary possible').

Excellence is evident in ambitious and high-quality work; breadth is evidenced in type of task and content; depth through rigour and accuracy. All such successes should be clearly and generously celebrated as pupils are encouraged to do their very best and are duly recognised when they succeed. I remember the pleasure of seeing a shiny silver star placed in my exercise book as a young child; stickers, merits, stars and certificates all have their place, and are enjoyed by children now every bit as much as in my memory.

In the areas of the arts and sports, although not typically book-based, output is often even more visible than in the academic subjects. Musical concerts, play performances and sports matches are all high-profile performance opportunities, a potent combination of seeing the children's work in evidence as it actually happens. For teachers working in these areas, as well as pupils, triumphant match results or a standing ovation may be the measure by which they feel judged. Feedback from colleagues needs to be supportive and empathetic, recognising the pressure brought upon teachers by such high-visibility events. Mutual support occurs when team spirit extends beyond the players and their coaches in such situations and spreads supportively through the whole school community.

Departmental review

A third and final way to foster collegial response to teaching and learning is through regular discussion and departmental review. Schools will determine for themselves how often and in what format such reviews can most usefully take place, but talking about teaching with colleagues is always informative and instructive.

Table 11.3 shows how a maths department could draw up questions based on the four-dimensional model to stimulate departmental discussion. The very act of setting aside time for such reflection is hugely beneficial in reminding us of our mission.

Follow-up to such discussion could be to reflect on and respond to each of the following questions individually:

- What am I going to do differently in a lesson next week?
- What I am going to reflect on at half-term?
- What end of year outcome would I most like to see?

SUMMARY BOX 11.3: The components of collegial review

Characteristics of collegiality:
lesson observations + assessing output + departmental reviews

---

Innovation, excellence and IT

There is no point in spending time on reflective practice as teachers if we are unwilling to change what we do. Consideration was given in Chapter 7 to the contribution that innovation makes to a school in ensuring excellence, through its judicious blend with tradition. The same principle applies in the classroom: innovation keeps teaching fresh, but tradition keeps it grounded. How can the best balance be achieved between the two?

The use of IT in the classroom makes a useful example here. In ascertaining the best use of embedded IT in classroom teaching, the guiding principle must be to ensure that children are 'gainers and not losers'. In other words, innovation should always be seen as a means to an end – and judged on that basis – rather than as an end in itself. To what extent does embedding IT in the curriculum enable higher levels of attainment or rates of progress across the four areas?

IT is an integral part of life, and as such is already an integral part of teaching, but the nature and extent of its benefits need to be articulated in order to ascertain its best use. Using electronic presentation to highlight key points, display visual material to provoke discussion or inspire a creative piece can be

TABLE 11.3 Questions for teaching colleagues to discuss in a spirit of collegiality

AREA TO REVIEW	QUESTIONS TO DISCUSS
The expectation of excellence	Are we clear on how we define excellence? Is our focus on producing really high-quality work? Do the pupils know what they have to do to do any given task well? Is excellence achieved, and if so how do we know? Is knowledge progressing at a good rate? Do we let pupils choose how hard their tasks are?
Learning habits	Are creativity, curiosity and collaboration actively being fostered? Are pupils showing short-term grit and long-term drive? Are listening skills strong?
Achieving ambition	Is academic and mathematical ambition explicitly valued, encouraged and promoted? What opportunities are there for the ambitious pupil? How is ambition fostered if absent? Do we reach as high and go as far as we possibly can with every pupil in every lesson?
Including innovation	To what extent is material used in lessons off-the-shelf or tailored? If material is off-the-shelf, are we fully confident that it is excellent? How varied in type are the tasks in each lesson? How tailored are the tasks to the group we are teaching? How much fun is the lesson?
How to trigger rigour	Are mathematical foundations laid with absolute clarity? Are pupils absolutely clear as to what they have to do to and what constitutes a right answer or correct solution? Are we clear on what the foundational points of understanding are that must be explicit and understood by all? Do we make a clear distinction between foundational points and their application to problem-solving that can be innovative, creative, varied and tackled at different levels?
Building confidence	Are all pupils mathematically confident? Is this appropriately based on a secure knowledge and understanding of foundational principles and their application? Do we encourage the growth of confidence through the stimulus of success? Is confidence consciously cultivated for every pupil in every maths class? Do we target any under-confidence strategically?

very effective, but lessons taught through preprepared slides alone can be as dull as any other repetitive approach. How can the one be implemented and the other avoided? As should be expected, with such a powerful tool as IT, the benefits are significant and numerous, but each positive attribute inevitably also has its limitation or drawback. The guiding principle must be to know both the upsides and downsides of using IT and ensure that it is used when, and only when, it is the very best way to teach.

The promotion of engagement

Benefit: Material can be presented to children in all manner of visual and interactive ways using IT, making lessons accessible and interesting. Engagement is often cited as a major advantage of using IT with children, drawing them into a subject through varied, attractive, intriguing and accessible portals.

Caution: Although engagement is an essential component, it is only part of the learning process. As a teacher I have not succeeded merely by engaging children, but need to press on to ensure that their knowledge, understanding, skills and appreciation of the subject matter are all being enhanced, as well as their desire and ability to grapple with concepts and challenges.

Access to information

Benefit: The opportunities provided by the Internet for pupils to access information are unimaginably great; pupils can readily access a virtually limitless stock of facts and figures, images and archives, reports and blogs. The chances are that whatever information they need, they should be able to find.

Caution: Information *per se* is obviously neither an end in itself, nor a substitute for knowledge and understanding. A clear distinction needs to be made between working and simply appropriating the fruit of someone else's labour. Foundational knowledge, held by pupils themselves for context and reference, is essential; multiple layers of personal understanding are vital; individual creativity is key. Teachers have a critical role in directing pupils towards useful sites and sources which support, rather than in any way undermine, academic rigour, and which promote their active learning. They also have a serious responsibility to teach children how to source true, reliable information rather than mischievous misinformation, and how to develop their own discernment and critical faculties in this regard.

Virtual reality

Benefit: Simulation and communication technologies enable virtual access to sites, communities and artefacts otherwise inaccessible, children being able to experience a virtual tour of the Taj Mahal, enjoy a real-time link with children in Spain or virtually turn the pages of Handel's original manuscript of Messiah. These are wonderful opportunities to be embraced, and provide a breadth of experience otherwise impossible to conceive.

Caution: Virtual reality must not be at the expense of real-life experience. Thus there may be a time for a virtual tour of the Taj Mahal, but not to the exclusion of a real tour of King's College chapel, or wherever else may be at hand. Pupils may have a web-based link with a Spanish school, but visiting a community and meeting its residents in their home situation is always a deeply enriching experience. Children may sometimes turn virtual pages but must also – self-evidently – be able to read and interpret what is written on them.

Whole-class teaching

Benefit: IT can be an excellent tool in whole-class teaching, and has revolu-tionised certain elements. Data-loggers in science enable efficient collection, information and analysis of experimental results. An interactive white board for maths equipped with graphical software readily enables children to see graphical display of functions or observe mathematical transformations. Software exploiting the use of shape, movement, colour, video, animation and sound can assist enormously in the understanding of concepts.

Caution: There is no substitute for high-quality content of children's and teachers' work, and teachers always need to be cognisant of the risk that tech-nically sophisticated presentation packages become a distraction from substance, rigour, depth and quality.

Individual support

Benefit: In recognising and celebrating individual differences and aptitudes, and aiming to cater as closely as possible for both the needs and strengths of pupils, IT already has much to offer in facilitating individual learning opportunities; this is likely to widen. Provision can be highly individualised as each pupil can interact independently with his or her digital device, particularly useful in promoting and developing speaking and listening skills in modern languages, for example.

Caution: A balance needs to be sought and struck between individualised and group learning. Heavy IT use can lead to children working in isolation from peers, interacting primarily with their digital device rather than their neighbour. Teamwork, the sharing of ideas and group discussion are all hugely fertile learning opportunities, lost at a cost: intellectual creativity is more often spawned through discussion than through isolated working.

Benefit: There is particular value for a Learning Support department in the use of IT, children with a dyslexic profile possibly finding a laptop useful for extended writing as well as software applications that support the organisation and display of information. The application of voice recognition software can be a valuable tool to support the acquisition of reading skills, albeit alongside the help of supportive adults.

Caution: Some children may instinctively enjoy and benefit from more IT-heavy delivery while others thrive less readily. It needs to be borne in mind that, as with employing to excess any one methodology or approach, some pupils will be disadvantaged or disengaged through excessive use of IT.

Benefit: One regularly cited advantage of IT-based learning, particularly for some children who find reading and writing very problematic, is the participation in activities, access to information and assessment of learning, made possible without the necessity of reading and writing. In such 'literacy-free learning', images on screens, audio instruction and click–mouse responses replace the written or spoken word.

Caution: It remains essential for all pupils to develop the strongest possible verbal communication skills, both written and oral, and to exercise these widely. One of the key ways in which literacy skills are refined and advanced is through application across a range of subjects. Caution should still be exercised in 'literacy-free learning', particularly for assessment purposes. Instead, children should be encouraged to develop their ability to formulate, explain and express ideas verbally for themselves and to others across the range of subjects – with or without the help of IT.

Innovative outcomes

Benefit: IT can facilitate otherwise impossible learning outcomes using various pieces of digital hardware and software, particularly in the creative arts, where children can make and edit their own animated films for example, or use computer-aided design to visualise and create three-dimensional models. IT allows varied recording and publication opportunities, using audio, video, photography and text, thus enabling sophisticated standards of presentation in pupils' work, to each other and more widely. It also facilitates greater immediacy of self-assessment, as pupils watch their gymnastics technique or listen to the development of their French accent, for example.

Caution: In the search for breadth and variety in both curriculum content and delivery, it is a truism that the use of IT provides variety in the curriculum, only if it is not used all the time. New digital technologies are not a substitute for teacher creativity and imagination, or for knowing pupils' needs and sharing teachers' personal expertise and enthusiasm. There are many ways in which teachers can be creative and innovative in their pedagogy, only some of which involve the use of technology.

Furthermore, it is self-evident that anything, including IT, is only novel when it is new or rare. Perhaps this is why the most recent training in the use of interactive white boards encourages teachers to switch off the boards for long periods of the day. With emerging concerns over the increase of mental health problems in young people, and the suspicion of links with excessive use of screens, some schools now have regular screen-free days or sessions, or choose to limit screen use in other ways. Teachers need to model turning off screens when they are not required, and actively demonstrate a lack of dependency on them.

Distance learning

Benefit: A virtual learning environment (VLE) enables children to access remotely their schoolwork and related Internet sites and resources. It is one way of supporting a school policy of teachers, children and parents working in partnership. Access to homework assignments, background material of interest related to a topic, games to reinforce learning, and discussion forums are all possible with a VLE. The posting of practice exam papers on a VLE enables pupils to work in their own time, and answers provided mean that parents are able to support at home. More broadly, a VLE also enables pupils to be directed towards, and have access to, courses taught by other institutions; for children with a particularly strong personal interest or aptitude in one part of the curriculum, this could prove to be a significant learning opportunity. The exploitation of social networking sites for educational purposes is a further area likely to grow in importance, safeguarding considerations notwithstanding.

Caution: All that said, it remains the case that there are no substitutes for teachers' knowledge of both pupil and subject, and their pedagogical expertise in bringing the two together in creative, imaginative and affirming ways.

IT and the allocation of resources

Teachers need to use their limited time for that which is of most benefit to pupils, and reference should be made to the law of diminishing returns when it comes to perusing developments in IT. The hidden time cost of sifting websites, trialling software and preparing digital resources is not to be underestimated. The bigger a VLE grows, for example, the more time is needed for modification and monitoring to ensure that the referenced sites remain up to date and safe for children to access. Teachers, however, need to have the freedom to focus on teaching, rather than become primarily purveyors of IT resources.

The rapidity of change in the field means that digital devices have a limited shelf-life, swiftly being superseded by superior models and alternative products.

An aspiration to having the latest or best device has financial and time–cost implications in terms of researching, purchasing, training, implementing and supporting technically. Although emerging technologies become less expensive as markets grow, a desire to remain up to date can lead to an ever-increasing IT budget. Increasing numbers of potential apps will also place demands on budgets and necessitate ever more careful and informed stewardship of resources.

The manufacturing, maintenance and operational costs of electrical and electronic devices and their supporting networks have sustainability implications. For all administrative purposes within teaching (and the support services across a school), IT will continue to be the major component. Pupil details, assessment scores, records of attainment and schemes of work – everything that previously would have been stored in paper files – will for the foreseeable future be stored digitally. The required capacity for such information is likely to continue to increase in all aspects; it will therefore be necessary to ensure continually improving systems for ease of navigation and access, and for data security and protection. As schools seek to promote a green agenda, they want to be responsible by seeking to minimise the use of material resources and power consumption inherent in the purchase and operation of devices – as well as paper resources inherent in traditional media.

As the examples above indicate, as a medium for teaching, like any other technology, IT in itself is value-neutral, and is only good insofar as it improves the quality of learning compared with intrinsically simpler and less costly media. It is clear that IT needs to be used judiciously in teaching and learning across the broader curriculum, if and when it facilitates higher attainment. There is no rationale for any subject other than Digital Literacy and Computer Science being taught exclusively in computer suites or through the medium of IT (and even these subjects will not always be taught using hardware), but all subject areas benefit from having some flexible access to such facilities, laptops or mobile devices.

The use of IT serves as a helpful example of assessing the value of innovation in the classroom. Implementation of IT-dependent pedagogy must be as a result of informed judgement of teachers and heads of departments who have weighed up the relative merit of using digital technology over other media, both traditional and innovative. Devices and applications need to be thoroughly explored for their potential to improve learning outcomes, and not judged simply on the basis that they can deliver the curriculum in novel ways. Close attention must be paid to the considerable body of research published on the comparative benefits of teaching with and without technological devices. Once purchases are made, training opportunities continue to be needed for staff for familiarisation of use and in order to gain maximum potential from the technologies.

The four-dimensional principles of education can be applied as much to the use of IT as to any other pedagogy. IT should be used in teaching if and when it facilitates heights of excellence (in terms of ambition and quality), ensures breadth of attainment and approach (both within and between subjects), fosters depth of engagement (in terms of rigour and interest) and promotes, as far as we can tell, length of endeavour. In any given subject, the judicious and expert implementation of embedded IT will, in all probability, do this some, but not all, of the time.

SUMMARY BOX 11.4: The components of IT use in lessons: benefits and cautions

promoting engagement + information access
+ virtual reality + whole-class teaching + individual support
+ innovative outcomes + distance learning + allocating resources

---

This chapter has focused on the way in which an individual lesson, its qualities and impact contribute to the four dimensions of learning, and specifically to ensuring depth of engagement. These are very high ideals for teachers to work towards, and their realisation requires both high levels of support and clearly articulated vision. The fourth principle, that of length of endeavour, is considered finally as attention is turned to the implications of the model in the creation of such a vision for education – and not just the creation of vision, but its implementation and bringing to fruition.

Notes

1 www.suttontrust.com/wp-content/uploads/2014/10/What-makes-great-teaching-FINAL-4.11.14.pdf, accessed 28 July 2017.
2 www.searchingforexcellence.co.uk/, accessed 28 July 2017.
3 www.philosophy4children.co.uk/, accessed 28 July 2017.
4 See, for example, www.thinkingschool.co.uk/resources/thinkers-toolbox/six_thinking_hats, accessed 28 July 2017.
5 See for example, www.thinkingschool.co.uk/resources/thinkers-toolbox/blooms_taxonomy, accessed 28 July 2017.
6 www.thinkingschool.co.uk/, accessed 28 July 2017.
7 www.jamesnottingham.co.uk/learning-pit/, accessed 28 July 2017.
8 http://mindsetonline.com/whatisit/about/index.html, accessed 28 July 2017.
9 www.suttontrust.com/wp-content/uploads/2014/10/What-makes-great-teaching-FINAL-4.11.14.pdf, accessed 28 July 2017.
10 See for example, https://giantworldwide.com/duct-tape-matrix/, accessed 09.11.2017.

12

A four-dimensional vision

Fostering length of endeavour

The adventure of learning is never over for anyone in receipt of a good education, because length of educational endeavour, both short and long term, is its goal. Having established the characteristics of the four-dimensional lesson, the cultivation of the fourth dimension, length, can finally be considered. It is in creating, supporting, implementing and sustaining educational vision that length of endeavour is achieved.

Grandma Moses and Mrs Delany

The iconic inventor and businessman, Henry Ford, once said, 'Anyone who stops learning is old, whether at twenty or eighty. Anyone who keeps learning stays young'.[1] Ford's compatriot, Anna Mary Robertson Moses who died in 1960, at the age of 101, lived out his words. A renowned American folk artist, the *New York Times* said of her: 'The simple realism, nostalgic atmosphere and luminous color with which Grandma Moses portrayed simple farm life and rural country-side won her a wide following. She was able to capture the excitement of winter's first snow, Thanksgiving preparations and the new, young green of oncoming spring . . . In person, Grandma Moses charmed wherever she went'.[2] Her paintings hang in the museums of the world, and in 2006 one was sold for over a million US dollars.

Mary Delany died at the age of eighty-seven, some hundred years before Grandma Moses was born. Born into an aristocratic English family, as a young woman Mary learnt English, French, history, music, needlework and dancing, and eventually became a close friend and supporter of the composer Handel. Later, she developed a passion for creating decoupage (finely cut paper) representations of plants and flowers, producing works which were exceptionally detailed and botanically accurate. King George III and Queen Charlotte, great supporters of her paper-cutting, 'always desired that any curious or beautiful plants should be transmitted to Mrs. Delany when in blossom'.[3] She created over 1,700 such works, each one from hundreds of minute particles of coloured tissue paper used to represent the petals, stamens, leaves, veins and other parts of the plant, using lighter and darker paper to form the shading. Today her ten volumes reside in the British Museum.

What these two formidable ladies, separated by century and continent, have in common is that neither started on their career as an artist until in her seventies. Grandma Moses started painting in earnest at the age of 78, and Mrs Delany, having twice been widowed, in her early 70s as a way of dealing with her grief. Both reached extraordinary heights of achievement despite the advanced years at which they started the work for which they are remembered.

I learnt about both women during my own adult years, Grandma Moses through my mother who had seen and admired her work, and Mrs Delany through a neighbour who was writing her biography. I find them both inspiring and encouraging, always holding out hope that it is never too late to develop a skill, to start a new career, to make an impact or indeed to learn. It is apt that my learning of them occurred well after my own formal education had finished.

Lifelong learning

'When I do not know, neither do I think I know', says Socrates,[4] who thinks himself a little wiser in understanding his own limits of knowledge than the man who pretends to know everything. In the long term, one of the results of a good education, ironically enough, is a recognition that there is always more to be learnt – the more we know, the more we realise we do not know.

The Comenius Medal, one of UNESCO's most prestigious awards in the field of education, is named after the seventeenth-century Czech educationalist. 'What differentiated Comenius from all others in the Europe of his time who sought to reform education was his concept of education as a life-long process', writes Dagmar Capková.[5] The ability, desire, self-belief and capacity to go on learning are essential to our need to be adaptable creatures in an ever-changing world. 'Intellectual growth should commence at birth and cease only at death', Einstein reportedly said, and we might readily imagine that if anyone should know, he would.

Technologies of today were unheard of and undreamt of in the age of my grandparents; the technologies that today's children may be using when they are grandparents are impossible to imagine. As has been true for every generation, pupils now at school will have to be willing and able to keep on learning not just through the years of formal education, but into adulthood and through its years of both employment and retirement, in order to flourish to the full. The benefits of remaining active – physically, socially and mentally – into old age are increasingly being understood. Reading, writing for pleasure, learning foreign languages, playing musical instruments, taking part in adult education courses and playing tennis, golf or bowls are all listed by the National Health Service as being of potential value in reducing risk of Alzheimer's disease and other types of dementia.[6] Holistic education would seem to characterise the flourishing life from the cradle to the grave.

The pattern of learning set in the early years at school therefore carries a weightier impact than might at first have been imagined. Education sets a direction of travel, with mighty implications for longer-term personal health and well-being, the capability to contribute meaningfully to family and community, and the capacity to influence and impact society for the common good. While it is heartening to think that it is never too late to learn, it is also sobering to consider how the patterns of learning set in the years of school education continue to ripple their impact throughout our lives.

Consideration has been given as to how, within a good education, the curriculum needs to be conceived in order to achieve breadth of attainment, how each subject must be managed so as to guarantee heights of excellence, and how every lesson needs to be taught so as to ensure depth of engagement. It could be argued that the fourth dimension, length of endeavour, is both the end result of these being done well and the ultimate goal of a good education (Figure 12.1).

As was stated at the outset, formal education is not the end in itself, but equips and enables the young child, school pupil or college student to move forwards into new and challenging situations, capable and confident not just to cope, but to prosper and thrive. 'Formal education', said the Quaker headmaster, Robert

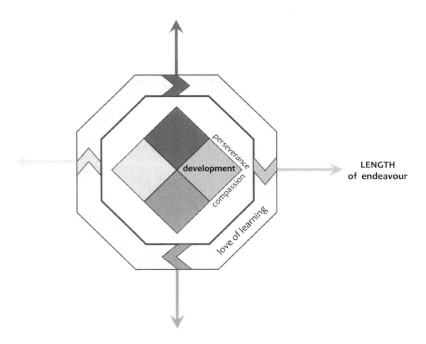

FIGURE 12.1 The principle of length and its elements

Lawrence Smith, 'is only a jumping off point for a lifetime of learning and doing, and what concerns good schools and good teachers is how students apply the learning they acquire to living their lives'.

Perhaps this is partly what is meant by the aphorism also attributed to Einstein: 'Education is what remains after one has forgotten everything learned in school'.

A vision of good education

The process of building this educational model started with a consideration of the stated aspirations of traditional English prep school education, the system chosen for analysis because of personal professional experience, and the choice justified by the significant proportion of time pupils spend at these schools including the critical pre-public examination years. By identifying their key characteristics, the ethos of such schools was articulated: individual pastoral care, within a strong community, and a striving towards excellence for all, within and beyond the curriculum. This ethos pointed to a holistic principle of education which places the individual pupil as a whole and multifaceted person at the centre of the educational enterprise.

From this point, a model of education started to take shape. At the heart of the model lies every individual child, each inherently precious, uniquely gifted, mutually dependent and continually learning – values which themselves arise from a broad, inclusive, Christian world-view. From these values, a learning community begins to take shape, characterised by individuals of integrity, distinction, initiative and perseverance, who hold each other in mutual respect and with shared positivity, and treat each other with an attitude of service and a compassionate spirit. Four key educational principles arise from this view of the individual within the community, which form the crux of the educational model: heights of excellence, breadth of attainment, depth of engagement and length of endeavour: the four dimensions of education. The practical outcomes evident are experience of success, love of learning, good habits of study and variety of achievement.

Having established an idealised model of good education (Figure 12.2), consideration has been given to how this can be translated into principles that apply at the whole-school level, across a broad and balanced curriculum, within a particular subject and even in an individual lesson.

Every part of the educational process contributes to the principle of longevity of learning, from the individual lesson that fosters good habits of study, through the various subject specialisms that enable pupils to experience success, across the broad curriculum that cultivates variety of achievement. All of these practical outcomes contribute to a love of learning, and thus longevity of endeavour characterised by short-term grit and long-term drive.

But just as the outcomes of a good education stretch far beyond the confines of the school years, so too the input to ensure a good education stretches far beyond the immediate confines of the school day. Many individuals and groups,

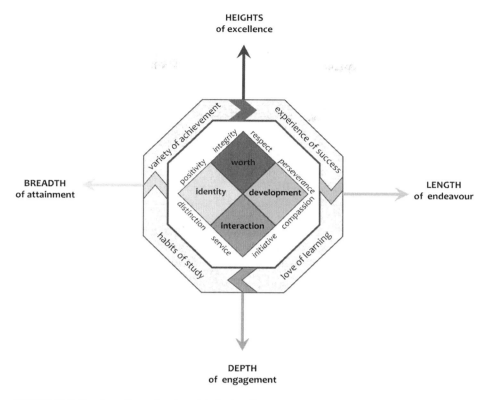

FIGURE 12.2 The four-dimensional model of education

from policy-makers to practitioners, bring education into effect; in order to do so successfully, each needs a clear educational vision, and a clear understanding of the part they must play in its realisation. At each level of contribution, considering the implications of the four-dimensional model can inform such vision. It is therefore to a consideration of vision that we now turn.

Conceiving vision: policy-makers

Earlier chapters have already touched on the extent to which policy-makers have tended to direct recent focus towards systemic reorganisation and structural change. I have been a huge beneficiary from educational reorganisation: I was in the first year of women admitted as undergraduates to my college at university. The expansion of higher education to include women reflected a fundamental change of attitude and approach for which I will always be enormously grateful: structural change is necessary. But in itself, structural change is not sufficient for ensuring a good education. My admission as a woman to the educational opportunities I received was only as useful as the education I received was good.

Educational policy-makers, such as nationally and locally elected representatives, civil servants and academy sponsors, need to have a vision of what good education is in order to inform large-scale decisions about provision, allocation of resources, educational organisation and structural reorganisation. This is especially so when resources are limited, as is inevitably the case. This contrasts with a 'value for money' approach which simply seeks the lowest cost option as its aim. Such a national or local educational vision may be inspired by or draw on some description, definition or model of good education such as the one presently under consideration. Policy should then reflect and facilitate the vision in as far as resources allow. Structural change and systemic policies should be implemented in order to facilitate the good education that has been envisaged, rather than changes be introduced in the hope that better education will follow.

Such vision may be couched in many different ways, and at policy-forming level needs to be precise on the essential principles, without being prescriptive on context-specific detail. The four-dimensional model might suggest an educational vision at policy-forming level, such as that given below (Vision box 12.1).

The articulation of a broad vision of what good education looks like, such as this, gives a point of reference against which suggested provision and specific policies can be assessed.

VISION BOX 12.1: A four-dimensional vision for policy-makers

WHAT IS A GOOD EDUCATION?

Our vision of a good education is one in which every individual child is known and cared for as a whole person within a strong and supportive learning community. This will entail the provision of strong pastoral care through which individual and community character development is actively fostered.

Pupils should be enabled to discover and develop their gifts through a broad curriculum of opportunity with high expectations for every pupil and provision for academic, artistic and sporting excellence.

Strong and secure progress in knowledge, understanding, skills and appreciation is expected across all the disciplines as pupils put down deep and secure roots of learning on which they can build over a lifetime.

Educational Excellence Everywhere, the UK government's 2016 educational White Paper, makes a strong and convincing case for the provision of excellent education for all, making the point, among others, that 'the better educated our society, the fairer, more cohesive, productive and innovative it can be'.[7] It goes on to propose seven ways in which such excellence will be achieved: through great teachers; great leaders; expansion of the academy system; prevention of underperformance; high expectations and a world-leading curriculum; account-ability which is ambitious for every child; and the right resourcing.

Some of these seven ways of achieving excellence are probably a matter of considerable consensus, at least at headline level, and would be held true irres-pective of the vision of education held. There are few who would argue that excellence in education is possible without really good teachers, and for the whole to be greater than the sum of the parts, good leadership is generally seen to be essential. Nonetheless, a clear articulation of educational excellence still needs to be agreed in order that good teaching and good leadership can be defined and recognised, and in order that appropriate arrangements can be made for their provision. The vision of good education above, derived from the four-dimensional model, provides an example.

The proposed expansion of the academy system provoked considerable reaction. I know from personal experience how wholesale upheaval impacts every single pupil in a generation, and the more seismic the changes (whether locally or nationally), the greater the potential disruption affecting individual children. In the four-dimensional model, the learning community, made up of past, present and future members, is regarded as a sensitive eco-system of inherent value. A vision derived from the model, such as that above, would protect and promote the strength of the learning community, suggesting that change should be managed in such a way as to protect educational heritage. A diet of change that is constant, fast-paced and untested is likely to be less educationally bene-ficial than that which is slower, more careful, more gradual and more considered. It may write fewer headlines, but evolution is almost always preferable to revolution. Where change is needed, even retaining the name of a school enables a degree of continuity which can otherwise be so easily lost: in most situations, there is some strength to be found in preserving a connection with the past.

Given the inevitable upheaval of change, it is hard to justify restructuring or re-designating a school which is already providing a good education. But that said, the four-dimensional model argues the strongest case for the prevention of underperformance and for the improvement of education where needed – the fact that every child being educated is inherently precious. And of course, new schools do have to be created: self-evidently every school was new once. A comprehensive vision of what constitutes a good education should precede all decisions about a new school from its size and site, to the shape of the build-ing, and provision of outdoor space.

I spoke with one newly appointed head teacher recently whose academy was going to provide musical opportunity for all its pupils through links with a local *conservatoire*; such provision can be made if and when educational vision informs planning. This confident, positive attitude is one of the community character traits directly arising from the four-dimensional view that each child possesses a unique combination of gifts; it is explicit in the vision of education articulated above.

One proposal in the White Paper for ensuring a world-leading curriculum is that funding be made available to 25 per cent of schools to extend their day so as to include a wider range of activities, such as sport, arts and debating. Under the heading of 'character and resilience', the Paper states that

> education should prepare children for adult life, giving them the skills and character traits needed to succeed academically, have a fulfilling career, and make a positive contribution to British society. The country's leading state and independent schools instil these character traits throughout school life and other schools can learn from their example. So we will introduce more support for schools to expand the range of evidence-based, character building opportunities they provide to pupils . . .[8]

The four-dimensional approach defines a world-class education as being permeated by character development and identified by heights of excellence, breadth of attainment, depth of engagement and length of endeavour. The vision stated above makes character development the starting point of a good education. This vision comes first, informing policy, which in turn determines practice. Curriculum innovation follows the same pattern, new subjects being judiciously introduced because they enable pupils to discover and develop their gifts, make strong and secure progress in knowledge, understanding, skills and appreciation, and put down deep, rigorous roots of learning on which they can build securely in the future.

The sixth principle, ambition for all, is self-evident in the model. In the White Paper, 'fair, stretching accountability' is called for to ensure its occurrence. The four-dimensional model starts with the even more fundamental principle of the worth of every child, and therefore the principle of ambition for all, and consequent experience of success, is indispensable. The vision here clearly sees good education as being that which enables pupils to discover and develop their gifts to the full – that is true ambition.

The seventh element contributing towards excellence referred to in the White Paper is that of resourcing. It is of course the case that adequate resources should be supplied to deliver educational vision. But with resources being of necessity limited, there is all the greater reason for ensuring that vision is crisply and clearly articulated so that money is intentionally directed. To be effective, allocation of resources, like each of the other six White Paper elements, requires an articulated and shared understanding of what excellence is, in order for it to be achieved, or at least promoted and encouraged in a systematic way everywhere.

Of course, a key responsibility of policy-makers at the highest level is the adequate provision and support of the teaching body. To teach well is extremely hard work. It requires mental, physical, emotional and intellectual stamina. The provision of good education depends on committed teachers who know their subjects, know how to teach and who care deeply about their pupils, demonstrating good will in going the second mile. These are the kind of teachers who need to be recruited into and retained in the profession. The respect they should be given as professionals should extend to devolving to them the responsibility to prioritise and focus on what is really important in ensuring excellent provision for the children in their care. Although such education cannot be prepared and provided in a predefined, fixed number of hours, nevertheless, teachers' time is by nature precious and limited; teachers must be able to use it in the best possible way and external demands kept to a necessary minimum. It is a role of policy-makers to understand the demands that delivering a good education makes on its teachers, and to support them in the fullest possible way in doing so.

White Papers, Green Papers, Bills and Acts do not create educational vision, but should reflect it. This model of education provides fertile ground for conceiving a vision for education on which policies can grow that support and promote such a vision in practice.

Establishing vision: governors

In effect, an academy board, or school governing body, defines what a good education is for its own institution, the key roles of a state school governing body in England being to set the aims and objectives of the school, and to set policies – and then targets – for achieving those aims. The process of articulating vision and values can bring stakeholders together to discuss what they believe is important, and can help to develop common purpose. Some schools may emphasise particular aspects more than others, a factor which may inform parental choice.

In addition, governors are expected to monitor and evaluate the progress the school is making towards its aims and be a source of challenge and support to the head teacher (who, together with the deputy head, they also appoint). With oversight of school finances, governors are expected to provide strategic leadership and accountability.[9] Recruiting good, appropriately experienced, governors and trustees is a vital task in securing the leadership that can enable a good education. Identifying and training people who will take up this role in the future will also require time and resource.

The four-dimensional model can readily be used to create a version of vision which reflects its elements, if such is desired, as shown below (Vision box 12.2). If there is a wish to emphasise particular aspects, it can readily be amended to reflect this. Overarching aims and objectives can be set to achieve it, and school policies written to support implementation.

The articulation of a vision for good education helps to avoid the tendency which might otherwise develop to focus solely on administrative matters such as compliance and the completion of risk registers, or on micro-managing parts of the curriculum, to the exclusion of assessing and considering educational priorities. Without educational vision, it is surely difficult to know what to try and implement, but with educational vision the direction of travel can be set.

The role of governors is critical in helping a school to set its direction by formulating its vision and then holding the school to account, as a critical friend.

VISION BOX 12.2: An example of four-dimensional vision for governors

WHAT IS A GOOD EDUCATION?

We aim for every child in our school to be individually known, cared for and valued as a whole person who has unique gifts and abilities to contribute to the learning community. This aim will be supported by strong systems of pastoral care. Every part of school life will support the development of good character, emphasising individual integrity, distinction, initiative and perseverance in a community characterised by mutual respect, shared positivity, an attitude of service and a spirit of compassion.

Excellence is sought and valued across academic subjects, the creative and performing arts, and team and individual sport. We recognise and support the sustained hard work that this requires from all members of the school.

By the time children leave this school our aim is that they should have experienced personal success, achieved significantly in their learning, developed strong habits of study, and found genuine joy in their educational endeavours which will stand them in good stead for the future.

Governors can ensure that the vision, once established, is being implemented to the full, or that steps are strategically being taken towards doing so, through the use of development plans with specific, measurable aims and goals for the short and longer term. Governors can provide a useful perspective for a school: they have the school's best interests at heart but avoid getting caught up in the detail of day-to-day life which can so easily obscure or skew perception. Governors can remind schools of what is important, when they are in danger of only seeing the urgent. As big decisions are made, from the appointment of the head teacher to deciding whether money should be set aside for a new science block or a new sports facility, they will be informed by and dependent on their educational vision.

The four-dimensional model can be used to assist in the implementation of vision as well as its formulation, through suggesting questions for governors to ask, such as shown in Table 12.1.

Referencing the elements of the four-dimensional model provides a framework for checking provision. Rather than being reactive, and responding to the demands of the latest pressure group, be that to introduce mindfulness or happiness, craft or computing, the model can readily help a governing body to be proactive, determining the next area for development and so informing the school's strategic development plan.

Any resultant changes will be made on educational grounds and local need, driven by a clear vision of what a good education is, and what needs to be done to provide it for all pupils.

TABLE 12.1 Questions governors might discuss in thinking through vision

AREA OF EDUCATION	QUESTION TO CONSIDER
General	How clearly articulated is our educational vision?
Foundational values	How is the individual child viewed in our school? How well do we feel that individual children are known? How good are relationships within the learning community? How could we create a stronger sense of community?
Character traits	What character traits matter to us for the individual and for our community? Which of these would we regard as particular strengths/areas to develop in our pupils: integrity, distinction, initiative, perseverance? To what extent is our community characterised by mutual respect, shared positivity, an attitude of service and a compassionate spirit, and which need to be prioritised for development? How respectful is the community? Are there equally positive expectations in all areas? How well do pupils persevere in their learning? What opportunities do pupils have to show grit and develop drive? How well is kindness valued?
Educational principles	Do we achieve breadth and balance in our use of time across the curriculum? Have we achieved the best balance of time in each year group for the academic, arts, sports and pastoral care? What would we expect excellence to look like in each curriculum area? How enthusiastic are pupils to learn? What are the long-term learning outcomes of our alumni? Which alumni do or could come back to inspire the pupils?
Practical outcomes	What are the school's greatest successes? What is being celebrated in this school? How are we gauging achievement? In what parts of the curriculum is achievement at its best? In what curriculum areas could achievement develop next? How do we or could we gauge pupil engagement in their learning? How well are habits of study being developed – what are the strengths or areas to develop next? Are there groups or individuals who work less hard? If so, how could they be supported?

By considering such questions, or any others that the model suggests, a governing body might decide that its school needs to provide greater opportunity and resource for the performing arts, or for participation in maths challenges, or for sports fixtures against other schools. Alternatively, it may be that it needs to give its teachers more training in pastoral care, support an initiative promoting good manners or introduce opportunities to serve the local community.

Implementing vision: school leadership

It falls to the head teacher and other senior leaders within a school to oversee, organise and manage it in such a way as to ensure that the vision established by the governing body is implemented on a daily basis. School leadership must promote excellence in every way possible, including, of course, through example.

Forging community and ensuring individual care

It also falls to the head teacher to forge the community in which this vision can be realised, lived out in practice on a daily basis. The first way in which school leadership does this is by setting the tone. The values and principles upholding an educational vision must be genuinely lived out in practice with passion, energy and commitment, by the head teacher and all in positions of senior leadership.

The way in which the head teacher thinks about, acts towards and speaks to pupils, parents and teachers establishes the standard for relationships within the school. The culture is set at the top. Therefore, although those in leadership may be very busy and potentially preoccupied, the individual child at the heart of the education always warrants respectful attention, and time will be found for teachers, or parents, who need it. Leaders will be servant-hearted.

Within good educational provision, a head teacher ensures that processes are in place so that no child is overlooked, whether this is through a tutor system, with houses, by year group or in some other way. Community is created and crafted in which everyone is known, and everyone is valued. Good alumni relations forge a school community healthily connected to its heritage, just as school uniform can reflect a unity in the now.

Pupils whose gifts have not yet been identified warrant special attention, as do pupils with particular need. Communication between staff needs to be excellent, and weekly meetings or some other such method may be employed to ensure that good communication and care takes place.

A culture of care and a committed community spirit is established and upheld by the school leadership.

Strategy: plans, goals, assessment and initiatives

As well as implementing and practising the governors' vision for community, the head teacher and senior leadership also have the responsibility of translating educational vision into particular plans, specific goals and agreed initiatives for teachers. There needs to be joined-up thinking between whole-school priorities and strategic plans, which in turn will be reflected in teachers' collegial and individual practice. Clear lines of management and communication need to be in place so that the articulated vision can be rolled out practically and effectively. Teams need to be built up that work well together towards shared and ambitious goals. Within such teams, individuals must have the freedom to catch and run with the vision in their own idiosyncratic ways: inspirational teachers always have plenty of ideas and such creativity must be welcomed and encouraged.

Part of building a team and planning for its success is ensuring that teachers new to the school are provided with mentors, and that experience and expertise are shared so they are given all the support they need. Even in schools where behaviour is good, children can seem surprisingly territorial, and new teachers need the full support of their senior colleagues in all aspects of teaching and classroom management until they are fully secure in post. School leadership can seek out the teacher who is innovative and encourage them to share their ideas with those who may be less imaginative or confident. The model can provide a means of encouraging individual staff to develop expertise or finesse practice, as it provides a point of reference for the whole school but also the individuals within it.

It also falls to school leadership to ensure that adequate provision is made for the assessment of learning. Standardised tests in reading, spelling, maths or English may be used to ensure that progress is being made at or above the expected rate by each individual and that additional support is provided where needed to ensure excellence for all in these key areas. If necessary, strategic plans should be developed to ensure that more time or improved resources are made available for specific curriculum areas or other parts of school life. Subject-specific assessments may review acquisition of knowledge, understanding, skills and appreciation in science, languages or the humanities, for example, which can enable teachers to see in which areas pupils might benefit from additional support or stretch.

At an appropriate age, and at least a year before any public examinations will be sat, pupils need to experience school examinations. The impact of success in public examinations is so important that school leadership needs to plan for pupils' first experiences of examinations to be as positive and helpful as possible. From the provision of clear advice on how to prepare, to careful timings of examinations, pupils can be helped to approach them with a healthy assurance: strategic means of maximising confidence must be found, and setting papers which are accessible for all pupils is particularly important in the early years of school exams. Like every aspect of school life, the experience of success is achieved through purposeful planned provision, and thorough strategic preparation.

More broadly, the model can provide a mental check-list for annual review, useful in considering areas to develop or that need additional support, training or resources. Excellence will be sought through weighing up the merits of a school's traditional mode of operation in any given area, with new opportunities provided through innovation, change and development.

Managing dynamic tension

Head teachers have the joy of managing dynamic tension in a school, of which tradition and innovation is one example. The two principles may appear to be in conflict, pulling in opposite directions, but in fact both need to be held and valued concurrently, as each is essential in its own right but also in keeping the other in check.

Another example of dynamic tension occurs in the staff common room. Strong teams are essential within the teaching body, but all the different groups need to work together for a harmonious result and leadership needs to encourage and facilitate this.

Similarly, in schools where everyone is striving for success, the school calendar has to be carefully managed to ensure that a balance of opportunities is provided for varied enrichment and extra-curricular activity, without compromising the integrity of the timetable.

Within the model itself, the tension between the four areas of the curriculum (academic, arts, sports and pastoral) has to be managed, as does the striving for balance between heights of excellence and breadth of attainment, or between ambition and quality, or knowledge and skill. In each of these, the leadership in a school needs to see this tension as creative: there is more, not less, to be found by embracing each of these ideals, in regarding them as complementary rather than contradictory. Grappling to find the right balance or to reconcile two ideas which pull in opposite directions is productive, generates new ideas, brings teams together and results in change and growth.

School leadership has to take responsibility not only for grasping the governors' vision, but for implementing it well. Heads, senior managers and departmental leaders can ask themselves whether heights of excellence are being achieved and celebrated across the board for example, whether breadth and depth are being achieved and whether long-term learning is healthy. Are the values that the school promotes evident in daily life and celebrated publicly?

Members of a leadership team need to model the character traits they desire for the whole school, both collectively and individually, and this means treating teachers with respect and compassion as well as children. It means senior leaders working with integrity and perseverance. It means providing verbal encouragement, relentless positivity and continuous thanks, while balancing such support with appropriate challenge. Like any good management, it means willingly absorbing disappointment when things do not work out well, as will inevitably sometimes be the case, and generously giving the credit to others when they do.

Delivering vision: teachers

The four-dimensional model of education strongly suggests that a good education depends upon teachers having the right attitude towards the children in their care. Their great privilege and daunting responsibility is to value every child and look for the gifts they may have, to understand that they need help to learn and that the learning process will go on for a very long time. These are the kind of teachers children remember with gratitude: what one parent described to me as 'the passionate, learned, caring, decent, engaged teachers'.

In all this, the joy to be had is in knowing that the enterprise, although daunting, is so very worthwhile. The American novelist John Steinbeck said, 'I have come to believe that a great teacher is a great artist and that there are as few as there are any other great artists. Teaching might even be the greatest of the arts since the medium is the human mind and spirit'.[10] It is indeed a very high calling.

Teachers as classroom leaders

Beyond setting out with this attitude, what are the other implications for the teacher? Teachers set the tone for their class – they are the class leader. Teachers are in the best position to be role models to their pupils in terms of punctuality, preparedness for lessons, personal presentation and manner. Teachers must model the very character traits believed to be important in the children: integrity (being utterly trustworthy), distinction (teaching as well as possible), initiative (being imaginative and proactive) and perseverance (which all teachers need in abundance). Equally, teachers must demonstrate respect for all pupils in their classes, expect the best of them, have the attitude of being there to serve the needs of their pupils, and demonstrate compassion, remembering that all pupils are still learning and need to be shown kindness and patience. This is another example of the need for dynamic tension, as high standards are expected and yet compassion is exercised.

When consideration was given to excellence, it was noted that excellence has to be an aspiration across all parts of school life, not just something that is expected of the pupils. So here too, a teacher can demonstrate this attitude in numerous seemingly insignificant and mundane ways, such as keeping a tidy classroom with fresh, up-to-date displays and tidy bookshelves; children need to be allowed to leave for break only when the desks are straight, chairs pushed under and surfaces clear. It follows of course that lessons need to be thoroughly prepared, bearing in mind the specific needs of the class. Good lesson planning meets the needs of the pupils to progress in knowledge, understanding, skill and appreciation, and well-marked books are one way of teachers gauging progress and communicating with pupils about it.

Clearly within the model, teachers will see their role as enabling their pupils to reach up as high as possible in terms of the ambition and quality of their work to attain excellence. They will also embrace breadth, valuing the contribution of other teachers and subjects, and rejoicing in the successes of pupils wherever across the curriculum they may shine. Teachers have a tremendous role in encouraging pupils to dig deep in their learning, to encourage grit and develop drive, but also to foster creativity and collaboration, and ensure strong, rigorous habits of study, all with long-term love of learning in mind. They have a responsibility to make learning enjoyable, even though at times it is also hard.

Teachers have key interactions with pupils as they deliver the vision of education formulated by governors and implemented under the direction of the school leadership. Individual teachers make all the difference. They set the standards for the children, and must insist on high quality in terms of punctuality, good manners and politeness. They are in a position to ensure that content and presentation of written work in class is good; that homework is prompt and complete (and to follow up in appropriate ways if it is not); and that as children work, they are happy and studious. In all this, teachers will motivate through praise and encouragement as much as possible, using kind words, positive personal feedback and no end of classroom, departmental or whole-school reward systems.

It is subject teachers, pastoral tutors and teaching assistants – the adults working most closely to individual children – who are in the best position to notice their need. It is said that you cannot love unless you notice. Teachers are called to put the needs and best interests of their pupils before their own, and they have a crucial role in ensuring that no one is overlooked, remains unnoticed or is not cared or catered for, whatever their ability in the class or mode of working.

Teachers as team players

While many teachers spend much of their time working in isolation from their colleagues, teachers must never forget that they are team players, part of a bigger enterprise (a year group, department, faculty or whole school) and that within this context, consistency with children, parents and colleagues matters, not least because within a school there is an entitlement to fairness and equality of opportunity. If excellence in any area is to be achieved, things need to be done in an orderly and planned manner, working closely with colleagues to ensure consistency of approach and provision.

In small schools, the team a teacher works in may be all the other staff in the school, but in larger schools, such teams may be departmental. In either situation, teachers are members of the wider school community made up of the pupil body, teachers, leadership, support staff, governors and parents. As such they have a great responsibility to demonstrate the character traits sought in children. As members of an educational community, teachers need to model respect, demonstrate positivity, work with a serving attitude and treat fellow members of the community with care and compassion.

A shared aspiration and commitment to excellence means recognising and valuing the traditions of a school but also working innovatively where appropriate. Entailed in this will be adherence to departmental plans and making good provision in order that agreed learning objectives for pupil progress can be met. Teaching resources must be of high quality, either those provided by senior colleagues or, if provided by a teacher, approved by departmental heads and shared as relevant. New ideas should always be welcome in a learning environment, and teachers should be encouraged to contribute innovative suggestions to colleagues on how to teach a topic. They should be encouraged to come up with ideas for off-timetable enrichment, or commit to sharing a hobby through a new after-school club.

Consistency comes through teachers following agreed protocols on marking, setting homework, setting (or not setting) holiday work, achieving balance in the types of task set and ensuring that the material is suited to the individuals within the class. New teachers need to accept the support of mentors, follow the leadership of management and endorse the vision established by governors if the community is to function effectively and happily. Assessments and tests must be done without help, following school guidelines and results recorded as required.

Teaching assistants are an invaluable resource and support, and they too need to be fairly managed, both for their own sake and that of the children. Teaching assistants often work very closely with pupils and have great opportunity to lead by example too.

Teachers are often the main communicators with parents and as team players, it is clear that they need to communicate as well as possible, with honesty, clarity and precision. If a problem occurs, the best approach is to be ready with a solution to suggest.

Reflective practice

The four-dimensional model provides a mirror which individual teachers can use to reflect on their own teaching, as shown in Table 12.2.

Being a teacher is about being both a leader and a team player, valuing the community as well as the individual. But it is also important to remember what teaching is all about: it is not primarily about pleasing parents, cooperating with colleagues or impressing management. First and foremost, it is about putting the child at the heart of education at the heart of all that we do.

Supporting vision: parents

Beyond the school gates, it is parents, of course, who have the greatest vested interest in education, and certainly have a huge part to play in the success or

TABLE 12.2 Questions teachers might reflect on in thinking through vision

	REFLECTIVE QUESTIONS TO CONSIDER
General	How clearly articulated is my educational vision?
Foundational values	How do I view the children I teach? How well do I know my pupils, their strengths and needs?
Character traits	How do I encourage integrity and distinction? Do I reach for the best in myself? Do I look for it in others? What opportunities do I give pupils for taking initiative? How determined are my pupils and how could I encourage them more? How respectful is the atmosphere in my lessons? Do I always expect and achieve a high standard? How do I encourage my pupils to serve and learn from each other? Do I always model positivity?
Educational principles	In which areas of my pupils' work do they demonstrate excellence? Do I foster both ambition and quality? Do I achieve good variety in types of activity and outcome? Do my pupils demonstrate curiosity and creativity? Do my pupils work well both independently and collaboratively? Could I enthuse them more? Am I cultivating short-term grit and long-term drive? What are my former pupils doing now?
Practical outcomes	Have all my pupils experienced success in some area this week/term? Have I provided opportunities for them to achieve in different ways? Are my pupils forming good learning habits? If so, which? Do they love their learning? How do I know? How engaging are my lessons? Am I providing appropriate challenges for all? Where is rigour hardest to achieve? What do I need to do? Are my lessons fully supportive of all pupils in their learning? Is my planning as thorough and creative as it needs to be? What progress do I see in knowledge, understanding, skill and appreciation?

otherwise of their children's school career. The most successful learning takes place when school and home have shared aspirations and approach. Prospective parents need to understand the educational vision of a school they are considering and see whether they agree with it, and can be supportive of it. No two schools are the same, and assumptions cannot and should not be made about a school's educational vision.

Here again, the four-dimensional model can act as a point of reference for prospective parents, and they can ask school-relevant questions based on its elements, such as those shown in Table 12.3. Such questions, and others suggested by the model, help prospective parents to know whether their values resonate with those of the school, and whether they share the vision of education the school holds. A visit to a school will rapidly show whether children are engaged in their learning, whether they are enjoying a sense of success in their endeavours and whether their studies are occurring in a harmonious, positive and respectful environment which promotes high standards.

Once a child is at a school, parents can play a huge part by sharing and supporting the educational vision, whether by helping their child, attending events, following advice or ensuring good two-way communication between home and school. Parents can also continue to ask such questions once their children are at a school, not critically, but supportively, on the grounds that the best education will be collaborative, with values and vision shared between home and school in an atmosphere of mutual trust and support. Parents sometimes even find it useful to ask themselves similar types of questions.

Much of what has been written may seem to apply only to school education, which is not surprising since that is where most education takes place. Approximately 3 per cent of American children are home-schooled,[11] and although no official figure is available in the UK estimates put the proportion at less than 0.5 per cent, but rising.[12] The principles of four-dimensional education apply equally to home-schooled children as to those in a school setting. Heights of excellence, breadth of attainment, depth of engagement and length of endeavour are all achievable in a home-schooling environment. The educational community, rather than being the school, will instead be the family, any clubs, groups or home-schooling cooperatives that children participate in. With many home-schooled children, joining in sports teams and music lessons, enjoying visits to museums and trips to historic sites with their parents, there is no reason why home-schooling cannot provide a good education within the four-dimensional model. The values concerning the child, the cultivation of character, the educational principles and practical outcomes are all possible within a home-schooling setting.

Receiving vision: children

The only thing that really matters in education is what the individual child takes home at the end of the school day. In considering a model of education that has the individual child at its heart, it feels apt that the child in receipt of this vision is the final point to be considered. At the end of the school day, term or year, what has the child in receipt of the educational vision received in practice?

The four-dimensional model suggests that the well-educated child is one who has acquired a love of learning which will last through their years of formal education and beyond, colouring their whole life as a continual learner. Such a

TABLE 12.3 Questions parents might ask in thinking through vision

AREA OF EDUCATION	QUESTION TO CONSIDER
General	How would you view my child? What values do you hold concerning children?
Foundational values	How do you celebrate different types of ability? How do you make sure that no child is overlooked? What provision do you make for the academically able? What support is available for any who find learning more challenging? What do you do for a child who does not seem to have strength in any particular area? What traditions does this school have? How do you foster community? What systems do you have in place for pastoral care? How important do you think it is that children are happy? What happens to a child who does something wrong? How do you make sure that everyone can get on with their learning?
Character traits	How do you encourage good behaviour? How do you develop confidence? How important are manners? What happens in assemblies? How do you balance collaboration and independence? How do you celebrate success? What opportunities are provided to develop leadership skills? What charities does the school support and how? How do you support your local community?
Educational principles	What is excellence? How have you been innovative in the curriculum recently? How important is detail in learning? How do you ensure that the classroom environment is studious and happy? Do you ever go off-timetable and, if so, what do you do? What opportunities do you provide for extra-curricular activities? What opportunities are there in the performing arts? My child loves sport: what opportunities would you provide? How do you allocate time between the academic, sports, the arts and pastoral time? How do you promote reading? What are the academic areas of strength in the school?
Practical outcomes	What notable successes have your pupils enjoyed recently? What opportunities are there for achievement across academic/ arts/sports/pastoral areas? How much contact do you have with former pupils? Do children enjoy their learning here? How can I be involved as a parent? What have some of your alumni gone on to do?

person has gained, and will continue to gain, a deep and broad appreciation of the world in which they live, its science and its heritage, its culture and its art, and the finesse and expertise across a whole range of endeavours of those by whom it is, and has been, inhabited. Well-educated children have developed a sense of responsibility for their choices and the decisions they make concerning their contribution to the world in which we live. They will function with a spirit of compassion to those around them, particularly those in need, and a spirit of humble perseverance in their own endeavours, recognising that each of us is continually learning and has a need, and the room, to change and grow.

A well-educated child has developed strong habits of study. Not only will they enjoy their learning, and see their need for it, but they will be able to learn well. They will have developed the skills and approach necessary to engage deeply, valuing and exercising intellectual curiosity and rigour, and appreciating the importance of detail. To be well educated also means to understand the place of collaborative effort, valuing the work of others and accepting responsibility to make their own positive personal contribution to the human endeavour, in whatever sphere. A good education enables children to grow into adults with a healthy understanding of the complexities of community, and an attitude of generosity and service, energised by personal initiative and creativity of thought.

In this model of education, well-educated children are achievers, not in a narrow sense, but within a wide-ranging arena, able to respond positively to living in a competitive world. Having had high standards set for themselves, each has found one or more areas in which they can attain particular levels of distinction whether academically, within the world of the arts or sports, or concerned with areas of human interaction, need and endeavour. But to be well educated also means to have gained a broad understanding which spans the disciplines, joining the dots, making connections between ideas, concepts and knowledge. Being in receipt of a good education therefore not only means having developed the wherewithal to make a unique contribution, exercising one's own inimitable and irreplaceable gifts, but to be able to do so in an intellectually and emotionally sensitive manner, within a broad and informed context.

In these ways, a good education means that in some sphere or other, its recipients will have tasted success. They will have acquired the necessary knowledge to have reached heights of excellence characterised by ambition and quality in a context that values both tradition and innovation. Such excellence of endeavour should be matched, however, by personal integrity and mutual respect. Otherwise, as St Paul says, although I may have 'all knowledge' if I 'do not have love, I am nothing'.[13]

Such love – respect, generosity of spirit, and attitude of service – is a direct result of individual children along with their peers being treated as being inherently precious. Within this model of education, the well-educated child will know that they are valued and appreciated for who they are. Each recognises that they are different from everyone else, and that this is something to be cherished and celebrated. As a result, such children will have confidence in themselves and know that they have a real and unique contribution to make to their community and to society more widely, as does each of their peers.

There may be many ways to formulate educational vision, but in the four-dimensional model the vision arises from a clear articulation of values concerning the individual child. Every child is a uniquely gifted, multifaceted individual who is inherently precious; those individuals make up a learning community whose members are mutually dependent and continually learning. The sense of worth associated with each child and the desire to do the best for every individual within the community is the beginning of creating an ethos-based vision. The development of character is central, and the educational principles of height, breadth, depth and length follow on. Experience of success, variety of achievement, good habits of study and love of learning are the end products. A good education should, I believe, contain all these elements in one form or another. The end results of such an education are flourishing children and young people who are equipped intellectually, emotionally, physically and morally to make unique and positive contributions to the world in which they live. Such people are able to move strongly, confidently and happily forward, intellectually engaged and curious, morally and spiritually alert and aesthetically sensitive. This is four-dimensional education, and I believe it to be a good education.

Notes

1   www.henry-ford.net/english/quotes.html, accessed 28 July 2017.
2   *Obituary: Grandma Moses Is Dead at 101; Primitive Artist 'Just Wore Out'*, *New York Times*, 14 December 1961.
3   Vulliamy, C.E. *Aspasia: The Life and Letters of Mary Granville, Mrs Delany* (London: J. and J. Gray, 1935), p. 254.
4   Plato's *Apology of Socrates*, 21d.
5   *Comenius and Contemporary Education*, UNESCO, 1970, p. 20: http://unesdoc.unesco.org/images/0013/001319/131996eo.pdf, accessed 28 July 2017.
6   www.nhs.uk/Conditions/Alzheimers-disease/Pages/Prevention.aspx, accessed 28 July 2017.
7   www.gov.uk/government/uploads/system/uploads/attachment_data/file/508447/Educational_Excellence_Everywhere.pdf, page 5, accessed 28 July 2017.
8   *Ibid.*, p. 20.
9   Further detail on the role of governors can be found here: www.nga.org.uk/Be-a-Governor.aspx, accessed 28 July 2017.
10 McKenney, J.W. 'John Steinbeck Says a Great Teacher Is One of the Great Artists'. San Francisco, CA: California Teachers Association, 1955. Archives & Special Collections PS3537.T3234 Z734 1955.
11 https://nces.ed.gov/fastfacts/display.asp?id=91, accessed 28 July 2017.
12 www.theguardian.com/education/2016/apr/12/home-schooling-parents-education-children-england, accessed 28 July 2017.
13 *The Bible*, St Paul's first letter to the Corinthians, Chapter 13.

Afterword

At first people refuse to believe that a strange new thing can be done, then they begin to hope it can be done, then they see it can be done – then it is done . . .

Frances Hodgson Burnett, *The Secret Garden*

Pre-empting possible objections and potential obstacles

The four-dimensional model of education defined and described in this book cares and provides for the whole child both as an individual and as a member of a community. That entails fostering good character traits in the individual and community. It leads to the principles of height, breadth, depth and length of educational experience. Effectively implemented, it results in success for the individual, achievement across the community, strong habits of study and a lasting love of learning.

By setting out the essence of a good education, this model is intended as a helpful frame of reference for different stakeholders in the educational arena, including teachers and parents, as they think through what a good education means. It is intended to have relevance in a variety of contexts.

However, while commitment, effort, energy, time and resources are always required to make good educational provision anywhere, it must be recognised that in some contexts, this is exceptionally challenging. It is therefore perhaps helpful to consider and counter possible reservations or objections.

There's not enough money

It should be acknowledged that if head teachers have serious worries about the financial viability of their school, they will not be able to focus on providing a good education. It is, of course, essential that adequate funding is made available. Education is too important for it to be inadequately funded.

Nonetheless, it might be assumed that independent schools can adopt a version of four-dimensional education because they are better financially resourced than state-maintained schools, and that the model therefore only has relevance in that sector. Fees for a term of independent education are quite likely to equate to the money spent in a year on a state school education. The financial factor is therefore real and must be taken seriously. It can be considered from a number of angles.

Class size

A significant financial factor is that classes are typically larger in state-funded schools than in independent schools. According to one report,[1] about 90 per cent of children who attend state schools in England are taught in classes with thirty pupils or fewer, but over 17,000 are taught in classes with more than thirty-six pupils. Clearly, this makes it harder to get to know children as individuals than in schools which have smaller classes. The average size of a state primary school class in 2011 was just over twenty-six, and just over twenty in secondary schools.[2] Many (but not all) independent schools try and keep their classes nearer twenty in number.

Nonetheless, a primary school teacher who spends much of the week with his or her class still has every opportunity to get to know each pupil individually. It may take longer, and it will be harder, than if classes are smaller, but it is both achievable and achieved in many, if not all, primary schools.

On the other hand, the secondary school drama teacher, for example, who may see twenty classes each of thirty pupils through his doors each week, will obviously be in a more difficult position to get to know pupils individually. In this context, the key principle derived from the model is that every child should indeed be known and cared for individually – but not necessarily equally by all teachers. Many secondary schools successfully operate a form tutor system whereby pupils are the pastoral responsibility of their tutor who will get to know them, look out for their needs, consider how they might best be met and communicate such points to other teachers as required. Such systems work very effectively in many schools.

Care of the individual child is a central tenet of the model, and must extend to ensuring that opportunity is given to every child to succeed. One inspirational head, who had worked in a particularly deprived area, explained to me her commitment to ensuring that every child in her primary school was able to read and write, no matter what effort had to be put in to support them in doing so. She was convinced that not only were their lives potentially going to be transformed, but so were those of their families. 100 per cent success was the only goal for her, and that meant tenacious commitment to caring for those individuals who might not succeed without considerable additional input.

It is hard to see why other elements of the model – cultivation of good character or ambitious, high-quality lessons, for example, or the deep roots of collaborative and creative learning – should be absent due to class size. Many schools with classes of thirty deliver lessons of the highest calibre in terms of excellence and rigour, as evidenced by inspection reports, which indicate that 86 per cent of England's schools were judged to be good or outstanding in 2016, with 18 per cent of primary schools and 22 per cent of secondary schools judged as being outstanding.[3]

Moreover, academy schools have some degree of autonomy over class size: one primary academy teacher recently explained to me that his head teacher had chosen to use her funding to keep all classes to a maximum of twenty-six.

School size

The Greater London secondary school that I went to had three classes in each year, each of thirty-three pupils, making a school of just under seven hundred pupils. Economies of scale make larger schools more financially efficient, however, creating a move towards increased size.

That said, the UK government's statistics of 2012 indicate that of the 3,268 state-funded mainstream secondary schools in England, just under half were like my secondary school, in being of between 501 and 1,000 pupils in size, with slightly fewer having between 1,001 and 1,500 pupils, while there were only around 300 with more than 1,500 pupils, and about the same number with fewer than 500.[4]

In 2014, London primary schools were reported as having an average of 399 pupils, while in some regions the figure is nearer 200. A few primary schools have as many as 800 pupils. Independent junior schools fall within very similar size parameters, and many independent secondary schools have over a thousand pupils.

It would therefore seem that a larger school need not necessarily negate the possibility of four-dimensional education: the size of a school need not have any impact upon its efficacy in valuing and caring for the individual pupil, which is at the heart of the four-dimensional model. Knowing and caring for pupils and their development, in the richest sense, is more a function of will, priority and organisation, than size. In one state secondary school the headmaster made it his priority to learn the names of all his pupils when they arrived in September. That may not perhaps be altogether unusual, but his next priority was to learn the names of the parents: the school had over a thousand pupils at the time. Knowing and caring for individual pupils is a matter of culture.

The key to care of the individual child then, is neither the size of classes nor the size of school, but rather, the recognition of the need for pastoral care and its organisation within the school. It is about recognising and valuing the individual. Different schools facilitate this in different ways, such as through 'schools within schools' in some larger academies, house systems or tutor groups. The key point is to make pastoral care a priority – in terms of organisation, time and personnel.

One state primary school acknowledges its 'primary responsibility for the care, welfare and safety of the pupils in our charge', stating that it will 'carry out this duty through our pastoral care policy, which aims to provide a caring, supportive and safe environment, valuing individuals for their unique talents and abilities, in which all our young people can learn and develop to their full potential'.[5] Another Church of England primary school simply states: 'Pastoral care is at the heart of our school. Our vision, ethos, mission and aims incorporate this'.[6] Such a culture is obviously achievable, even if at present the perception created by an Internet search is that pastoral care remains largely the preserve of the independent sector, and the church schools.

In some ways, the larger the school, the more readily it might be expected to be able to supply breadth of opportunity, given the range of expertise available on the teaching staff. Similarly, the size of a school should not, in itself, make any discernible difference to the quality of teaching in lessons, and the striving for a culture of excellence. Height, breadth, depth and length are the principle elements of educational ethos, rather than a function of size.

Limited space and resources

Allied to the issue of financial resourcing are those of space, facilities, teaching resources and consumables. Clearly, a larger fund of money to draw on can be used for more elaborate and luxurious facilities and to provide more expensive equipment. Is this what facilitates four-dimensional education?

One of the key elements of four-dimensional education is that of breadth: academic, artistic, sporting and pastoral elements are all essential within a four-dimensional curriculum. In terms of breadth, one key impact of financial limitation is most likely to be the impact on sport, because of the space required. As already recounted, my own school was one which lost its sports fields, as did many in the later decades of the twentieth century, and the impact was considerable. The loss was not simply, or even primarily, in terms of space, however: the greater loss was the gradual disappearance of interest in, and support for, sport.

It is true that many independent schools can support their sports programmes through the use of extensive and expensive facilities. But equally, there are other independent schools – particularly in the big cities – which have very limited outside space, or none at all, yet nevertheless ensure that sporting opportunities are provided. Sometimes children may be bussed to sports grounds at a distance, but even this is not always feasible, and provision for physical activity is reliant on the use of local parks or other open spaces, as is often the case with state-funded schools.

Once again, the key point is fostering a culture which values and therefore affords priority to physical activity. Schools do not have to – and usually cannot – provide a wide range of sports. It is not essential to field teams in everything from athletics to Zumba, as some independent schools may aim to do, but rather importance lies in recognising the significance of sport and making provision for it as well as possible.

Limited resources and lack of space can of course introduce challenges of their own, but small classrooms in converted buildings are the norm in many schools, which nevertheless provide education which could be described as four-dimensional in substance, not least within the fee-paying independent sector.

Providing additional teaching opportunities, along with the necessary materials and resources for a broad curriculum, is of course harder the scarcer the money. It is not a challenge which, it seems, is necessarily insurmountable, however. One state-funded primary school states on its website that 'Creative Arts are a particular focus within the school and specialist Dance, Drama, Art and Music teachers ensure that children develop skills to a high standard. The school has a specialist music and dance/drama studio and a film studio'.[7] The school's website continues by explaining that all children from Year 1 learn the violin and recorder, and from Year 4 they may select other orchestral instruments to learn. 'In Years 5 and 6 children may join the orchestra and there are lots of opportunities for them to perform in music concerts and plays'.[8] Four-dimensional education is alive and well in some state-funded schools, just as it is in some fee-paying schools.

There's not enough time

Is it then, perhaps, time which is more of a limiting factor?

Providing a genuinely rounded curriculum, which includes academic, artistic, sporting and pastoral elements, requires time to be allocated carefully. If the school week has thirty one-hour teaching units, as some independent junior schools have, these can be divided up in such a way as to provide two hours of English and maths each day, two hours of other academic study each day (including humanities, sciences, languages and technology) and two hours each day of non-academic lessons (artistic, sporting and pastoral), creating a timetable allocation along the lines of that shown in Table A.1.

As already noted, some schools have a significantly shorter day, in which case a different approach needs to be taken. Lessons could, of course, be proportionately shorter but follow exactly the same pattern.

TABLE A.1 Thirty-hour timetable option

	MONDAY	TUESDAY	WEDNESDAY	THURSDAY	FRIDAY
1	English	English	English	English	English
2	Maths	Maths	Maths	Maths	Maths
3	Science	Computing	Science	Engineering	Science
4	Humanities	Languages	Humanities	Languages	Humanities
5	Pastoral	Sport	Pastoral	Sport	Pastoral
6	Art	Sport	Music	Sport	Drama

TABLE A.2 Twenty-hour timetable option

	MONDAY 1	TUESDAY 1	WEDNESDAY 1	THURSDAY 1	FRIDAY 1
1	English	English	English	English	English
2	Maths	Maths	Maths	Maths	Maths
3	Computing	Science	Humanities	Science	Languages
4	Sport	Pastoral	Sport	Art	Drama
	MONDAY 2	**TUESDAY 2**	**WEDNESDAY 2**	**THURSDAY 2**	**FRIDAY 2**
1	English	English	English	English	English
2	Maths	Maths	Maths	Maths	Maths
3	Humanities	Engineering	Humanities	Science	Languages
4	Sport	Pastoral	Sport	Pastoral	Music

An alternative used by many secondary schools if the week is shorter but the term is longer, is to operate a two-week timetable, such as that shown in Table A.2.

A third approach would be to have a larger number of off-timetable days devoting time to those subjects not regularly timetabled. Either way, breadth should be achievable.

There's not enough expertise

It was not unusual when I was a child for classrooms to have an ageing upright piano in the corner, and for music lessons to consist of the class teacher playing the piano and the class singing along. Those days seem to have long since gone, but I do believe that all schools should seek out, and make the most of, the interests and expertise of their teachers beyond the purely academic.

The prep school pattern from which four-dimensional education is derived, typically has subject specialists teaching the upper years on a secondary school model (perhaps from age nine or even younger), whereby the children move from class to class and have different teachers for each of their different subjects. Subject specialists may also provide some teaching for the younger years too. Such a pattern could be adopted in primary schools, but is not essential.

An alternative hybrid model of staffing can be envisaged, with each teacher contributing a specific area of non-academic (or academic) expertise to the school as a whole, enabling greater provision for areas such as languages, music or sport. There is no reason why a primary class needs to have the same teacher for all subjects. As children get older, a flexible, hybrid model of subject specialists or some rotating of teachers between classes could help share available expertise. Similar recommendations were made in the Cambridge Primary Review.[9]

Ideally, teachers need to be recruited who can bring a high level of relevant knowledge and understanding, interest and expertise into school. They need to be trained to become experts in understanding children and how they learn best, thereby learning how to teach, but also experts in a field of study, subject or domain of learning which they can contribute to their school. High-level training also needs to be provided to ensure that they are fully equipped for the challenges they will encounter. Recognising that recruitment and retention of teachers in some areas and schools is particularly difficult, and needs to be addressed, such factors might be borne in mind in any future review of teacher recruitment, training and retention.

At secondary level, concerns are raised about schools making economies through a narrowing of the curriculum, which can cause subjects such as music to suffer, through reduction in teacher time or complete removal. The children of course still need to be taught for the same number of hours, and it would seem that every effort should be made to ensure that this is not seen as the way to balance the books, but that imaginative approaches, perhaps including collaboration with other schools, are considered instead.

Much benefit can also be gained in schools by welcoming local volunteers, whether from among the parental body, the local community, industry, higher education or outreach groups linked to professional or charitable organisations. There is often a great willingness among such experts to come and speak to classes or run sessions in schools. Although this entails time in organisation and paying attention to safeguarding, much benefit can be had and shortfall in in-house expertise ameliorated.

What about exam results?

With the publication of so-called league tables of schools since 1992, schools have become increasingly sensitive about being judged by their performance, at primary level in English and maths, and in secondary schools in public examination results. Indeed they have a rightful obligation to ensure the highest possible results for their pupils at these points.

Four-dimensional education values much in addition to, and beyond that, which is measurable and rankable. A good education will indeed enable pupils to perform well in examinations, but it does so not by focusing solely on such performance indicators.

An analogy may help. The increasing height and weight of a child are important indicators of growth, but they do not tell the whole story and indeed to focus solely on them would be to miss the point altogether if we were seeking to ensure a child's good development. A child's good health, indicated in part by these measurable outcomes, is not achieved through their direct pursuit. Rather, it will be forged through a combination of less measurable factors including good diet, fresh air, exercise and sleep. And it will also be the result of factors which are immeasurable: security, safety, well-being, good humour, laughter and love.

Just so with educational outcomes: we may, and should, measure performance in English and maths, acknowledging the key importance of progress in these areas and working hard to ensure it. But the less easily measurable components of good education – scientific and linguistic appreciation, proficiency in the arts and sport – and the immeasurable components such as cultivating respect and integrity, imagination and creativity, perseverance and initiative, all play their part in contributing to a good education. They cannot be dismissed or disregarded simply because we cannot or do not measure them.

In addition, however, it is worth reiterating that allowing pupils to achieve in a variety of areas, including the arts and sports, can in fact be very beneficial for their academic exam performance at the time and in the longer term. The experience of doing well in one area of school life, and finding an area of real strength, has a positive impact across the board as children see that hard work pays off and success tastes sweet.

One advantage of having a fixed year-round timetable even for primary-age children, with or without subject specialist teachers, is that of protecting those areas of the curriculum not under scrutiny through public examination.

Does this model only work for compliant, affluent children?

Another objection sometimes raised concerns the transferability of four-dimensional education to contexts in which children are unresponsive, disruptive or violent. How can this model of education possibly be applicable to schools where children throw chairs across the room, I have been asked. If the model is derived primarily from a private school context, should it not be confined to that arena?

I would argue two points. First, no education is going to succeed if children are inattentive, disorderly or aggressive. Pupils must behave in school and not disrupt the learning of others, and good classroom management is essential. To ensure that this is the case, teachers need to be trained and they need support, especially at the start of their careers or when new to a school.

I met a young teacher some years ago from a tough inner-city school who had suffered the trauma of having a chair thrown across the room at her by one of her students. I asked what her senior managers did to support her, and she said that they told her to improve her classroom management skills. Classroom discipline must be an absolute priority, but its achievement takes a strong resolve by senior leaders to actively and visibly support all teachers, making expectations clear to pupils and following up any inappropriate behaviour with commensurately serious responses. There is no place in schools for children to throw chairs across the room, and senior leaders are the ones who need to make this clear, backing their junior colleagues to the hilt rather than leaving them to their own devices. A clear framework for order needs to be in place for education to succeed. Interestingly, I met the same teacher a couple of years after my first meeting with her. I somewhat tentatively enquired whether she was still in teaching. She was, she said. And she added that new senior leaders were in place who had taken behaviour firmly in hand; the school was being transformed and standards were rising across the board.

Second, I would argue that a rich educational experience should not be the preserve of the socially or materially advantaged. If an education is good at all, it should be good for all. There is no justification for withholding the best possible education from children who are already underprivileged or deprived in other ways, although it must be acknowledged that it is very much harder if a lot of teacher energy is expended in behaviour management.

In fact, four-dimensional education may be exactly the thing that is needed in the most challenging of situations. I remember speaking to a young man in his second year of teaching. He was working in a school for young people who had been excluded from mainstream education due to their extreme behavioural problems, in a city which has seen more than its fair share of organised crime and extreme violence. The young people in his care were certainly not without their talents, but alongside tenacious individual care he was clear that they needed a rich, varied and imaginative curriculum which was flexible enough to treat them as individuals and cater for them as such. Four-dimensional education is not a system which should be confined to leafy-location private schools, but a model which can find application in any context – that is the point.

Does this model only work with supportive parents?

Children may be in school for approximately a thousand hours of teaching a year, but that leaves well over seven thousand hours under the jurisdiction of home. Education is not something that parents can merely subcontract out, but rather always remains the joint responsibility of home and school. The more input and support that home provides for education, the greater the likely impact education will have.

Schools need to help parents to understand the vital role that they can play in their children's successes. Parents can do an enormous amount to maximise the effect of education, from engaging in conversation with their children, to hearing them read and providing a table in a quiet space on which homework can be done. Using local sporting facilities or parks, or visiting places of interest or museums are also of immense value. Again, schools need to know their pupils as individuals so that they can have intelligent and informed conversations with parents about how the children's learning can best be supported.

More generally, a school needs to encourage its families to understand two things: first, that a good education matters, and second, that everything about a good education can be provided by home as well as school, to at least some extent. This is true for parents of all socio-economic groups: parental support, interest and involvement is beneficial to every child, and will make a positive difference to their futures, whatever their financial or social background. Equally, apathy, cynicism and antagonism are also damaging whatever the background, as is unhealthy pressure.

The pursuit of excellence is undoubtedly aided by the support and expectation of parents; where parental expectations are lower, or non-existent, education is more challenging and, sadly, likely to have less successful outcomes. Schools repeatedly need to engage with parents, reiterating the vital role that they have in their own children's futures.

That said, the fact that educational outcomes will depend to some degree on the level of parental support provided is all the more reason for input to be as good as possible across all groups of children in school, and most particularly for those who may receive little or no support for their education at home. In this way, schools should see themselves as major contributors to the common good of the wider communities they serve and not just to the children who come through their doors.

Is it too good to be true?

A final objection must be addressed: does this model pretend a perfection which does not and cannot exist, thereby negating its validity? Is it overly idealistic and simplistic, glossing over the flaws and imperfections of the private system, from which it originates, and the wider world in which it sits, wishfully but mistakenly thinking that if only all schools were like private prep schools, there would be nothing left to worry about?

The four-dimensional model is a construct, an abstraction, which tries to describe clearly and simply the essential elements of a good education; as such it is an ideal. But while it is true that it is a model which exudes positivity, it is also realistic. It rests on the belief that children are highly complex, both individually and socially. Children will not always respond as positively to prompts and opportunities as we would wish. They will not take all that they are taught on board. Sometimes they will exercise their free will in defiance of instruction. Sometimes they will do things that are wrong, through deliberate choice or weakness of character, and this will continue throughout their lives. Truly, no one reaches perfection either in character or in examination, and indeed some crash sadly and spectacularly in one or both regards. This includes some who have received the best of educations.

This model recognises this trait, and acknowledges that this reality applies to every member of the human race. Indeed, just as no pupil is perfect, so too no teacher is perfect, and by extension, no school is perfect and no model of education is perfect. No input is perfect and no output is perfect. This need not depress or discourage us, but simply helps us to be realistic, and not give up the pursuit of excellence when we encounter inevitable disappointment. We cannot and need not discard a good education just because it is not a perfect education – or indeed a good model because it is not a perfect model.

Any model of good education has to have built into it a recognition of, and response to, flawed human nature. Poor execution of educational ideals does not discredit the ideals, and disappointing outcomes of an education do not nullify it; they should, however, serve as a prompt to a healthy humility for all of us, reminding us that while we need to strive for excellence we will never reach perfection.

And the other side of the coin is positive. The model also recognises that everyone can continue to learn throughout their lives. We are continually developing, responding to new opportunities and stimuli and there is always time to change for someone who finds that their direction of travel is misguided. Indeed, for everyone, identifying the next opportunities to improve further are important, since the very point at which a pupil, teacher or school is performing at the very top level is when the seeds of decline can be sown. Both our lives as teachers and the lives of those we teach should be characterised by compassion and humility, seeking an honest and regular questioning to check that our own personal values are as good, intentions as honourable, and actions as characterised by integrity as they could be.

For all of us, as long as there is openness to continual learning, it is never too late to change. The four-dimensional model is intended as a useful framework for thinking through educational policy, provision and practice, but in doing this, among other things, it also offers a certain hope that the past can always be redeemed, the present embraced with positivity and the future anticipated with confidence.

The minimum requirement for implementing the four-dimensional model is an attitude of mind. It is an approach which recognises the individuality and present worth of every child while acknowledging the significance of their interactions and future development. Everything else flows from that simple foundation: integrity and respect, distinction and positivity, initiative and service, perseverance and compassion. Aspiring to excellence means knowing that it really matters to do things well, and that doing things well is possible. Encouraging breadth means valuing gifts in whatever area they lie, and fanning them into flame. Developing depth reflects an understanding of the importance of rigorous and vigorous roots of learning, which underpin the enterprise. Appreciating the whole endeavour fosters lifelong learning which will bear fruit in due season.

I once heard of an artist who visited a far-off land. In the course of his travels he met a child who had an extraordinary gift of drawing. Entirely untutored, and with just a ballpoint pen and torn piece of paper, she recreated astonishing likenesses of herself, her friends and her family which silently communicated beyond any barrier of language, age or culture.

What would a good education look like for her? She would be respected and valued and so would her evident gift. She would be encouraged to reach as high as she could – certainly in her art, but as broadly as possible too, to gain all that she needs to have a flourishing life, and make a successful and positive contribution long term, in whatever way she believes right, to her community and beyond. She would be taught to study well, with perseverance and, with others, to find joy and purpose in the endeavour.

The principles apply irrespective of context, because a good education rests on universal values. These values themselves are centred on goodness, and the outcomes are also to do with goodness.

Writing of her grandfather Ruben, the science historian and philanthropist Lisbet Rausing tells how he spoke to his grandchildren 'about substantive issues – how to feed the world, how to improve agriculture, how to package food, how to cure illnesses. He never doubted the family had an important role to play in solving the problems of this world, and he was sure, too, that we would do well by doing so. "Doing well by doing good", Ruben reminded us grandchildren, "doing well by doing good"'.

When taken full advantage of, in the best possible way, the opportunities provided by a good education result in flourishing societies in which individuals thrive, each contributing in his or her way, to the success and well-being of the wider community.

Ultimately, the truly well-educated child will do well, or put another way, the child who has benefitted from a good education will do good. A good education: doing well, by doing good.

Notes

1   www.bbc.co.uk/news/uk-england-3850630,5 accessed 28 July 2017.

2   www.gov.uk/government/uploads/system/uploads/attachment_data/file/183364/DFE-RR169.pdf, pages 20 and 21, accessed 28 July 2017.

3   www.gov.uk/government/statistics/maintained-schools-and-academies-inspections-and-outcomes-as-at-31-march-2016, accessed 28 July 2017.

4   www.gov.uk/government/publications/number-of-secondary-schools-and-their-size-in-student-numbers, accessed 28 July 2017.

5   www.stjohnspsmoy.com/cmsfiles/items/downloads/PastoralCAREPOLICY.pdf, accessed 28 July 2017.

6   www.newnhamstpetersschool.org.uk/pastoral-care/, accessed 28 July 2017.

7   www.lhpa.co.uk/admin/resources/1442316727-lhpaprospectus.pdf

8   *Ibid.*

9   *Children, their World, their Education*, published by Routledge, Oxford, 2010. See p. 506.

Index

Taylor & Francis eBooks

Helping you to choose the right eBooks for your Library

Add Routledge titles to your library's digital collection today. Taylor and Francis ebooks contains over 50,000 titles in the Humanities, Social Sciences, Behavioural Sciences, Built Environment and Law.

Choose from a range of subject packages or create your own!

Benefits for you

- » Free MARC records
- » COUNTER-compliant usage statistics
- » Flexible purchase and pricing options
- » All titles DRM-free.

Benefits for your user

- » Off-site, anytime access via Athens or referring URL
- » Print or copy pages or chapters
- » Full content search
- » Bookmark, highlight and annotate text
- » Access to thousands of pages of quality research at the click of a button.

REQUEST YOUR FREE INSTITUTIONAL TRIAL TODAY

Free Trials Available
We offer free trials to qualifying academic, corporate and government customers.

eCollections – Choose from over 30 subject eCollections, including:

Archaeology	Language Learning
Architecture	Law
Asian Studies	Literature
Business & Management	Media & Communication
Classical Studies	Middle East Studies
Construction	Music
Creative & Media Arts	Philosophy
Criminology & Criminal Justice	Planning
Economics	Politics
Education	Psychology & Mental Health
Energy	Religion
Engineering	Security
English Language & Linguistics	Social Work
Environment & Sustainability	Sociology
Geography	Sport
Health Studies	Theatre & Performance
History	Tourism, Hospitality & Events

For more information, pricing enquiries or to order a free trial, please contact your local sales team:
www.tandfebooks.com/page/sales

 Routledge
Taylor & Francis Group

The home of Routledge books

www.tandfebooks.com